DEADLY FORCE

UNDERSTANDING YOUR RIGHT TO SELF DEFENSE

MASSAD AYOOB

Published by

Gun Digest® Books, an imprint of F+W Media, Inc.
Krause Publications • 700 East State Street • Iola, WI 54990-0001
715-445-2214 • 888-457-2873
www.krausebooks.com

To order books or other products call toll-free 1-800-258-0929
or visit us online at www.gundigeststore.com

ISBN-13: 978-1-4402-4061-4
ISBN-10: 1-4402-4061-2

Cover Design by Dave Hauser
Designed by Tom Nelsen
Edited by Corrina Peterson

Printed in the United States of America

10 9 8 7 6 5

Dedication

To Gail Pepin, producer of the ProArms Podcast … my girlfriend, shooting partner, and Adult Supervisor, without whom this book would have taken a lot longer to put together.

Table of Contents

Foreword

– by Atty. Jeffrey Weiner, former president, National Association of Criminal Defense Lawyers

In all professions requiring high levels of specialization, there are those who "talk the talk" and then there are those who "walk the walk." Massad Ayoob is unquestionably among the rare few who fall in the latter category.

If you carry, be competent with your gun. You don't need to be able to shoot this perfect qualification score with a Glock 30 and 45 hardball, but you want to come as close as you can. Confidence and competence intertwine, says Ayoob.

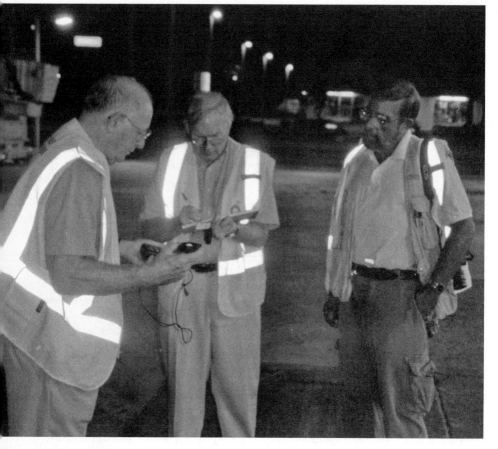

Ayoob, right, observes as lighting experts determine ambient light at a crime scene. This could be a critical element for the jury to weigh.

Massad Ayoob is the real McCoy. I know. I trained with him for years and I survived a gunfight because of his teaching and training. (More about that later...)

Having attended college, law school, and dozens of legal courses and seminars, both as a student and teacher, I have seen many people instruct. Simply put, Mas Ayoob is the best teacher and instructor I have ever learned from. Mas Ayoob is extremely knowledgeable – just ask anyone in the profession of firearms. Mas is a top shooter and true expert in all the mental and physical aspects relating to weapons.

Mas is a superb lecturer and writer. In fact, having read gun publications for almost four decades, I often shake my head in disbelief when I see how other "gun writers" essentially take Massad's comments and even his phrases, as well as his teachings, an re-phrase them in an attempt to use them as their own.

I smile each time I think of my training with Mas in weapons retention and disarm techniques. I vividly recall how, in each class, he would select the biggest, toughest student and say to him, "I am little and weak and you are big and strong." Mas would hand him a replica of the gun that the student carried and would tell him to grip the gun any way he wished and to hold that gun as tightly as if he had just drawn it in a threatening situation.

Then, Mas would tell the student that he was going to take the weapon away from him – so there would be no surprise. Usually, the student would laugh as he firmly gripped the gun with both hands. Mas would ask, "Are you ready?" And when the student acknowledged that he was, Mas proceeded to disarm him within about two seconds. I witnessed this over and over, even when the students were highly trained police officers or Federal agents (who were smart enough to attend Mas's courses at their own expense).

I learned handgun retention techniques that work in the real world, and had the pleasure of listening to Mas's lectures and answers to questions on virtually every aspect of self defense using handguns, Kubotans, knives, long guns, and other weapons.

Several years ago, Mas and I, along with two other folks, were panelists in a video produced by the American Bar Association's American Law Institute. The video was for lawyers and judges and the topic was the judicious use of deadly force. The video has been played around the country and has been widely used as an educational source. Mas is not a lawyer, but he is extremely knowledgeable about the law in this area.

With Mas's experience and qualifications, as a champion shooter – a police captain and a highly-qualified expert witness – I can't think of anyone better to write the book which you are about to read.

I speak from first-hand knowledge of Mas's credentials as an expert witness. I am a Board-certified criminal trial lawyer, a former president of the Na-

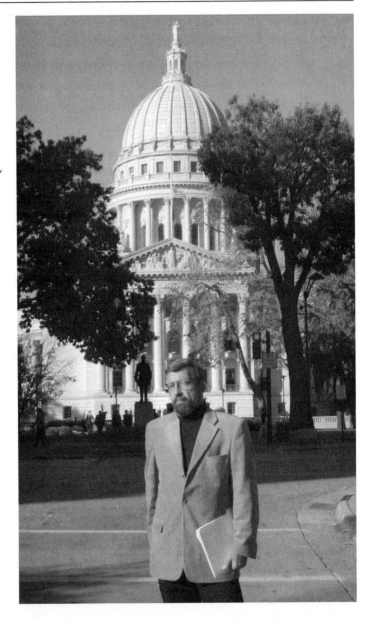

Where the laws aren't right, work for change! Ayoob leaves Wisconsin State House in Madison after testifying for shall-issue concealed carry. Bill passed Legislature, but when anti-gun governor vetoed it, gun owners' civil rights forces fell one vote short of over-ride. Wisconsin later passed shall-issue carry, however.

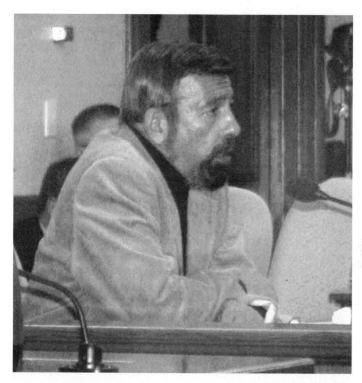

Ayoob testifies on behalf of shall-issue concealed carry legislation at a State House. If we don't fight for our rights, he warns, we'll lose them.

tional Association of Criminal Defense Lawyers, and a practicing criminal defense lawyer for forty years. My clients and I have benefited from Mas's expertise in several high profile, murder, shooting, and self defense cases through the years. When I need an expert witness whom I know has rock-solid credentials and credibility and who is untouchable under cross-examination by prosecutors, I call Massad. He is "The Man."

So, when Mas asked me to write this foreword, I immediately accepted. I am genuinely honored by his request.

Okay, I promised details of why I so fervently believe in Massad's training. In 1991, my former wife (who also trained with Mas) and I drove home with another couple returning from a wedding party at a fancy hotel in Miami. Everyone was dressed up for the occasion. I wore a tuxedo and a SIG P220 (.45 caliber) in a Milt Sparks's Summer Special holster (under my cummerbund!).

When we arrived at my home, my former wife and I exited the car. As we said "goodnight," my ex-wife yelled, "Home invaders!" and she dove for cover under the car. I was in front of the car and saw a tall man with a ski mask running toward the rear of the car that my law partner and his wife were still in. The gunman held a semi-automatic handgun in what was essentially an isosceles position aimed directly at me.

Thanks to my training, I immediately drew my SIG and fired first, over the roof of the car I was facing as he stopped behind the car. The violent attacker got the surprise of his life when I fired my .45 directly at him. He returned fire with what we later learned was a 9mm.

Whether I actually hit him is not known, but he spun around and crouched and stumbled into the getaway car, which was waiting and then pulled up to get him after the shots were fired. And that was it. It was over.

No time to think – only time to react. No time to retrieve a gun from an ankle holster or a "man purse" or briefcase. All the training and hours of practice kicked in, and it was over in an instant.

None of us were hurt. The police recovered the 9mm bullet from the dashboard of my law partner's vehicle (who, along with his wife, wisely ducked down as they saw me draw my weapon). The brand new Lexus (which he had picked up that afternoon) had a cracked rear windshield where the 9mm bullet had entered. The 9mm had then traveled forward, hit the front windshield and ricocheted into its final resting place, the dashboard.

When it was all over and the police finally left my home in the early hours of the morning, I made three calls: one to Mas, one to John Farnam and one to

Quique Fernandez. I thanked them for saving four lives that night. Had it not been for their excellent training, for which I was and am so grateful, the outcome would certainly have been different.

If it sounds like I'm a huge fan of Massad Ayoob, it is because I am. After all, because of my training with him, I am here to write this. And, after forty years as a practicing criminal defense attorney, I know that what Mas says, teaches, and writes is the best, state of the art knowledge you can get.

I would be remiss if I did not mention that it is essential that every gun owner make contact with a

trained and gun-knowledgeable, experienced criminal defense attorney so that, if the unthinkable happens, you will have someone who knows you ready to take your call and advise you *before* you talk with police.

Jeff Weiner, Former President, National Association of Criminal Defense Lawyers www.jeffweiner.com

So, read and enjoy this and all of Massad Ayoob's books – he is an excellent writer – and feel good about what you will have learned. You never know when your life could depend on it.

All the best, and stay safe.

– Jeff

Acknowledgements

I cannot list all the attorneys, judges, law professors and master police investigators with whom I've worked and from whom I've learned over the decades without forgetting a name and hurting some feelings. But a piece of each of them is in the book you hold in your hands, and I profoundly thank them all for the experience and hard-earned wisdom they have shared, to make this book a reality.

– Massad Ayoob

Chapter 1:

Introduction

My first book on use of deadly force by the private citizen in defense of self and others came out in 1980. The title was *In the Gravest Extreme: the Role of the Firearm in Personal Protection*. It has been a bestseller ever since, and remains available through Police Bookshelf, PO Box 122, Concord, NH 03302. Many have been kind enough to call it "the authoritative text" in its field.

The book you now hold in your hand was not written to replace *In the Gravest Extreme*, but to augment it. Deadly force is one of the most mature bodies of law that we have, and there is relatively little in it that significantly changes over time.

Author, 3rd from left, at the scene of a shooting involving the three policemen shown in photo.

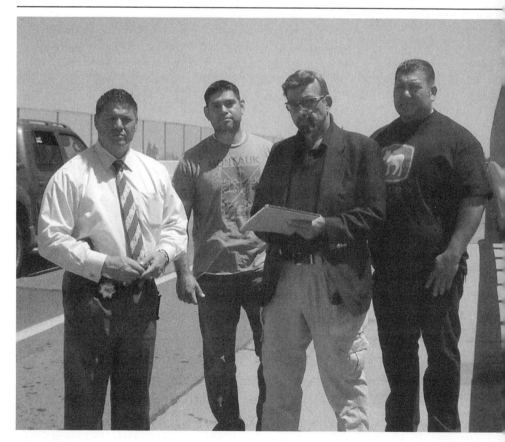

Since writing that book, I've been able to gather more research and experience. I've been an expert witness in weapons and deadly force cases both criminal and civil for three and a half decades now. Any veteran attorney will tell you that law school teaches you law, but experience teaches you trial tactics. It is from that experience that many of the lessons shared here have been drawn.

> "Any veteran attorney will tell you that law school teaches you law, but experience teaches you trial tactics."
>
> 🟅🟅

Author, right, prepares for direct testimony by defense attorney John Colley, left. The defendant was acquitted in the criminal trial over a fatal self-defense shooting.

That experience between books has included nineteen years as chair of the Firearms Committee of the American Society of Law Enforcement Trainers, eleven years on the Advisory Board of the International Law Enforcement Edu-

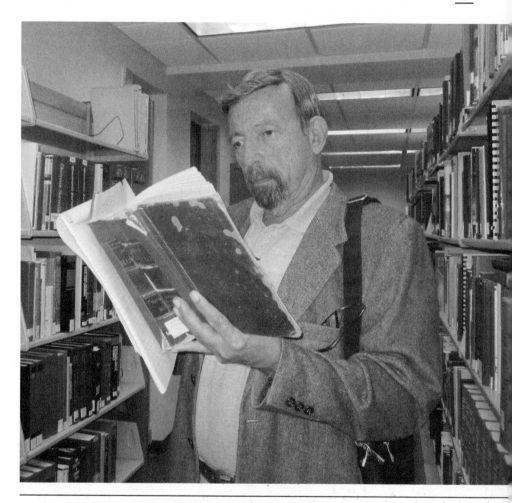

cators and Trainers Association, and presenting at regional, national, and international seminars of the International Association of Law Enforcement Firearms Instructors. I've attended several advanced homicide investigation and officer-involved shooting investigation courses, and taught at some of both. Part of my teaching load includes Continuing Legal Education courses for practicing attorneys doing firearms and use of force cases. Since writing *In the Gravest Extreme*, I founded Lethal Force Institute in 1981, and taught there through 2009, after which I established Massad Ayoob Group (http://massadayoobgroup.org), through which I now teach nationwide on related topics. My time carrying a badge is now at four decades, all in a part-time but fully-sworn and -empowered capacity.

Author has spent a substantial part of his life in law libraries absorbing and deciphering deadly force law.

Author's first book on this topic, In the Gravest Extreme, *remains in print.*

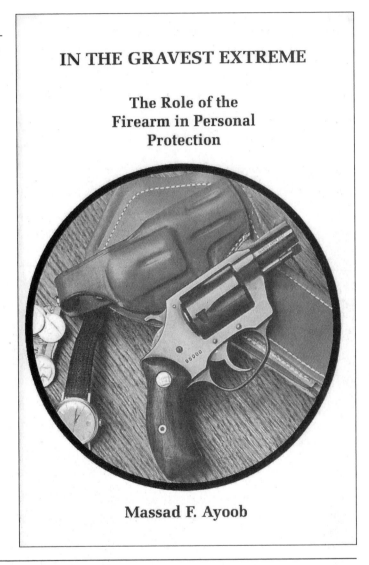

IN THE GRAVEST EXTREME

The Role of the
Firearm in Personal
Protection

Massad F. Ayoob

There have been changes in some jurisdictions' laws as regards the Stand Your Ground and Castle Doctrine principles, but while these changes have been hugely controversial, they have also been very widely misunderstood. As we'll discuss in these pages, once we get past the misunderstandings there's not anything of substance that has changed all that much.

In the areas of gun laws, as opposed to self-defense laws, there certainly *have* been changes. At the time I wrote *In the Gravest Extreme*, there were seven states in the USA where there was absolutely no provision at law for the private citizen to legally carry a concealed handgun in public; now, there are none. In 1980, most jurisdictions offering carry permits were "may issue," meaning that the issuing authorities could pretty much grant or deny the permits at their own discretion. In many places, "may issue" came to be a code for "we'll issue you the permit if you're white, male, rich, and politically connected." Today,

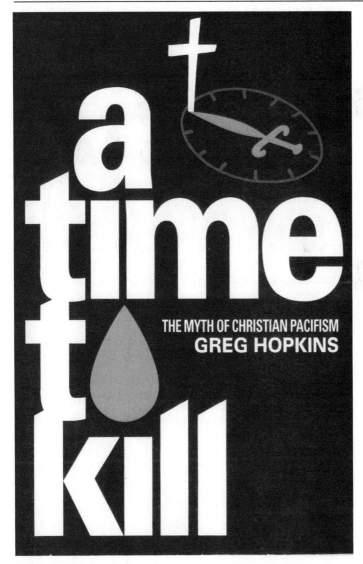

For devout people troubled by the idea of using deadly force in self defense, the excellent book A Time To Kill *explains why it is justified in the* Scriptures.

the majority of the states are "shall issue." This has come about through reform legislation that mandates the issuing authorities to grant permits to all law-abiding private citizen applicants who meet certain simple requirements. Back in those days, there were only two total reciprocity states, Indiana and Michigan, where a permit from another state was recognized there; today, reciprocity is *vastly* wider. There was only one state, Vermont, where a permit wasn't even needed to carry loaded and concealed in public; people were merely forbidden to do so if they had a criminal record, were adjudicated mentally incompetent, or could be shown to be doing so for malicious purposes. At this writing, Vermont has been joined by Alaska and Arizona in permitless carry, and by Wyoming, which limits it to Wyoming residents.

> "While that decade-long exercise in futility is thankfully past at this writing, such limits remain on the books in several states."

Gun laws have come a long way for armed citizens. But there have also been setbacks. I can't think of a jurisdiction that had magazine capacity limits when I wrote *In the Gravest Extreme*. From 1994 through 2004 our country lived with the Clinton Assault Weapons ban that limited new magazines to ten-round capacity. While that decade-long exercise in futility is thankfully past at this writing, such limits remain on the books in several states. In my opinion this can hamper the defensive capability of law-abiding armed citizens in general, and the physically challenged among them, in particular.

It's been a long ride, and a most instructive one. I've been able to learn a lot, and I'm honored to be able to share some of that learning with you here.

— Massad Ayoob
June, 2014

Chapter 2:
Standards

If forty-some years working and teaching in the justice system has taught me anything, it is this: If you act to the standards by which you know you will be judged, you should not be found wanting in the judgment.

No two use of force incidents will be exactly the same in every respect. There is a virtually infinite potential for branching of circumstances. Because of this, the courts will hold us to standards, to a formula if you will. For the same reasons, it behooves all of us to use a formula to analyze each situation we face to determine whether lethal force is justified.

No matter how justified the shooting was, some will mourn the slain criminal and seek revenge in court. Here, from one of author's cases years after the shooting, is a shrine to a man who died trying to kill a cop.

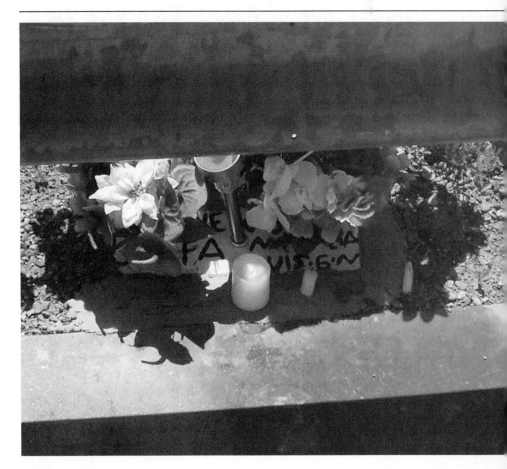

Lethal force (or deadly force; the terms are interchangeable) is that degree of force which a reasonable and prudent person would consider capable of causing death or great bodily harm. Various laws use the terminology "great bodily harm," "grave bodily harm," "serious bodily harm," etc.; the easiest way to remember it in layman's terms is "crippling injury."

The set of circumstances that justifies the use of deadly force is a *situation of immediate danger of death or great bodily harm to oneself or other innocent persons.* Since deadly force is normally only allowed as a last resort, the danger should be otherwise unavoidable and not created by the defender himself. This brings in an element called *preclusion,* which can vary according to jurisdiction and circumstances, and will be discussed separately in this book.

Warren on Homicide is widely considered the "bible" of homicide law.

Part of gun owner's responsibility is keeping weapons secure from unauthorized hands. However, quick release feature of many gun safes allows door to pop quickly...

That situation of immediate danger of death or crippling injury is normally determined by the simultaneous presence of three criteria. Different schools use different terminology, but the most widely used and court-proven standard has been in use for decades: *ability/opportunity/jeopardy.* "Ability" means that the assailant possesses the power to kill or cripple. "Opportunity" means he is capable of immediately

...and put the already-loaded weapon into an AUTHORIZED hand in time to interdict a home invasion.

Experience in court has taught author, "If you act to the standard by which you know you will be judged, you should not be found wanting in the judgment."

employing that power. "Jeopardy" means that his actions and/or words indicate to a reasonable, prudent person that he intends to do so and is about to do so. We will discuss each of these in great detail in this book.

Throughout, the law-abiding armed citizen must maintain *the mantle of innocence*. Think of the mantle of innocence as a legal cloak that shields the wearer from successful accusation of wrong-doing. The defender must not have

> *Think of the mantle of innocence as a legal cloak that shields the wearer from successful accusation of wrong-doing.*
>
> **"**

provoked the encounter, must not have started the fight, or an element of guilt and wrong-doing will accrue. If it lay within the defender's power to end the argument or abjure from the conflict, but instead he "kept the ball rolling" and things predictably escalated, he may very likely be held to have been at least partially at fault.

Those who don't know their rights to self-defense, or are unprepared and unequipped to defend themselves, can end up here.

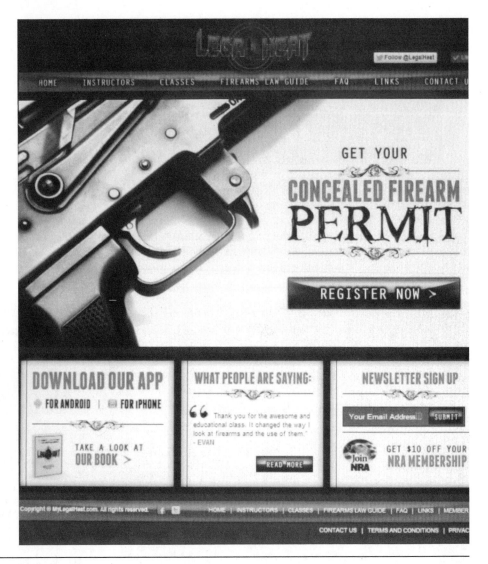

Know the laws where you go. This Legal Heat app is useful for checking that on handheld electronic devices.

Some states, but not all, have provisions for *excusable homicide* as well as *justifiable homicide*. In essence, a finding of excusable homicide means that the deceased probably shouldn't have been killed, but any reasonable and prudent person under identical circumstances would likely have made the same mistake as the person who killed him. By contrast, a finding of justifiable homicide says in essence that the person who killed the deceased acted correctly in doing so. In either case, the person who is responsible for the killing is held harmless.

Author's CLE teaching partner Jim Fleming, a veteran criminal defense lawyer, notes sagely, "You don't have to like reality, but you do have to face it."

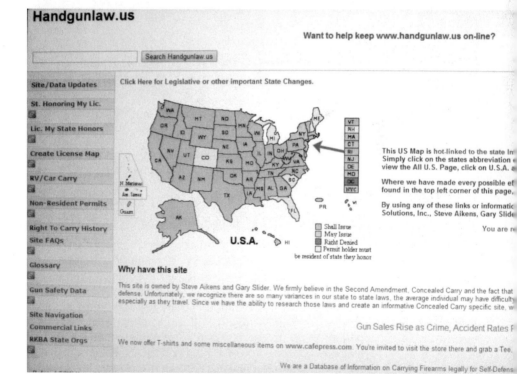

Website handgunlaw.us is author's favorite internet site for up to date state-by-state gun laws, including reciprocity.

Seasoned criminal defense lawyer Jim Fleming tells a class of attorneys how to handle a deadly force case.

We must have *reasonable fear* of death or grave bodily harm when we employ this level of force. Reasonable fear is starkly distinct from what the law calls *bare fear,* which never justifies harming another. Bare fear is naked panic, a blind and unreasoning fear. It is understood that when panic comes in, reason departs. The necessary reasonable fear doesn't mean you're soiling your pants or running away screaming; reasonable fear is simply that apprehension of danger which any reasonable, prudent person would experience if they were in the same situation as you, knowing what you know at the time.

General Rules of Engagement

Each state has its own statutes and codes, colloquially known as "black letter law." The laws are interpreted through the prism of case law, decisions by appellate courts which essentially nail down the fine points. Some of the clearest, most easily understood legal definitions and interpretations may be found in the given state's recommended jury instructions on the various issues. All of these may be researched at a legal library. In every county seat, at or near the county courthouse, you will find a legal library that is open to the public. The legal librarians, I've found as a rule, are delighted to help ordinary citizens look up these things.

Much – but not all—about deadly force law can be learned on-line.

Lawyer, police chief, and tactician Jeff Chudwin reminds his students, "You don't have to be right, you have to be reasonable."

Because ours is the most mobile society on Earth, we are constantly moving between jurisdictions. No lawyer can memorize the vastness of The Law in its entirety; that's why every law office has its own legal library. No police officer can memorize them all; that's why the patrol car has a mobile data terminal with the capability of looking things up. It follows that the law-abiding armed citizen can't hold all the laws in his head, either. For that reason, in this book as in my classes, I teach generic principles that are common to the law of all fifty states.

Now, let's move forward and examine these matters in greater detail.

Chapter 3:
The Ability Factor

In this context, *ability* means *your assailant possesses the power to kill, or to inflict crippling injury.* This power most obviously takes the form of a weapon, but it also may manifest as something called disparity of force. Let's look at weapons first.

A gun, obviously, is a deadly weapon. So is a bow and arrow. So is a bludgeon, whether it was designed to be a club or is some ordinary object being used as a makeshift striking weapon. So, of course, is a knife, a sword, an ice-pick, a razor, a broken bottle, or any other edged or pointed object which can be used to stab and/or slash.

The Opponent's Gun

How could opposing counsel ever allege that the gun your attacker was wielding or reaching for *wasn't* a deadly weapon? As counterintuitive as such an allegation might seem, it crops up all the time. "The gun wasn't loaded, so you weren't in danger, ergo it wasn't really self-defense when you shot him." "The gun in the hand of the deceased wasn't a *real* gun, so shooting him wasn't justified."

The law doesn't see it that way. The reasonable and prudent person is not Superman and does not have x-ray vision. He or she has no way of knowing whether the gun is loaded. In one case in which I testified, the defendant was charged with murder for shooting a man who, in a state of screaming rage, pulled a 9mm semiautomatic pistol on him. The

Photographed in evidence, this knife was used to attempt to slash a policeman to death. It's wielder was killed, justifiably, by police gunfire.

defendant drew his own nine-shot 9mm, and had to empty it into the attacker before the latter fell and dropped his weapon. The dead man's unfired pistol turned out to have a full magazine but an empty firing chamber, and the prosecution tried mightily to use that fact to convince the jury that the defendant was not in real danger and therefore could not be justified in shooting.

In addition to pointing out that the defendant could not possibly have known that his opponent's chamber was empty, the defense attorney used me as an expert witness to show the jury that the assailant could have racked the slide of his pistol and fired in a fraction of a second. Nonetheless, the exoneration of the defendant took a long and arduous court battle.

For a very long time now, toy guns and Airsoft guns have been manufactured to so closely replicate real guns that they can't be distinguished from the genuine article without detailed examination. When things happen quickly in the real world, even in broad daylight, it is no trick to show the jury or the grand jury that these realistic toys look exactly like the real thing. When the incident occurs in poor light, as is often the case, it is even more likely that no reasonable person could have been able to tell the unshootable "clone gun" from the deadly genuine article. This does not, however, keep clueless people and those with certain agendas from organizing protest marches and orchestrating a blizzard of letters to the prosecutor's office demanding criminal charges against the man who "shot the poor guy who only had a toy."

After the toy industry agreed to make toy guns transparent or brightly colored, or at least put a Day-Glo™ orange tip on the barrel so they hopefully wouldn't be mistaken for real ones, criminals and children alike proved to be adaptable. In both cases they simply removed the orange tip, or painted it over, or painted the whole toy gun flat black. Conversely, there are documented cases of criminals painting real guns orange, in hopes that police will think they're toys and hesitate to shoot, giving the criminals time to murder them and escape.

A few years ago I did a murder case in Baltimore. The shooting scene was a workshop that had been burgled many times. The owners were working late one night when they heard sounds indicating that it was happening again, and armed themselves. They soon found themselves facing an intruder in dim light, who turned toward them suddenly with what appeared to be a long-barreled revolver. Both shop owners opened fire simultaneously, one with a 12-gauge shotgun and the other with an HK pistol. Their double-0 buckshot and .45 caliber hollow points killed the intruder, who turned out to be armed with a long-handled hammer. He had been holding it by the head with its long handle protruding as he spun toward them. I was able to show in court how this looked exactly the same as a large revolver (I used a blue steel Smith & Wesson Model 29 .44 Magnum with eight and three-eighths inch barrel for the demonstration). The judge in the bench trial "got it." His verdict was not guilty for both defendants, on all counts.

You may even encounter the allegation that you were out of range of the opponent you shot, even though he had a real gun that was fully loaded. Many years ago the brilliant Miami attorney Jeff Weiner, who would later become president of the National Association of Criminal Defense Lawyers, hired me as expert witness on behalf of one of his clients charged with manslaughter. The deceased had the proverbial "record as long as his arm," if you unrolled the printout showing his arrest and conviction history, and on his last day on earth had decided to use a loaded, stolen gun to commit armed robbery on the wrong victim. He had terrorized the owner of a real estate office and his secretary, and when he fled the scene, the owner told the secretary to call the police and tell them what happened, because he was going after the robber. There was a 12-gauge pump gun he kept loaded in his office; he grabbed it, and sprinted out the door after the perpetrator.

A few blocks away, he caught up with the perpetrator and ordered him to halt. Instead of complying with that lawful order – the victim did, after all, have the right of citizen's arrest – he swung on his now-armed victim with the stolen gun. The victim did the logical thing: he fired. Twenty .30-caliber pellets from a 12 gauge Magnum #1 buckshot shell struck home simultaneously, and the gunman was killed instantly.

However, the shooting pushed some politically incorrect buttons. There had been a spate of killings of criminals by armed citizens in that community at the time this shooting went down, and the anti-gun newspaper was loudly crying for the anti-gun chief prosecutor to "do something" about this "outbreak of vigilante justice." The robber had been black (as was one of his victims, the secretary, whom the robber had called a "nigger" during the robbery), but the man who shot the robber was white. Because the gunman had been aiming over his shoulder at the robbery victim when the latter fired, the buckshot pellets had entered his body behind the lateral midline, so the prosecution characterized the armed robber as having been "shot in the back." Finally, the prosecution took the position that in chasing the felon, the victim had become the aggressor.

In the course of my sworn pre-trial deposition, it became apparent that the prosecution was going to make another huge issue out of the fact that some fifty feet separated the men at the time the fatal shot was fired. The assigned assistant state's attorney took the position that the defendant was out of range of the stolen, fully loaded snub-nose .38 with which the decedent was trying to shoot him. In deposition, I explained that both men were in range of each other, which was obviously how the armed robber had come to his death in the first place. The visibly skeptical prosecutor asked me how far away I would have to be to feel safe from a man armed with a short barrel .38. I resisted the urge to say, "Oh, maybe Kenosha, Wisconsin," and instead replied that I would consider myself in deadly danger from a man so armed even at 100 yards. Noticing my examiner furiously writing in his yellow legal pad at that point, I made a "note to self" to prepare demonstrative evidence.

Upon returning home, I went to a shooting range with a notary public and four exemplar snub-nose .38 Special revolvers, and set up Colt police targets depicting a human silhouette, at a hundred yards. With a Charter Arms Undercover revolver, a duplicate of the dead robber's stolen weapon, I was able to nail the silhouette with two of the five shots in the cylinder, and did the same with a similar five-shot .38, a Smith & Wesson Chief Special. With six-shot, two-inch barrel revolvers, I was able to hit with three out of six from a K-frame Smith & Wesson, and with all six shots from my wife's Colt Detective Special. Attorney Weiner shared this experiment with the prosecutor before trial, and for this and other reasons, the prosecutor's office decided that it would be inexpedient to take the case to trial.

It might be helpful, if you ever faced such a bogus allegation, for you to be able to articulate that you knew beforehand that there is a shooting sport, the International Metallic Handgun Silhouette Association, in which competitors in Production Class use handguns to shoot targets much smaller than a human being at distances up to 200 meters.

And never let those who judge you forget that since you were obviously close enough to your opponent to shoot him with your gun, he was, *ipso facto,* close enough to shoot you with his.

If, as demonstrated above, opposing counsel can make such far-fetched arguments as "the gun you faced wasn't deadly enough," what do you suppose they'll do if your opponent's weapon can be perceived as less lethal than yours?

The Dangerous Myth of Hierarchy of Lethality

We live in a world where the entertainment media and the news media alike have demonized the firearm as a frightening, high-efficiency killing machine. A myth has arisen that I call "hierarchy of lethality." It is the false belief that the firearm represents the nuclear level of hand-held weaponry, and is somehow more lethal than other deadly weapons. The general public sees the knife as something less: after all, they'll open their mail in the morning with something very much like your opponent's knife, and will slice the roast at dinner tonight with something virtually identical to the blade your opponent wields. Because it's an accoutrement of everyday life, they just don't see the knife as a weapon, even though they know cognitively that it can be turned from culinary aid to murder weapon in a heartbeat. An impact weapon, a "club"? Well, they may see that as even less deadly.

Now, the night comes when you are attacked by a homicidal perpetrator wielding bludgeon or blade. You are forced to shoot him in self-defense. I can almost guarantee where the subsequent attack on you is going to come from:

"He *only* had a knife!"

"He *only* had a baseball bat!"

Opposing counsel may attempt to paint you as the bully and coward who used a deadlier weapon than your assailant, and will attempt to convince the jury that your shooting of a man with "a less than lethal weapon" is unfair and therefore improper. Of course, this flies in the face of the legality of the matter, which is that within their range, the club and the knife are every bit as deadly as the gun…and, in some situations, can be deadlier.

Knife Lethality

I've been cross-trained with the knife, and over the years have had the privilege of having trained with some of the finest instructors in the field. That list includes Graciela Casillas, Michael deBethancourt, Marc Denny, the late Grandmaster Jim Morell, the late Grandmaster Remy Presas, the late Hank Reinhardt, Paul Vunak, and others. The experience left me with a very strong sense of just how destructive this simple, seemingly mundane tool can be.

A knife never jams. A knife never runs out of ammunition; you rarely see a gunshot murder victim who has been shot more than a few times, but any homicide investigator can tell you how common it is for the victim of a knife murder to bear twenty, thirty, or more stab and/or slash wounds. "A knife comes with a built-in silencer." Knives are cheap, and can be bought anywhere; there used to be a cutlery store at LaGuardia Airport, not far outside the security gates. There is no prohibition at law against a knife being sold to a convicted felon. Knives can be small and flat and amazingly easy to conceal.

Anywhere on the human body where you can take a pulse, the knife only has to slice a few millimeters in to cause exsanguination, or death by loss of blood: it will just have cut open an artery.

Common sense would tell you that a four-inch blade knife can only inflict a stab wound four inches deep, but in practical reality knife penetration is about twice that. Soft tissue compresses before the point of a knife: reach down to your own abdomen, and see how deeply you can press in. The two-inch blade can penetrate four inches into such parts of the body, the four-inch blade eight inches, etc.

Having been certified to teach disarming people of various weapons – gun, knife, club – I am convinced that the knife is the hardest to take away from another person. The gun projects its force in only one direction, so if you can control the barrel, you can keep it from hurting you as you twist it out of another person's hands. Against the stick, if

The knife can be deadlier than the gun, under some circumstances.

you simply grab it farther out than the other person is holding it, you're already ahead of the curve in taking it from
him, and if you can interdict the bludgeoner's arm or wrist
you've minimized the impact he can deliver with his club.
But where do you grab a knife without getting cut?

A gunshot has a finite amount of power in terms of the
wound it can create. The knife is limited only by the strength
and range of movement of the person wielding it. In all
these years of going to court in homicide cases and graduat-
ing many homicide investigation schools, I've never seen a
human being decapitated by a homicidal gunshot wound.
Decapitation by knife, however, is not terribly uncommon.
Anyone who has butchered animals on the family farm or
after a successful hunting trip can tell you that it takes only
a matter of seconds to cut the head entirely off the body of a
human size animal, such as a white-tail deer.

Impact Weapon Lethality

The club is the simplest and the crudest of deadly weapons, but that does not mitigate its lethality. It is also the most
readily available. In almost any fight in almost any environment, there is some object within reach which can be hastily
grabbed and used to bash another human being's brains out.
The death weapon may not have left its maker intended to
be a bludgeon, but any hard object with some mass to it can
be a makeshift bludgeon. The brick, the paperweight, and
almost anything it between can be "clubbed," or turned into
a striking instrument.

That seemingly harmless icon of innocent childhood,
the baseball bat, is a common tool of assault and murder.
Legend says notorious crime lord Al Capone used a ball bat
to murder two associates he no longer trusted.

Common tools turn into remarkably efficient death
weapons, some more readily than others. Police batons have
rounded surfaces in hopes of reducing fractures to underly-
ing bone and minimizing lacerations, while still delivering
a stunning impact to stop the recipient's physical assault.
Many common tools and other objects have rough, irregular
edges which are *conducive* to shattering bones and splitting
flesh. The common claw hammer is a particularly deadly
murder weapon. In blows to the head, it often punches
completely through the skull wall and into the soft, vulnerable brain tissue beneath. Hammer murderers have told in
their confessions how the hammer became stuck inside the
victim's skull so deeply that they had to step or even stomp

on the head to break the hammer free for the next blow. Crowbars are also associated with particularly destructive blunt force injuries. The list goes on.

Anyone would recognize a broken bottle held by its neck as a deadly, edged weapon. It's easy to miss the fact that an *unbroken* bottle, made of heavy glass, is more than sufficient to beat someone to death. If it is unopened and still full of liquid, it is all the more deadly once it is clubbed and turned to assaultive purpose.

Many years ago I took the Medico-Legal Investigation of Death class at the Metro-Dade (now Miami-Dade) Medical Examiner's Office. The legendary forensic pathologist Dr. Joe Davis was still the CME (Chief Medical Examiner) then, and indeed, was the man who had created that training program. At one point, the homicide investigators and forensic pathologists who were taking the class were asked to look at slides of certain injuries, and try to diagnose the cause.

One slide that came up on screen was a headless man whose neck came to a stop in a thick puddle of blood and brain matter spread flat across the kitchen floor. Hypotheticals abounded. "The stove exploded while he had his head in it?" "A hand grenade in his mouth?"

When we all gave up, Joe Davis said, "None of those things. I'll show you." He clicked the next slide up: a tiny woman five feet tall or less, weighing no more than a hundred pounds, her hair and clothing covered with gore. He clicked again: a claw hammer, thick with drying blood and hair and bits of brain matter. "She said she couldn't take his beatings anymore. She hit him in the head with the hammer. He fell to the floor. She was so afraid he'd get back to his feet and hurt her, that she hit him again, and again, and again..."

Like the knife, the bludgeon doesn't jam or run out of ammunition. The sound of the brutal blows it inflicts is louder than a knife piercing flesh, but is still much more quiet and

> *In a typical year, more people will be murdered with bludgeons than with so-called "assault rifles" in the United States. In one recent year, the FBI listed 323 people as killed with rifles of all types, including ordinary hunting rifles as well as "assault rifles." The same study showed **496** people killed with blunt objects such as hammers, bats, etc.*

stealthy than a gunshot. A cop or parole officer who finds a convicted felon carrying the readily available knife can arrest him for illegal possession; not so if the same convicted felon is carrying the classic heavy, ridged glass bottle of Coca-Cola™.

The "Unarmed Motorist"

There are out-of-control people in our society who use their vehicles as weapons. Police run across it more than ordinary citizens, but it can happen to anyone who becomes a victim of "road rage" or finds himself in the path of a criminal desperate to escape. It is not unknown for an angry spouse to use their vehicle as a death weapon and run over the partner who has incurred their rage.

If in your community tonight a violent criminal attempts to run down a police officer and is shot, it is all but guaranteed that tomorrow morning's newspaper will have a headline reading "Unarmed Motorist Shot by Police."

Unarmed? A full-size automobile traveling fifty miles an hour generates approximately half a million foot-pounds of energy. Far from being unarmed, the violent man who turns his automobile into a guided missile has armed himself with the most crushingly powerful of bludgeons. Deliberately driving at a person on foot is a serious crime, delineated in some jurisdictions as "assault with a deadly weapon, to wit, a motor vehicle." That angry spouse who runs over the significant other is culpable for murder in every jurisdiction.

I was in Austin, Texas, on the day in 2014 during the South by Southwest Festival when a suspect being pursued by police deliberately drove his vehicle into a large crowd of people. He killed two and injured twenty-three, and was charged with capital murder.

The United States is the world's most motorized nation. Our vehicles become extensions of our home in daily life, complete with cushioned "armchairs" and elaborate sound systems. Indeed, the laws of some states treat the vehicle as an extension of the home. We simply don't see ourselves as being armed during what may be hours a day when we hold a steering wheel in our hands. Thus, the "unarmed driver" meme is an easy sell to the general public and the jury pool. When a driver turns his car into a weapon and someone has to shoot him to stop him and prevent the death of themselves or another innocent person, it's going to take some logical explanation to educate a jury that at the moment he was killed, that rogue driver was in fact exerting unlawful deadly force with a terribly destructive weapon.

There is an interesting dynamic at play in auto-pedestrian assaults, and perhaps to some extent in all "road rage" incidents. Look to the movie "Aliens" which starred Sigourney Weaver. The athletic, six-foot-tall Weaver played a female astronaut in the future, doing constant battle with a huge and almost indestructible monster from another planet. To defeat the creature she gets inside a powerful robot designed for cargo loading, which allows her to equal the alien's greater power. In the fight that follows, she flings the monster into infinite space, winning the fight and saving the day.

That movie scene is an allegory to the mentality of the angry person who turns a vehicle into a weapon. Perhaps feeling inadequate and weak on their own, the vehicle becomes their powerful exoskeleton, vastly multiplying the force they can exert and the damage they can inflict.

Life imitates art, though art more often imitates life. We've all met the person who chooses a vehicle to make up for his perceived personal inadequacies. The man who chooses a "young" car when mid-life crisis hits. The man who sees himself as weak, and compensates with a "muscle car" or "monster truck." In the popular comic strip "Rose Is Rose," the title character is a meek and mild housewife who develops a Harley-riding biker chick persona as her fantasy alter ego, to become the strong woman who takes no crap from anyone.

In similar fashion, the angry person who turns his (or her) vehicle into a murder weapon is much like Sigourney Weaver's character donning the robot exoskeleton to fight the otherwise unbeatable space monster, or the bad guy in the Iron Man comics and movies who steals that title character's supercharged metal suit to become invulnerable and super-powerful, and crush his enemies.

But in this real-life scenario, the vehicle is the powerful exoskeleton, the super-suit…and in his distorted perception, you are the enemy he is trying to crush.

The word "crush" is not an exaggeration. Any pathologist, any trauma surgeon or emergency room professional, any firefighter or paramedic or police officer who has seen the result of an auto-pedestrian collision can describe to you the sort of human wreckage which ensues.

I have seen total decapitation, and heads and faces so horribly mangled that the victim's own mother would not be able to identify the corpse. I remember one young man whose head and facial features were compressed into a hideously distorted egg shape by the automobile tire that went over him and fatally crushed his brain. I've seen intestines and other internal organs that burst out of the body from the internal compression caused when vehicle struck victim. I've seen genitals torn away from the body by the brutal friction of the spinning tires that went over the front of the torso lengthways. The emergency services professionals cited above can tell you that the person on foot being "strained through the grille" of the car that hit him is not a figure of speech. It is not unknown to find bits of human flesh inside the grille and bumper and even the engine compartment of the automobile or truck that struck the hapless pedestrian.

When this kind of murder attempt goes down, I've found more often than not that the intended victim will later say something like, "The car became a thing that was trying to kill me." The vehicle looms so large, it dominates the con-sciousness of the person at whom it is rushing. If the victim cannot simply move sideways and evade, instinct takes over and tells the intended victim to fight back with the most powerful weapon available. If that weapon is a firearm, it is natural to expect the victim to resort to it.

A vehicle bearing down on you is like a huge, dangerous animal charging you. To stop it by shooting it, you can't aim for its body or its leg; that won't stop it in time. Any experi-enced hunter of game would tell you to aim for the brain. On, say, a Cape Buffalo, your hunting guide would tell you to aim into the skull just below the boss of the horns, because that's where its brain is located. When the dangerous thing charg-ing you is a motor vehicle, its "brain" – the thing guiding and controlling its charge – is located behind the steering wheel. Therefore, with the strongest of logic, the intended victim of the run-down attempt shoots at the driver.

Why not simply duck to the side? This theory was actu-ally the paradigm in the early 1970s when I first became a sworn police officer and law enforcement instructor in firearms and deadly force. The theory was that gunfire might kill the driver but could not stop the oncoming vehicle, so the officer should duck to the side. The theory also held that a wounded driver might go a mile away and then pass out from his wound, sending the vehicle out of control and endangering the public.

Over the years and the decades, this theory changed on both counts, based on collective experience. Vehicles are surprisingly nimble, particularly motorcycles. It is not easy to maneuver out of the path of the oncoming vehicle when its driver has the power to "track" you with a touch of the steering wheel or handlebars, but neutralizing him with gunfire prevents him from doing that. Indeed, even if the bullet only wounds the driver or misses him entirely, his instinct is often to veer away from you, the source of the pain. Moreover, in most cases when the driver is neutralized, his vehicle comes to a halt in a relatively short distance.

Because the public, many plaintiff's lawyers, and even some prosecutors do not see the motor vehicle as a weapon, these cases often go to trial, if only in civil court. One day in Miami, a two-time loser for drug dealing named Clement Anthony Lloyd was fleeing from the police on his high-powered motorcycle, one cargo pocket of his pants filled with the cocaine he was selling, and the other with the cash he'd received from what he had sold that day. He wound up being pursued by police through the Overtown district of the city. A Miami PD field training officer (FTO) named William Lozano was standing beside the street taking a crime report from a citizen with his rookie partner Dawn Campbell when they heard sirens approaching, and what was described by multiple witnesses as the "howling sound" of a motorcycle revving at red line. Stepping out into the street to see what was going on, Officer Lozano was instantly confronted by the onrushing motorcycle, whose driver saw him and turned deliberately toward him on course to run him down.

There was no time to run. As he desperately tried to turn away, in a movement witnesses described as similar to a bullfighter's *passata soto,* Lozano reflexively drew his department issue Glock 17 and fired a single shot. The bullet struck Lloyd in the head, killing him instantly. The vehicle traveled about a hundred yards and crashed head on into a Buick containing two felony suspects who had just been released from jail. (Welcome to Overtown.) While neither of those men were seriously injured, the crash killed a young man who was riding pillion behind Lloyd on the motorcycle, a tragic corollary casualty unusual for this sort of incident.

The officer had not seen the young man because he was directly behind the operator, who was hurtling the bike toward him, and he experienced the tunnel vision effect that is so common in life-threatening encounters. The bike was a Kawasaki Ninja 600 café racer. The crashed bike was found to be in third gear, and the 115 grain 9mm Silvertip bullet from the officer's weapon had killed Lloyd so quickly he could not have changed gears. When Lozano was charged with manslaughter and I was hired as an expert witness by his defense lawyers, Roy Black and Mark Seiden, one of the first things I did was call Kawasaki. Their engineers told me that if their Ninja 600 was "howling at red line" at the top of third gear, it would have been doing approximately 93 miles an hour.

Florida v. Lozano went through two tortuous trials. During the second, my suitcases were packed in the front hall and I was about to drive to the airport to fly to Miami to testify, when I received a noontime phone call from Mark Seiden. I wouldn't be needed, he told me, with an incongruously cheerful tone in his voice. When I asked why, he said "Turn on Court TV after the lunch break." That channel was broadcasting the trial live, in real time.

I watched on the tube as the lead prosecutor, a highly competent trial advocate, told the court "The state rests." At that point the cameras cut to Roy Black at the defense table, who stood up and said with a big, confident smile, "Your Honor, given that the state has presented no case, the defense rests also."

It was a stunning courtroom ploy, rather like a jump-spinning back kick in a karate tournament. You're either going to score a spectacular knockout, or you're going to fall ignominiously on your butt.

In this case, it was a spectacular knockout. The jury soon returned with a total acquittal on all counts.

I was retained in another case of a similar nature in Sanford, Florida. A violent teenager had driven his car savagely at two private security guards, both of whom drew their 9mm pistols and fired, killing him. The cross-racial shooting of a teenager created great furor in the community, and a cry for the blood of those who pulled the trigger, and a homicide charge resulted. Attorney Chris Ray hired me as an expert witness. The prosecution objected furiously, and I had to go to Sanford for a hearing before the trial judge, in which I laid out the testimony I planned to give. The judge determined that it would be of value to the triers of the facts, and ruled that I would be allowed to testify.

On the day the defense was scheduled, I was already in the courtroom. Usually, all witnesses are sequestered outside the courtroom until they have testified, but apparently the prosecution saw no point in arguing when Ray asked if I could be present earlier. The prosecution rested. It was just before lunch. Before the court went into recess, Ray stood and performed a common ritual of defense attorneys: he made a motion to dismiss on the grounds that the state had not proven its case. This is normally a *pro forma* gesture, done if nothing else in hopes of perhaps preserving some grounds for appeal if a conviction results. But Chris Ray didn't make it as a routine motion. He made it as one of the most eloquent, heartfelt arguments I've ever heard in a courtroom, detailing every flaw in the state's theory and every reason why the bullets fired by his client, Billy Swofford, were fired with absolute justification. The judge said he would take it under consideration, which was surprising; as routinely as it's made, the motion to dismiss is just as routinely rejected by the bench. The judge declared recess and we all went to lunch.

When we returned, the courtroom and the halls were literally *swarming* with Seminole County deputies. I heard someone ask, "Has there been a bomb threat or something?" But what went through my own mind was, "Oh, my God – *he's going to grant it!*"

And he did. In a no-nonsense voice and in no uncertain terms, the judge made it clear that while the decedent was a fleeing felon in any case, his actions in running the car toward the security officers could only be construed as an attempt to murder them, and that his death at their hands was absolutely justifiable. He then dismissed the case with prejudice, meaning that it could never be brought again.

While most such cases involve police (or security, as the one above), it is not unknown for them to involve private citizens who fire in self-defense.

While there can always be negative outcomes, acquittal seems to be by far the most common outcome when the shooting of an "unarmed motorist" who attempts murder by motor vehicle meets death by defensive gunfire. Unfortunately, requiring a trial to sort out the facts and achieve this just outcome also seems to be "par for the course," if only in civil court in lieu of criminal court.

Less Lethal Weapons

When a police chief pinned my first badge on me in 1972, what we now call "intermediate force options" such as the police baton were referred to as "non-lethal weapons." If it seems unfair that such a thing would be "a deadly weapon, to wit a bludgeon" when wielded against an ostensibly unarmed man by a private citizen, but was merely a tool of arrest in similar circumstances for the sworn officer, it was because there were differences in purpose and application. "Clubbing a man about the head and shoulders" does indeed constitute potentially lethal brute force. Police have in modern times been taught to strike at motor nerve complexes, hit the limbs to reduce mobility and "defang the snake," or thrust into the abdomen to fold the suspect, take his wind, and reduce his ability to continue fighting police. There was also the element of necessary force vis-à-vis equal force: the civilian was seen at law as needing only sufficient force to make an assailant stop attacking him, while the officer had a sworn duty to overpower all resistance, pursue if necessary, completely overpower and capture and manacle and transport the suspect. This being a much more difficult sequence of events to accomplish than merely convincing the opponent to abjure from the conflict, greater latitude in the use of that intermediate force was granted to the law enforcement officer.

Over the years, the terminology changed from "non-lethal" to "less-lethal" or "less than lethal." The reason was simple: in real world application, intermediate force weapons weren't always non-lethal. A fight is generally a rapid swirl of movement involving at least two people. Sometimes, for example, a swing of the baton intended for a suspect's shoulder or upper arm might hit the rounded deltoid muscle and skid off into the head as the suspect simultaneously tried to duck away from the stick. The result could be a blow to the temple with enough power to fracture the skull, and/or cause permanent or even fatal brain injury.

The same dynamic was seen with other intermediate force options as police technology advanced. Chemical Mace™ came out in the 1960s and was at first seen by the public as "a magic spray that makes the bad guys go away." It was essentially tear gas delivered by aerosol, and teaching protocol was to spray it at the offender's chest and allow the vapors to rise to his eyes or nostrils. This proved to be particularly spotty in its performance. Lawmen of the day were prone to comment bitterly that it only worked on cops and victims. In later iterations, the manufacturer issued the product with a warning to the effect of "Caution: this substance may not be effective on those under the influence of drugs, alcohol, or state of rage." (My reaction was, "Who the hell *else* would we ever have to Mace?")

Aerosol sprays got better, and soon we had pepper spray, known colloquially as OC for its active ingredient, oleoresin capsicum. It worked vastly better than the original tear gas sprays, but there were still some people who could resist its effects. Famed police martial arts instructor Phil Messina tes-

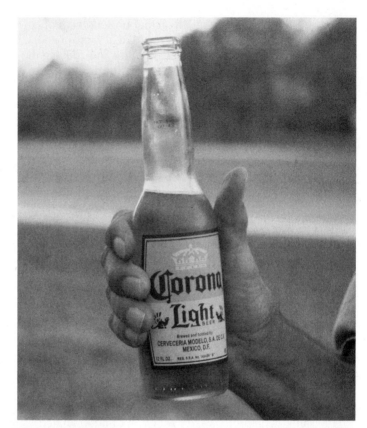

Tres cervezas. *What something is may be defined by what is done with it. In most settings, this is just a tasty bottle of beer…*

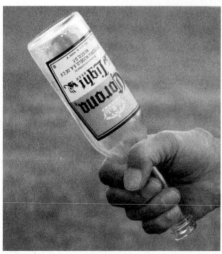

…but held like this, it can become a deadly bludgeon…

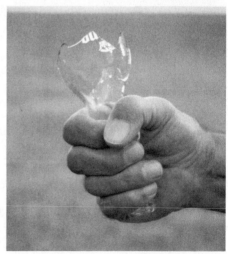

…and in this case, a lethal edged weapon.

tified in a case in the Pacific Northwest where pepper spray failed an officer so badly that the man he sprayed beat him to death with a chunk of wood. Most police departments soon learned that since their own people could be affected by the spray, they had to learn to fight through those effects, and it became a standard part of training. The cops came to realize that if *they* could fight through it, so could their criminal opponents on the street.

But, more to the point of the topic at hand, there were a proportionally tiny number of deaths involving those sprays. Usually, the victim was an asthmatic or a sufferer of some other serious respiratory disease who, unknown to the officers applying the spray, could not take that level of interference with breathing. When electronic restraint devices (ERDs) typified by the super-popular TASER came out, there was the occasional death. Most commonly, medico-legal investigation has determined that the cause of such deaths was a usually-drug-induced phenomenon known as excited delirium, though here and there a medical examiner did attribute the death in question to the TASER. (By the way, yes, it's TASER in all caps. It's an acronym for Thomas A. Swift's Electronic Rifle, believe it or not. Never let it be said that law enforcement and the industries which serve it are *totally* devoid of whimsy.)

So, we see why the "non-lethal" terminology went by the board in favor of "less lethal" or "less than lethal." Which brings us to the question: *What level of force may the private citizen use against a criminal who attacks them with intermediate force weapons?*

To answer, we must first parse the weapons involved. We have to separate out the striking instruments from the aerosol incapacitants and electronic restraint devices. We have already established that any sort of club or bludgeon, even a makeshift one, is considered a deadly weapon when in the hand of a law-breaking assailant, and one that absolutely creates the Ability factor in terms of the Ability/Opportunity/Jeopardy triad that makes deadly force justifiable in response.

Can a similar approach be taken when the robber or rapist is armed with Mace™ or OC spray, or with an electronic "stun gun"? The answer seems to be a qualified "Yes," and it comes more from Attorneys General at the state level than from case law.

Almost as soon as the incapacitating sprays came out, cops asked, "What do we do if the bad guy gets hold of our spray – or has his own – and sprays *us?"* This is a question street cops ask of their chief or department legal advisor, and it is a question that chiefs and legal advisors generally buck upstairs to their state's Attorney General. A State Attorney General is usually seen as the chief law enforcement officer of the entire state, and as far as cops are concerned, his opinion on the matter is very close to law. If I may be forgiven a comparison of the justice system with the Holy Trinity, a decision rendered by the Supreme Court of the United States is pretty much the word of God for practical law enforcement purposes. A ruling by a Federal Court of Appeals or a State Supreme Court may as well have come from Jesus Christ himself. By that analogy, an official opinion State Attorney General's Office carries the gravitas of a determination from the Holy Ghost.

Every such State Attorney General's opinion I've seen or heard of on the matter of responding to a criminal attacking with spray or stun gun is, "You can shoot him: it's a deadly force situation." The reason is that criminal use of something intended to render the recipient helpless creates an obviously reasonable belief that said criminal intends to do something nefarious to that recipient once the helplessness is achieved. Moreover, abuse of these tools can kill.

Yes, the incapacitating sprays are designed to be less than lethal, but they are designed to be used only until the suspect can no longer resist arrest. If the criminal sticks the spray dispenser in the victim's mouth and hoses it down his throat until it is empty, likelihood of death or grave permanent injury resulting is quite high for anyone. The manufacturers and instructors of the TASER would, I'm sure, be first in line to tie the noose around the neck of the abuser who held the device against the forbidden target of a person's head or cervical spine, and ran a constant series of drive stuns until the central nervous system was fried and irreparably damaged.

In 2013, at the height of public concern over group assaults on lone victims in violent flash mob attacks, and a "point 'em out, knock 'em out" game of violence that became popular among inner city youth, a teen with a stun gun attacked a victim with it. He suffered what I've come to call "sudden and acute failure of the victim selection process": His intended victim, licensed to carry, drew a Smith & Wesson .40 caliber pistol and shot him down. Not only did the armed citizen go uncharged, but the teenage assailant was convicted and sentenced to a year in jail, and publicly apologized to the man he had attacked.

Disparity of Force: The "Unarmed" Assailant

One of the least understood principles in deadly force law is that of *disparity of force*. It applies directly to the Ability factor in the Ability/Opportunity/Jeopardy equation.

Disparity of force is the principle that allows the victim, or the person defending the victim, to use lethal force against an unarmed person. It applies *only* when the ostensibly "unarmed" assailant has no "deadly weapon" *per se,* but within the totality of the circumstances has a physical/tactical advantage over the victim that is so great that if the assault continues, death or great bodily harm is likely to be suffered by said victim.

Disparity of force can take many forms. *Force of numbers* is one of the most common. A *significant disparity of size and strength* is another. *Male attacking female, adult violently attacking child,* and *able-bodied attacking the handicapped* also constitute disparity of force. So does *highly skilled hand-to-hand fighter attacking the less-skilled.* So does *position of disadvantage,* in which the law-breaking attacker has a huge tactical and/or physical advantage other than disparity of size, strength, or skill as the assault unfolds.

Because so few people among the general public, who constitute the jury pool, understand this – and because so many attorneys never even hear the term "disparity of force" in law school – it is important to discuss it here in detail.

Force of Numbers

The law has long since recognized that when two or more criminals attack a lone victim, their physical and tactical advantage is so great their single victim is likely to suffer death or grave bodily harm if the attack is not stopped immediately. (And, of course, the innocent victim has no prudent reason to believe that the attack *will* be stopped before that point by his or her violent assailants.)

A classic case in this vein was *Michigan versus Ossian Sweet,* in 1925. Dr. Sweet was a black physician in Michigan, in a time when segregation was law in the South, and "practice if not law" even in the North. He and his wife Gladys purchased a home in a Detroit neighborhood that was "all-white." Hellish racial animosity ensued, and rose to the level of deadly threat. On the day in question, Dr. Sweet had been so alarmed he had bought guns for the friends and relatives who came to his home to protect him. Hostile crowds formed, at first held back by local police. When the mob began to storm the house, first throwing rocks through the windows, the defenders inside opened fire. One white man was killed, and another wounded.

Murder charges resulted. Legendary attorney Clarence Darrow took the case for the defense. In the chain of trials that followed, all of the defenders were ultimately exonerated, either by verdicts of not guilty or by prosecutorial dismissal of charges.

Not long after this trial, the classic legal text *Warren on Homicide* appeared, in 1938. This was the authoritative text destined to become known as "The Bible of Homicide Law" among lawyers and judges. The author(s) made it clear that when an individual faced a mob bent on doing violence to him or his compatriots, each member of that mob shared the culpability of the entire organism of the mob…and, therefore, was equally and individually fair game for the defensive violence suffered at the hands of the lawful defender(s).

One would have thought that would have decided the issue…and one would be wrong. It has long been a societal norm in the entertainment media, from books to "moving pictures" to the entertainment and even news media of today that "only a cowardly murderer would shoot/stab/kill" an "unarmed man." We live in a society where media memes have so overpowered collective logic, and even long-established law and case law precedent, that it takes a full-blown trial for the truth to come out, and for law and justice to prevail.

Significant Disparity In Size and Strength, Which Favors the Assailant

The first and most obvious question is, "What exactly marks the borders of *significant?*" The answer is, in a buzzword of the Courts, it depends on "the totality of the circumstances."

In February of 2013, I testified in a first degree murder case in West Virginia, brought in as expert witness by Brian Abraham, a highly skilled defense attorney who had formerly been District Attorney in the jurisdiction where the shooting went down. In my continuing series "Ayoob Files" in American Handgunner magazine, where at press time my article on the case is still archived at http://americanhandgunner.com/fist-vs-gun-disparity-of-force/, at the request of the defendant I changed the names of the participants in the deadly fight to "Mr. Phist," the now-deceased attacker, and "Mr. Gunn," the defendant who shot him in defense of his own life and the lives of his wife and two little boys. To make a long story short, Mr. Phist was six-foot-three and Mr. Gunn had been told he weighed "300 to 350 pounds of solid muscle," and on the night in question, dressed in cold weather garb, "Phist" appeared to be all of that. "Gunn," by contrast, was an average size man.

Phist had threatened previously to "beat the life out of" Gunn, and when he showed up on Gunn's doorstep, the latter had the presence of mind to tell his wife to take the kids into another room, and tucked a Ruger P345 pistol into his waistband before he answered the door. (Arming himself would later be cited by arresting officer and prosecuting attorney alike as the "premeditation" element which justified a first degree murder charge. In court, I explained to the jury that the bailiff had armed himself with a .40 caliber pistol and the arresting officer who sat beside the prosecutor had armed himself with a Smith & Wesson .45, not because they intended to murder someone that day, but because they knew their duties might require them to defend innocent human lives, including their own…and the defendant had armed himself for the exact same reason, in light of his right to protect his own life, and his ethical duty to protect his wife and children from clear and present danger.)

Stepping out through the front door to talk to the man in hopes of calming his anger, Gunn was met by angry screams from his huge opponent, who soon repeated "I'll beat the life out of you" … and then proceeded to start to do exactly that. Phist landed a punch to the face so brutally powerful that it knocked Gunn's teeth loose and sent him rocking back, and knowing that this was his last chance to protect himself and his family, Gunn drew his .45 and fired as fast as he could pull the trigger. Not until his pistol had run empty to slide-lock did he realize that, in the dim light of a November evening, his opponent had turned and run…and then collapsed.

Several of the fatal bullets had entered behind lateral midline – "shot in the back" in the common parlance, yet another dynamic that the general public has been conditioned for centuries to associate with an innocent victim murdered by a vile killer who deserved severe punishment. I was able to explain the dynamics of that too, in the same way they are explained elsewhere in this book. There were other elements in play, but a key factor in the case was the unarmed man being shot by a man with "a .45 automatic loaded with extra-deadly hollow point bullets."

It turned out when the corpse was weighed at autopsy that Mr. Phist was only in the high 200s on the scale. Close enough. Remember the yardstick of judgment: "What would a reasonable and prudent person have done, in the same situation, knowing what the defendant knew?" Seen in the light most favorable to the prosecution, the deceased was *still* vastly larger and more physically powerful than the man who shot him. Seen in the light most favorable to the defense – what the defendant knew at the time he drew his gun and fired the fatal shots – the attacker was all the more advantaged over the defendant by disparity of force.

The jury came to what I consider to be the correct conclusion. They found the defendant not guilty on all charges. He went home that night to sleep in his own bed, in the same house as his two little boys. Sentencing guidelines in the state where it was tried would have sent him to prison for life without parole if he had been found guilty.

Attacker was where Ayoob is seen here in foreground when defendant opened fire. Much larger assailant was unarmed, but after disparity of force was explained to jury, defendant was found not guilty at trial.

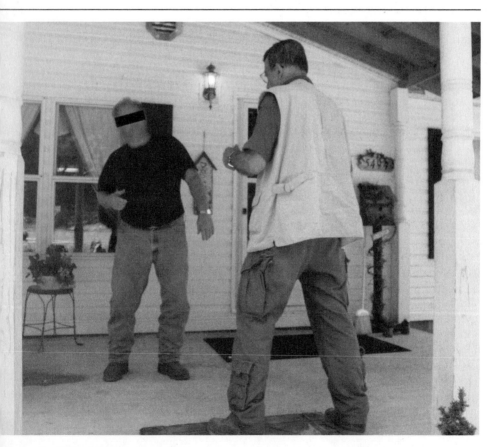

Male Attacking Female

It has long been understood at law that a man attacking a woman has a huge physical advantage over her. The male of our species tends, on the average, to run larger and heavier than the female. Any physiologist can tell you that, even if height and weight are equal, the man has dramatically more physical strength than the woman, and that this is particularly true in terms of upper body strength. *Human beings kill with their hands, whether or not those hands are holding deadly weapons.* When the "personal weapon" is the kicking or stomping foot instead of the punching or strangling hand, the greater weight of the male body driving the blow causes more damage. Moreover, it is well understood in logic and law alike that the cultural predispositioning of the male is toward combat and conflict, and that of the female is toward tenderness and nurturing. Throughout history, the males of our society have been taught to hit hard and play tough, and that aggressiveness is the sign of the "winner." The females of the same periods were taught, "My dear, no one likes a pushy, assertive bitch." It ain't fair, it ain't right, but it is what it is, and we'd all be fools not to recognize it. The law, in its wisdom, *does* recognize the differences between males and females, in terms of not only physical strength, but predisposition to aggression and ferocity of attack.

I had to deal with this for the first time in the 1980s, in the case of *Florida v. Mary Menucci Hopkin* in Miami, Florida. Mary was a tall, slender woman of 63, who suffered from acute arthritis. Her common law husband, James Yarolem, was 43 years old, weighed about 230 pounds, and liked to brag to Mary about having once murdered a man and gotten away with it. She worked, he didn't; he lived in her trailer like a parasite. He also beat her frequently and mercilessly. The day came when she told him, "Jim, you drink all my beer, you smoke all my cigarettes, you won't get a job..." and finished by telling him it was time to go. She didn't mention "You also beat the crap out of me," because that was pretty much a given.

Jim didn't take that news well. He began to beat the hell out of her *again,* and when she reached for the telephone on the wall of her trailer to call the police, he ripped it out of the wall before she could make the connection, and then wrapped the cord around her neck and strangled her until she became unconscious and he thought she was dead. Apparently satisfied with what he had done, he left the mobile home to go to the nearest bar. While he was there, she regained consciousness, and crawled out of the trailer to the nearest mobile home for help, where someone called the police. When Jim came back, police were there, and arrested him. The cops who made that arrest would testify at her trial that as they took him away, James Yarolem was screaming, "Mary, you fucking bitch, I'll kill you for this!"

Before long, James had bonded himself out of custody. Pausing only long enough to find enough booze to get him to the .18% blood alcohol content that autopsy would determine was in his bloodstream after he died, he made his way back to the trailer. Like the Big Bad Wolf he yelled threateningly, "Mary, let me in!" Mary, armed with a cheap little RG-14 .22 caliber revolver made out of pot metal – thank heaven, one of the few they ever made that worked – Mary answered that she knew what he was going to do, and she wasn't going to let him do it, and she begged him to stay away.

James Yarolem broke down the door – the jury saw the pictures of the shattered doorway – and came at her. Mary pulled the trigger three times. James turned and ran and got into the yard before he collapsed and died; one of the little .22 bullets had found its way into his heart.

Mary Hopkin was charged with murder in the second degree. At 63, if she was convicted, she would have died in prison. Living at poverty level, she qualified for a Public Defender or, in Florida, Assigned Counsel. In a stroke of great good fortune, the Assigned Counsel she drew was... Mark Seiden.

It was not the first case I would do with this gifted defense attorney, and would not be the last. The time would come later when Mark and I would serve two years as co-vice chairs of the Forensic Evidence Committee of the National Association of Criminal Defense Lawyers. He called me to see if I would take the case, since there was no money available in that time and place to pay for expert witnesses. After reviewing the evidence, I took the case.

There were other elements besides the obvious disparity of force in terms of size, strength, gender, and predisposition to extreme physical violence, but the disparity of force was in my opinion the primary issue. Mark took his time at trial taking me through direct testimony explaining why she couldn't effectively retreat, why there was no time for her to call the police, etc...and, perhaps most important, why the jury could believe that this time, the man who had left her for dead once before could finish the job and make certain that she was dead.

My testimony under Seiden's questioning – he has always been detail-oriented, and always knew enough to leave no stone unturned and no issue on the other side still intact – took quite a while. Cross-examination, on the other hand, was a personal best for me, probably about 45 seconds.

I don't have a transcript to quote from. Transcripts are expensive, and when neither side appeals the issue, testimony need not be transcribed. But just going from memory, it went like this:

Q: Mister Ayoob, you're normally paid for your testimony in cases like this, aren't you?
A: I'm paid for my time, sir. My testimony is not for sale.

Q: How much do you charge for your time?
A: (What I charged in the 1980s). (NOTE: at this point, the prosecutor was conspicuously rubbing his thumb against his forefinger in front of the jury in the age-old gesture that says, "For Money.")

Q: And how much have you already been paid in this case?
A: Nothing, sir. I took this case at no charge.

Q: *Why?*
A: (Going from courtroom voice to teaching voice) Because this case is an outrage.

Q: Your honor!
(Brief digression for explanation: when you are testifying on the witness stand and lawyers on either side say "Objection," you are supposed to be silent until the judge has ruled on the objection. However, if they have NOT uttered the magic word "objection," that does not hold true.)

A: (Same hard voice): I've seen injustice before but nothing like this.

Q: (finally): Objection:
Judge: Overruled. *You* asked him the question!

Q: Sidebar, your honor?
Outside the hearing of the jury:

Q: (by prosecuting attorney) I didn't know he was going to say that!

A: (by attorney Seiden, for the defense) I knew he was going to say that.

Judge: *I* knew he was going to say that.
Back on the record, within the hearing of the jury:

Q: No further questions.

The bottom line: the jury was out for approximately two hours including dinner before they returned a verdict of not guilty on all counts...

...and some of the jurors waited outside on the courthouse steps to hug Mary Hopkin and tell her that they thought her being tried was an outrage, too.

This gives you an idea of how well recognized the male attacker versus female defender disparity is, as seen by a jury in a self-defense shooting.

Skilled/Highly Trained Fighter Versus Average Person

A professional boxer against someone who has never fought except in the schoolyard is recognized at law as someone who has a huge advantage over the ordinary person he attacks. Have you ever heard the phrase, "I'm a black belt, and my hands are registered as deadly weapons"? As stated, that's total BS, but in the case law (as opposed to most of the "black letter law" of the statutes and criminal or penal codes), there's actually some very strong truth to it.

The tricky part is, *how did you **know** your opponent had that advantage over you?* Once again, we must bear in mind that Reasonable Person standard: "What would a reasonable and prudent person have done, in the exact same situation, *knowing what the defendant knew?"*

In the case of *Tennessee v. Shawn Armstrong* just a few years ago, the defendant testified that she *knew* the violent, estranged husband who attacked her and beat her and kicked her when she was down – and was now apparently coming back toward her to "finish the job" – had been trained by the United States Army itself in advanced hand to hand combat to the point where he could kill adult male enemy soldiers with his bare hands. I was therefore able to speak to that as an expert witness for her defense, and it was a cornerstone of our winning an amazingly swift acquittal thanks to the masterful lawyering of her defense attorney, John Colley.

Perhaps you, the defendant, *didn't* know your opponent was a champion fighter, a black belt in this or that martial art, or whatever. But you have just seen him sidekick a six-foot-tall security guard through a plate glass window. That's probably close enough. Remember the standard of judgment: "What would a reasonable and prudent person have done, in the same totality of the circumstances, knowing what you, the now-defendant, knew?

I was a consultant in a case in South Florida that began when a young man was invited to a party a beautiful young woman was holding at her home. What the young man didn't know was that the home in question belonged to her live-in boyfriend. As the night went on, he perceived her as playing up to him, and he responded in kind. The live-in boyfriend took this in the same hostile fashion as you might expect, and since it was *his* place, he roughly ordered the young man in question to leave.

After taking a while to figure out what was going on, the young man did leave, escorted out by the angry boyfriend and the boyfriend's coterie of friends. The "escorting out" became more and more hostile. In the driveway, in his pickup truck about to leave, the young man in question came under attack: a bat was slammed against his car, and then, the angry boyfriend punched his fist straight through the safety glass of the side door window at his face. Absolutely terrified, the young man came up with a .38 and opened fire, killing the assailant. He then sped away, firing a warning shot to keep the others from following, which went harmlessly into an unoccupied part of the building.

To make yet another long story short, the young man in question was acquitted for the killing of his attacker, because a skilled defense team made it clear to the jury that a blow that could shatter side window safety glass was a blow that any reasonable, prudent person would conclude was likely to cause death or grave bodily harm if the same powerful fist had connected with the temple it was obviously aimed at. (Ironically, the young man in question was still sent to prison because of the shot fired from his vehicle which, in the prosecution's theory, could have endangered innocent bystanders…but that's a topic for another part of this book.)

Adult Violently Attacking Child

Here, we are not talking about the adult defender using deadly force against a large, strong teenager attacking him.

What we're talking about here is a full-size, adult-size human being attacking a small child who has not yet reached the age of maturity.

In Texas not long ago, the father of a very little girl came upon a man in the act of undeniable rape: forcing sexual intercourse upon the child. The father pulled him off his little daughter…hit him with his fists…and hit him again until he was dead. He literally beat the child rapist to death.

In Texas, any homicide normally goes before the Grand Jury. The Grand Jury in this case returned a verdict of No True Bill, which says in essence, "We, the Grand Jury, do not believe that a crime has been committed here."

I see no problem with that.

Do you? I didn't think so.

I haven't spoken with any of the people involved in that case, but I suspect that they realized that what was going on when the father happened upon the scene was so heinous a felony that it warranted a degree of force which rendered the offender incapable of continuing his horrible crime.

This book has elsewhere addressed the difference between *malum prohibitum* and *malum in se,* the difference between "It's against the law because a law was passed prohibiting it," and "It's against the law because it is a crime so horrible that throughout the history of human society it has been rigidly prohibited and severely punished."

It is hard for any member of society, including the jury pool and the judges who stand as referees of the law, to imagine anything more heinous and worthy of deadly force response than infliction of death or grave bodily harm (such as rape) upon a helpless young child.

Able-Bodied Attacking the Handicapped

Able-bodied attacking the handicapped is an absolute example of disparity of force, *even if the handicap has taken place in the course of the instant conflict!*

Let's suppose that the fight began with no weapons involved except your own gun, which was in your holster. Let's further presume, for purposes of argument, that your opponent is exactly the same height, weight, age, muscularity, and gender as you. It has been fist to fist until now.

But then, the opponent lands a kick which, at least for now cripples one of your legs, or one of your arms, or makes you reasonably believe that you are about to lose consciousness. Now it is no longer a battle of equals. Your ability to block or evade kicks or punches is now severely limited, and the likelihood of your being killed or crippled in the

continuing assault is so high that it becomes the equivalent
of a deadly weapon in your opponent's hands, warranting
your recourse to a *per se* deadly weapon.

One such case in which I testified for the defense as an
expert was *Minnick v. Shawn Joyce and Sacramento County.*
Shawn was a deputy with the Sacramento County Sheriff's Department, and had sustained a serious injury to his right wrist
that kept him off full duty at the time of the shooting. It happened at his parents' home in the countryside, where he and
his wife were visiting with their kids. There was an informal
shooting range on the property, and the family was out shooting .22s on a pleasant weekend afternoon. Suddenly a man
came charging through the bushes from an adjacent property
at the family, screaming like a maniac. He grabbed for one
of the target rifles, a semiautomatic .22. Identifying himself
as a law enforcement officer and following his Pressure Point
Control Tactics (PPCT) training, the off-duty deputy kicked him
in the common peroneal area of his thigh. The powerful blow
had no effect: the assailant, who would turn out to have a long
and ugly history with drugs, also had a high blood alcohol
content.

Shawn drew the off-duty gun he was carrying, his wife's
SIG-Sauer P230 semiautomatic, and ordered the man to halt.
Being right-handed, he had withdrawn the pistol with his
injured right hand, out of habituation. When the man lunged
for the gun, Shawn realized that he would not be able to effectively retain it against a man this large and strong with his
severely weakened wrist, and he opened fire. It took seven
of the eight .380 hollow points in the little pistol to stop the
forward charge. The assailant, a man named Minnick, stopped
as if pausing for breath with his hands on his knees as he
glared at the deputy. Then he slowly sat down…and slowly
laid down…and died. All seven bullets had hit him, most of
them "center mass" in the torso.

The shooting was thoroughly investigated by agencies other than his own, and ruled justifiable by both law
enforcement and the District Attorney's office. However,
that was no bar to a lawsuit by the family of the deceased,
against the officer personally and also against his department.

When I was called to the stand by the masterful Attorney Terry Cassidy, I explained the disparity of force issue
pretty much as I did here. The desperate plaintiffs had even
argued that it was negligence for a man who hadn't qualified on the training range with his off duty gun to carry it
at all, let alone use it, in light of the injury to the wrist of

his gun hand. I was able to dispose of that with one of the shortest answers ever in my career on the witness stand: "He fired seven shots, and hit him seven times. Marksmanship is not an issue."

Our arguments succeeded, the principle of disparity of force as it applied to the handicapped attacked by the able-bodied was understood, and the result was a total defense verdict.

Position of Disadvantage

Position of disadvantage is another element of disparity of force. My friend Chris Bird, author of the excellent books *Thank God I Had A Gun* and *The Concealed Handgun Manual*, has written splendidly of the first case in Texas in which an armed citizen used a gun to save his life after shall-issue concealed carry was signed into law by then-Governor George W. Bush. It involved a man of middle years who became the victim of a large, strong, violent young man in a road rage incident. It culminated when the younger man came to the driver's door of the older man's car and began raining savage punches upon him through the open window.

The driver was trapped in place by his seat belt; the lap and shoulder restraints held him in place as if the assailant had a criminal accomplice who was holding him from behind for the first assailant to mercilessly batter at will. The driver could no longer roll with a punch, or evade a punch. He had no ability to generate power in counterpunches because of the trapped position. In desperation, the Texas driver drew his .40 caliber Beretta 96 pistol and shot the larger man in the chest. The attacker staggered back – at which time, of course, the defender stopped shooting – and stumbled toward his own vehicle and then collapsed, dying.

As is normally the case with any homicide in the state of Texas, the case went before the Grand Jury. Hearing the facts, the Grand Jury returned No True Bill, effectively saying there was no reason to believe a crime had been committed by the innocent motorist who had shot and killed his attacker in self-defense.

Another example of position of disadvantage creating disparity of force is found in a case discussed in depth elsewhere in this book, the high-profile shooting death of Trayvon Martin at the hands of George Zimmerman. Evidence and testimony showed that Martin had attacked Zimmerman, had him down and was straddling him in a "mixed martial arts mount," and was smashing the back of his head into the sidewalk at the time Zimmerman drew his 9mm Kel-Tec and fired a single, fatal shot. Zimmerman was found not guilty by the jury.

Suggested Reading

It would be useful for any law-abiding citizen who carries a gun to own a copy of the authoritative text *Medico-Legal Investigation of Death*, from Charles C. Thomas Publishers in Springfield, Illinois. Don't just buy it, read it and absorb it! It is edited by Dr. Werner Spitz, one of the all-time great forensic pathologists. I testified with Dr. Spitz in a lawsuit arising from a fatal SWAT team shooting of a suspect in Port Huron, Michigan, and I can tell you the man is simply awesome in court.

The book explains – and, perhaps more importantly, photographically illustrates – death of human beings by all sorts of means. Gunshot, knife, bludgeon, stomping, strangulation, automobile collisions and auto-pedestrian strikes, death by fire, and more are thoroughly covered.

When opposing counsel says of your opponent, "He only had a knife (or stick, or bottle)"… "He was unarmed!"… "He was just driving his car!"…"He was only standing there with an ordinary can of gasoline and an ordinary Zippo lighter!"…

…I would like you to be able to honestly say, "Counselor, in that moment I knew what he could do to me. My mind flashed back to pictures I had seen of someone stabbed/ clubbed/stomped/run over/burned to death. I pictured my mother or my spouse having to identify me looking like that on a slab in the morgue, and I knew I had to stop him."

There is now an excellent chance that, since those images you had seen were germane to your mind-set, your attorney can introduce those photos to the jury. Those twelve people and their alternates will now see exactly what you were trying to prevent when you fired defensively. It would be a powerful way to get the truth of what you faced, across to the jury. "What would a reasonable and prudent person have done, in the same situation, *knowing what the defendant knew…*"

Ability, the power to kill or cripple, must be readily and immediately deliverable by the attacker to warrant the defender using deadly force against him. That brings us to the next chapter, the opportunity factor.

Chapter 4:

The Opportunity Factor

Another criterion which must be present in the AOJ triad that creates a set of circumstances that can warrant defensive deadly force is *opportunity*. "Ability" meant that the opponent possessed the power to kill or cripple; opportunity means that opponent has the power to carry out that ability in the immediate here and now.

The opportunity factor encompasses elements of distance, obstacles, and perhaps most importantly, time.

Distance Element

The most famous research on the distance element of the opportunity factor was published in 1983 in *SWAT Magazine*, in the article "How Close Is Too Close" by Dennis Tueller. Dennis at that time was a sergeant on the Salt Lake City, Utah, Police Department, and also an adjunct instructor at Jeff Cooper's famous shooting school, Gunsite. One of the Gunsite drills was to start at the seven yard firing line with hands clear of holstered weapon and, on the start signal, draw and shoot a silhouette target twice in the chest in 1.5 seconds. This is actually a good test of skill at what Gunsite founder Jeff Cooper called "pistolcraft." Gunsite students were usually working from an open-top holster worn exposed; it is more challenging when the pistol must be drawn from concealment, or from a typical police security holster, designed to be "snatch-resistant."

Dennis tells me, "I was running the Firearm Training program for SLCPD at that time, and was doing the (draw and fire twice in 1.5 seconds) drill … with a group of recruit officers. This led to a discussion of the use of deadly force, when one of my recruit officers asked about shooting someone who is attacking with a knife, club, or other contact weapon. He wondered how close the attacker had to be before you would be justified in shooting. I realized that I didn't have a good answer to that question, and that led to our experiments into reaction and response time."

He continues, "We actually did a role-play with an 'aggressor' and 'victim officer' with two observers with stopwatches to time the attack. I didn't have a rubber knife available, so I think we simply used a plastic pocket comb to represent a weapon."

Their average time to do so was roughly…1.5 seconds.

Tueller adds, "I was doing a class at Gunsite shortly after conducting these experiments at the SLCPD Academy, and was sharing this information with my fellow Gunsite instructors and discussing how to incorporate this into our training. Chuck Taylor was the Operations Officer at Gunsite at that time, and was also an editor for the new *SWAT Magazine*. It was Chuck who encouraged me to write the now famous article."

This was a stunning breakthrough at the time. Prior to Tueller's revelation, self-defense shooting investigations had often presumed that a man with a contact weapon such as a knife or club had to be within touching distance for his intended victim to be justified in killing him. A police training film produced by Woroner Films and distributed by Motorola Teleprograms, Inc. titled "Shoot/Don't Shoot" was in virtually universal use at police academies at that time. Incorporating the ability/opportunity/jeopardy standard, it was seen as the moving picture equivalent of what the courts call an "authoritative text." Early in the film, officers saw a violent man grab a woman and shove her against a chain link fence while he wielded a knife in such a manner that it was obvious he was about to stab her with it. The film explained that while this scenario would certainly justify deadly force, that might not be the case if the attacker was ten feet away from his victim.

SWAT Magazine, then and now, has always been widely read in the training community. I – and many others, including John Farnam and Manny Kapelsohn, to name just a couple – read Tueller's article. Most people's reaction was, "Twenty-one feet in a second and a half? From a standing start? It can't be *that* fast!" We went out and tried it ourselves…and discovered that Tueller had been absolutely correct.

We incorporated it into our own training immediately, giving attribution. Shortly after the article was published, I taught a Lethal Threat Management for Police class at the Tacoma, Washington, Police Department range. Of course, many Tacoma training officers were in the class. The "Tueller Drill" (more about that shortly) was an eye-opener. The instructors at the department took it so seriously that they incorporated it into their training, making a training film on the topic and running every officer through the drill.

Something happened thereafter which proved to be a classic example of what some in the training world call the "Oil Stain Effect." Akin to the "ripples from a rock thrown in

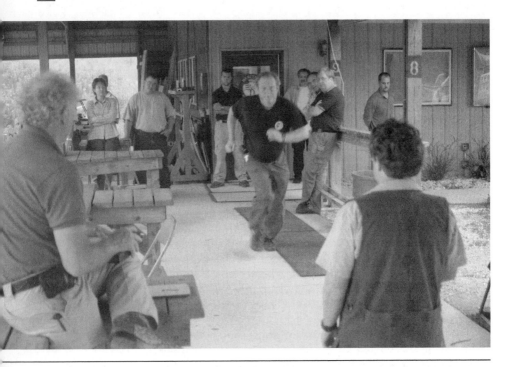

Tueller Drill in action. Student in Attacker role runs at student in Defender role, as a third student in Timer role wields the stopwatch

the water" metaphor, it means that if you place a tiny drop of oil in the middle of a piece of linen, the oil's stain will spread, wider and wider. One entity does the research. The result of that research is spread to several instructors. They in turn pass it on to far more practitioners, and in that last generation of the transmission, the research saves lives.

Soon, an incident occurred in Tacoma. A crazed man with a knife attacked a woman and absolutely savaged her. A BOLO (Be On the Look-Out) was broadcast to Tacoma officers. Soon, the suspect was spotted. He was hard to miss: naked, covered with blood, wielding a large knife in one hand and a bludgeon in the other. The first officer who spotted him called for backup and soon multiple officers were on the scene. They arrayed themselves in a semi-circle to prevent a crossfire, something their critics would later describe as "firing squad formation." All the cops, of course, had their guns drawn. The highest-ranking officer present, a sergeant, ordered the suspect to drop his weapons.

With a hostile expression on his face, the suspect moved toward the sergeant, who fired one shot. The 9mm bullet struck the madman center chest. The knife wielder paused for a second, then uttered an inchoate scream of rage, and lunged at the officer.

The cops all opened fire. The assailant went down in the proverbial hail of bullets, falling virtually at the sergeant's feet, stopped barely in time by multiple gunshot wounds.

The deceased attacker was African-American. There had been allegations of racism and police brutality against the department involved. The situation flared like kerosene on a fire. "Cross-racial shooting." "He ONLY had a knife." "Why couldn't five cops restrain one lone, nude man without killing him?" "Why did they have to shoot him so many times if malice wasn't involved?" "They shouldn't have killed him; he wasn't in his right mind, so it wasn't his fault!"

What seemed to be ignored in the whole matter was the dead criminal's victim, an African-American woman whom he had attacked and mangled like Jack the Ripper.

It became a major political issue in the city. The case went before a grand jury. The proceedings of a grand jury are normally secret, but in this unusual instance, it was made public.

Each of the officers who had fired testified. All but one stated in their initial reports that it was fresh in their mind from their (Tueller Drill) training how quickly the man could have reached the sergeant with his deadly blade if he was not stopped by gunfire. They all said the same to the grand jury.

The trainers were brought in to testify. They made the speed of closure clearly apparent to the grand jury. They demonstrated the drill live in front of the jurors. I was told later that, during their deliberations, the members of the grand jury went out into the courthouse hall and ran the drill themselves.

They returned No True Bill, which in essence means a determination that no crime had been committed by the officers who fired the fatal shots. The foreperson of the grand jury, a prominent African-American woman, stated publicly that at that point there was nothing else the officers could have done.

Oil-stain effect. First, Tueller completes and publishes his research. Second, his peers evaluate and accept it ("peer review" at its most effective level) and begin teaching it. Third, those they teach it to, share it with others who need to know it. And, at the fourth level of transmission, it saves the life of one law enforcement officer and the careers of more.

Grasping Tueller's Principle

That oil stain under discussion will always be most intense at its center. As it spreads, it can weaken. Remember VHS videotapes? People would copy them and copy them, and in each stage of copying, it became fuzzier and more indistinct and harder to interpret. So it was, unfortunately, with Tueller's research.

We came to see misinterpretations. There were those who said, "Okay, this means that if the guy with the knife is 20 feet, 11 inches away, you can shoot him, but if he's 21 feet, 1 inch away, you can't." *False! That simply is not the correct interpretation!*

Suppose the man with the knife is standing still, 21 feet away from you or his other victim. Suppose he is holding a knife but pointing it to the ground, and standing as if in a catatonic state. Would you be justified in shooting him? Of course not, at least not at that moment.

Suppose he is half again as far away, but has already attacked you twice, and is lunging at you with that knife after uttering threatening words? Are you expected to wait until he crosses an invisible 21-foot line before you press the trigger? Of course not.

This writer had to deal with that in the 1980s, in the case of *State of New York v. Frank Magliato*. To make a long story short, Magliato was attacked on a New York City street by a junkie who had threatened him with deadly force more than once earlier that night. The soon-to-be-deceased Anthony Gianni screamed, "I've been looking for you, fucker!" and, raising a two-foot police baton over his head in a ready-to-club motion, began to lunge. At that moment, Magliato – who had drawn the .38 Colt Detective Special revolver he was licensed to carry, unfortunately cocked the hammer, and shouted for the man to stay back – then unintentionally pressed the trigger. A 158 grain Winchester semi-wadcutter bullet struck Gianni in the forehead, killing him instantly.

NYPD determined that at the moment the fatal shot was fired, the two men were 32 feet apart.

Now, there were many issues in the Magliato case. One was "flight equals guilt," discussed elsewhere in this book; the panicked Magliato fled the scene, turning himself in later. Another was that the discharge was unintentional. A third was that in cocking the hammer and creating what the prosecution argued was a "hair trigger effect," the prosecution (and later, the appellate court) determined that there was an element of negligence.

But, on point to the topic at hand, the prosecution also argued that a man with a contact weapon who was 32 feet away, could not be considered a danger.

I was hired as an expert witness for the defense by Bob Kasanof, the original defense attorney retained by Magliato. When Magliato changed horses in midstream and hired famed defense lawyer Gerry Lefcourt to represent him, I came along with the package. I assembled a dozen or so men who fit the physical profile of the deceased, and timed them as they lunged 32 feet from a standing start to strike a silhouette target in the head with an exemplar Monadnock 24-inch Monpac police baton. Their average time to "crush the skull of the target and kill the victim" was…2.08 seconds. (My friend, colleague, and past student Michael DeBethancourt, who rose to prominence as one of today's top self-defense instructors, incorporated this case into his training and calls it the "Magliato Drill.")

There is another lesson to learn from this case, which is very much on point to this book. The case was tried in Manhattan. New York is a "trial by ambush" state in that, unlike most other jurisdictions in the US, the defense doesn't get to see everything the prosecution has until it is about to be presented at trial. Therefore, on each side of the courtroom fight, counsel *voir dires* the witness in court but outside the hearing of the jury and the judge determines whether the evidence can be presented to the jury or not.

During my *voir dire* for Magliato's defense, I explained the Tueller research, and the fact that in preparation for the case at bar, we had determined that someone like the deceased in that case could be expected to cross those 32 feet in 2.08 seconds or so. I explained ability, opportunity, and jeopardy. The question came up, would I have fired intentionally under the circumstances Magliato was facing when his Colt discharged. I replied in the affirmative. One of the New York City tabloids the next day headlined their story on the trial, "Cop: I Would Have Shot Him Myself."

The reporter was there to hear that; the jury, unfortunately, wasn't. Remember, that colloquy took place during *voir dire* of an expert witness, with the jury out of the courtroom. Judge Thomas Sullivan at that point addressed the defendant directly, and asked Magliato if he had known Gianni could have reached him and clubbed him that quickly. Frank Magliato replied honestly that no, at that time, he did not.

The judge ruled that he would not allow that element of my testimony to go in front of the jury. We can never allow ourselves to forget that the reasonable man standard encompasses "what would a reasonable and prudent person have done, in the same situation, *knowing what the defendant knew.*" If we did not know it at the time we took the action for which we are being judged, we are unlikely to be able to use it in our defense in court.

This was the first case I was ever involved in as an expert witness where the side I was testifying for lost. Magliato was convicted of depraved murder. The appellate court reduced it to manslaughter eventually, but he still served years of hard time and was branded a felon for the rest of his life. Of the many lessons from this case, one is, *Be Trained!* Training is discoverable, and therefore introducible to educate the jury. Magliato had not been trained in this. Had he been able to introduce this opportunity element from having been trained in it, I strongly believe that he might well have been acquitted.

The Texas Tower today. In 1966, when a mad sniper opened fire murderously from here, armed citizens hundreds of yards away justifiably pinned him down with return fire.

The distance element of the opportunity factor has been widely misunderstood in other ways. I have lost count of people who claim that "if you shoot a man more than 7 yards/ 10 yards/ 25 yards/ whatever yards away, you won't be justifiable." In and of itself, that statement is simply BS.

Let us go back in time to 1966, and the Texas Tower Massacre, the mass shooting perpetrated by Charles Whitman. His sniper's perch was some 330 feet above ground level, and he murdered helpless victims from hundreds of yards away with a telescopic-sighted, high-powered hunting rifle. History records that he was killed at fairly close range atop the tower by Austin, Texas, police officers. What you have to dig into history to find is that the murders were cut short well before that conflagration at the pinnacle of the tower…by armed citizens on the ground who returned fire with hunting rifles and at least one target rifle!

Far from being criminally charged for "shooting at a man too far away to constitute a danger," these citizens were lauded for their courage in pinning down the mad sniper and stopping the killing. While Whitman was thus held in check by armed citizens, another armed citizen named Alan Crum led Austin police officers Houston McCoy, Ramiro Martinez, and Jerry Day up through the inside of the tower to the roof where the mass murderer held forth. Finding a cluster of victims hiding from Whitman inside the tower, Day ushered them to safety. Crum guided the other two officers to the roof; they approached Whitman's position from one side, and Crum from the other. Crum was the first to see Whitman, lying in wait for the cops with a sawed-off semiautomatic 12 gauge shotgun. A shot from citizen Crum's rifle, a .30 caliber Remington handed to him earlier by a law enforcement officer, was the first round of the final shootout and it "broke the ambush," startling Whitman. This allowed

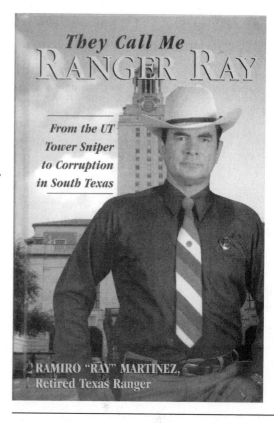

They Call Me RANGER RAY

From the UT Tower Sniper to Corruption in South Texas

RAMIRO "RAY" MARTINEZ, Retired Texas Ranger

Ramiro Martinez, one of the heroes of the Texas Tower incident, in his autobiography They Call Me Ranger Ray, *credits return fire from armed citizens on the ground with rifles for stopping the murderer's rampage.*

the officers to open fire. A blast from McCoy's Winchester pump shotgun mortally wounded the gunman; Martinez emptied his Smith & Wesson .38/44 service revolver into the killer, then snatched McCoy's shotgun and blasted Whitman one more time. The long, terrible nightmare was over.

In his autobiography, *They Call Me Ranger Ray*, Martinez later wrote, "I was and am still upset that more recognition has not been given to the citizens who pulled out their hunting rifles and returned the sniper's fire. The City of Austin and the State of Texas should be forever thankful and grateful to them because of the many lives they saved that day. The sniper did a lot of damage when he could fire freely, but when the armed citizens began to return fire the sniper had to take cover. He had to shoot out of the rainspouts and that limited his targets. I am grateful to the citizens because they made my job easier."[1]

Understanding and Interpreting the Tueller Principle

Some people lose sight of the fact that Dennis Tueller's work in this respect was geared to opponents armed with *contact weapons:* people who must touch their victims to kill them. This encompasses the opponent armed with a knife or some sort of bludgeon, and also in a disparity of force situation the attacker who is attempting to punch, strangle, or kick his victim. The person attempting to grab the lawfully-wielded gun of homeowner or cop, since he must lay hands on the gun to snatch it, should also be treated as a contact weapon assailant. In all these cases, Tueller's principle will be extremely relevant.

For thirty years, Tueller had to watch his work occasionally bastardized and misinterpreted by others. People began to refer to the "21-Foot Rule," and to read it as "shoot him if he's closer, don't shoot him if he's farther." Tueller, one of the great firearms instructors of his generation, never said that. Circa 1990 he and I did a training film on the topic, using the same title as his seminal article: "How Close Is Too Close?" Then, and before and since, he made it clear that the purpose of the exercise was simply to make the trainee understand how quickly such a distance could be closed, and to evaluate that as the courts would in the aftermath: in the context of "the totality of the circumstances" to determine whether defensive lethal force was

1   Martinez, Ramiro: "They Call Me Ranger Ray," New Braunfels, TX: Rio Bravo Publishing, 2006, Page 84.

or was not justified and necessary at a given moment in an encounter.

Today, Tueller adds, "We should also give credit to Calibre Press. They referenced my article in their *Tactical Edge* book, and incorporated and demonstrated some of the principles in their 'Surviving Edged Weapons' training film, correctly using terms such as 'proxemics' and 'the reactionary gap'."

Terminology is an issue in this discussion. The core research establishing that the average adult male can close seven yards in a second and a half from a standing start, I refer to as the *Tueller Principle*. Almost immediately after reviewing and confirming Tueller's seminal work, I began teaching what I called the *Tueller Drill*. This was experiential training geared to bring home the unforgiving speed of a potential assailant. One way to do it is to have a single person in place as the Timer, and another individual in place in the role of Defender or Intended Victim. Now, at a starting line seven yards from the latter, each student begins standing still. This student then lunges, and closes the distance as fast as he can.

We learned early that the Timer should *not* blow a start whistle, or shout "Ready, set, go," or otherwise issue a start command. The reason is that this creates a reaction time of a quarter second or so for the student in the Attacker role. This in turn falsely understates the speed at which the distance gap can be closed. In real life, the attacker does not have to deal with reaction time; he initiates the attack himself. Accordingly, we learned to have the Attacker start on his own command. The Timer would be ready, and would start the time as soon as the Attacker began to move, and stop the time when the Attacker made physical contact with the Intended Victim. Any "reactionary gap" on the part of the timer would be equalized and negated by the fact that reaction time on the start and stop button would be the same at the beginning and the end of the run.

When time allowed, I found early that the best way to implement the Tueller Drill was to break the students up into groups of three, and have each take turns in each of the three roles: Timer, Attacker, and Defender. They were instructed to bring their pens and notebooks to the exercise. Just before taking their run in the Attacker, each student would dictate the following for other students to write down in their notes: their height, weight, age, gender, footwear, and existing injuries or medical problems. (Ground surface would also be listed, and the same for all participants.) Momentarily, after the run, the entry in the notebooks would be completed with elapsed time, announced by the Timer. Tueller comments, "Early on, we also did a variation of this exercise using toy dart pistols and rubber knives."

This meant that at the end of the exercise, each student would have a comprehensive list of students with a broad range of physical attributes, at least one of which would probably be reasonably close to the physical description of a future assailant who might be coming at them. Having acted out all three roles would allow them to say the following in court: "Counselor, I knew how fast that person could close the distance and kill me because, in my training, they made me do that to another person. I knew it because in my training, they made another person do that to me. I knew it because in my training, they made me stand back so I could see the forest for the trees, and time another person doing it to someone else. And if need be, I can demonstrate that here in this courtroom."

In the course of more than thirty years of running Tueller Drills, I was able to observe thousands of people run it. Tall and short, male and female, ectomorph and endomorph and mesomorph, the "lame and the halt," as well as those in prime of life and health. I was able to share information with countless peers in the training world who had supervised a like number of drills.

Many people were *faster* than 1.5 seconds. I saw a very few people who could actually complete the Tueller Drill in under a second flat, usually in the high nine-tenths of one second. These tended to be accomplished athletes and martial artists, and they would often close the final part of the gap with a leap.

I saw two men with freshly broken legs in walking casts – Jan Stevenson in a class I taught in England, and Bob Smith at a class I taught in Idaho – hobble through a Tueller drill in two seconds flat.

I saw men in wheelchairs do it in roughly the same time. Our "wheelchair record" was set by a partially quadriplegic Vietnam veteran. He did it in 1.8 seconds.

A memorable moment in the history of Tueller Drills occurred in June of 1993 at an LFI-I class I was teaching for Lethal Force Institute at the Pioneer Sportsman range in Dunbarton, New Hampshire. Larry Anderson, age 43, was the participant. Larry suffered from recurring orthopedic issues in the lower limbs. I watched as he began his run; he appeared to stumble at first, then righted himself and completed the lunge. As he made contact, he fell to the ground with his next and last step.

He had suffered a spiral fracture of tibia and fibula. Surgery involving steel bolts was the result. Larry told me later, in the Emergency Room, that he had felt a bone in his leg crack as he began the run, but pressed onward.

His sacrifice was for all of us. Suppose that sometime in the future, you have shot your assailant in the leg, but he continues his attack and you have to shoot him again. In court, opposing counsel may say, "You can't believe he was in danger from a man who only had a knife and was seven yards away, because that man had a bullet in his leg and couldn't run." Thanks to Larry Anderson's experience, it is now a matter of record that a man with a freshly broken leg, untreated, can still close that gap and deliver what would be a fatal knife thrust in the time Larry was witnessed and recorded to do it that day – *1.8 seconds!*

We learned many counter-intuitive lessons over the years that we've shared with law enforcement and law-abiding armed citizens. The perception that "big equals slow" is an absolute myth. Tall people with long arms and legs are deceptively fast. Their higher center of gravity may allow them to gain momentum and speed slightly faster than their shorter brethren. Their longer legs definitely allow them to cover more ground with fewer steps. Their longer arms allow them to reach their victim more quickly. Even morbidly obese people are surprisingly fast. The reason is, the weight they are constantly carrying strengthens their leg muscles with every step they take in daily life, and it is leg muscles that drive a short-range anaerobic movement pattern such as a knife attack.

It would seem at first that the attacker with the heavy crowbar would be slower than the same man with a light, fast-moving knife. *Au contraire.* A long club-type instrument can add as much as another arm's length to the assailant's reach. This means he has one less step that he has to take to harm his victim, making him that much faster, not slower.

Similarly, assailants in poor physical condition for other reasons can still move with more speed than the average person would suspect. I testified in two trials on behalf of Mark Branham, an ex-cop in Virginia who shot and killed a man who was in the unprovoked act of clubbing him about the head with two weapons. In one hand, the attacker swung a heavy miner's lantern against Branham's skull, and with the other hand the assailant was pistol-whipping him with a loaded Smith & Wesson Model 10 .38 Special revolver. A special prosecutor hired by the family of the deceased alleged, among other things, that the assailant posed no danger to Branham because that assailant was known to

Branham to suffer from coal worker's pneumoconiosis, also known as "black lung disease" or "miner's lung." When I was called to the stand as an expert witness for the defense by Branham's brilliant lawyer, Eugene Compton, I was able to counter this by explaining that such brief, violent movements do not require a large aerobic reserve to carry out. "This is probably why there is no Olympic event called 'the seven-yard dash.' Almost anyone can do it," I pointed out. Branham was ultimately acquitted. He returned to law enforcement and completed a distinguished career, culminating as Chief of Police.

Fine Points of the Tueller Drill

One thing we observed over the years was that people would disadvantage themselves and slow themselves down by starting too far back at the beginning of the Tueller Drill. We learn to "toe the line" on the firing line at a shooting range, and to not let our toes get forward of the "do not cross" line when standing in queue at a security gate. In the real world, and in court, the distance between two people is generally perceived and measured "torso to torso" in this writer's experience. A person preparing to run – or an attacker standing in an aggressive posture – will generally have one foot ahead of the other, with the torso centered in between the spread-apart feet. Accordingly, we learned to have each student in the Attacker role begin with one foot forward of the line and the other behind, *and the torso centered over the line*. This gave a truer reading of potential speed.

Safety is critical in performing this drill. Shoes with smooth leather soles turn into something dangerously close to roller skates when attempting to run over smooth, hard surfaces. While it might be interesting to see how fast a woman in high heels could run, the likelihood of tripping and falling is so obvious and so potentially dangerous that we chose not to explore it, in the interest of student safety. We always made note of ground surfaces for the record. Sand and gravel, because they slip from under the feet, slow the run. So would wet grass. So, of course, would ice and snow; this is why we do not have data on running speed upon such surfaces. We had no right to endanger the students by asking them to do that.

We always lectured the students beforehand, "If you have bad back, bad knees, bad heart, high blood pressure, history of stroke, etc., *do not attempt maximum speed!* This is why we are making note of pre-existing injuries and medical conditions. If you fit any of those medical profiles, just walk it quickly. You'll still close the distance in three seconds or less, and that still isn't time for your life to flash before your eyes before you die if you don't stop the attack. You're not short-changing the other students by walking the Tueller Drill quickly instead of running it flat out. On the contrary, you are giving them knowledge they can use in court if their attacker happens to be disabled in a future, real encounter, and opposing counsel argues that the Tueller Principle only covers healthy, athletic police academy recruits."

Additional Safety Considerations

We have always been careful to have the students take off their guns before doing a Tueller Drill, even on a "cold range" where the weapons were unloaded. In the Defender role, we didn't want them to reflex to their weapons. If they fell and rolled, we didn't want them to have guns (or other heavy things) on their belts, which could cause a hip or lower back injury in the fall.

We discovered early that there was injury potential even with dummy knives. Those of us who train extensively with the knife know that a blunted "drone" knife made of metal or even edgeless wood can cause severe bruising or even broken bones. Even a rubber knife can leave nasty bruises or cause damage to eye or larynx with a hard blow.

Moreover, in the training environment, no one wants to slam full-speed into an inanimate target, let alone a human training partner. This caused the students to slow down in the instant before contact, which in turn falsely slowed their time to make contact. In the real world, we knew, the opponent would be *seeking* aggressive contact and would slam into their intended victim like a charging rhino.

The best way I found to have the students replicate "real world speed" without training injuries was to have the one in Attacker role run full speed *past* the one in Defender role, slowing only after contact had been made. Because even a light "strike" or pulled punch could unintentionally be made harder by the attacker's forward momentum, I would have the defender stand sideways instead of facing the Attacker. The Defender's arm would be somewhat (but not fully) extended, with palm of hand facing the Attacker, who would slap the Defender's palm like a "high five" as he passed. This kept the Attacker's hand away from the face and torso of the Defender, further avoiding injury. The sideways stance of the Defender kept a hard hand-slap by a strong man from dislocating his shoulder. I also recommend that all participants wear safety glasses, in case of an unintentional strike to the eye area.

When performing Tueller Drills, expect someone to take a fall. I've rarely supervised one of these where someone *didn't* go to the ground. It will generally be a male, who has been in a sedentary lifestyle for many years and hasn't sprinted full out since his school days. (The early warning is an awareness that your head is well forward of your feet, which are struggling to keep up.) Remind the students that should they fall, they want to catch themselves on flat palms and forearms, with palms and forearms in a straight line. Instinct will tell them to catch themselves with just the palms, and this tends to hyperextend the wrists, resulting in sprains or even fractures.

What if, subsequent to the training, the student is attacked by a knife wielder who trips and falls, or perhaps goes to the ground after the student's first defensive shot? Instead of staying down, the assailant now tries to rise with his knife, and the student, logically, shoots him again. Expect opposing counsel to argue, "The Tueller Drill training invoked by the defendant is irrelevant! This man wasn't starting on his feet when the defendant fired the fatal shot, he was starting from flat on his face (or flat on his back)! The defendant wasn't in immediate danger!"

When time permits, I like to proactively counter this by taking a volunteer student and having him or her start supine (on their back) or prone (face down). They can generally spring to their feet and sprint seven yards to contact in three seconds or so, and I've seen it done in two by the more athletic individuals. That's still more than sufficiently "immediate" to constitute the ability factor...and now it is provably known to the student beforehand in a way that will normally be court admissible.

Dennis Tueller retired many years ago from SLCPD at the rank of Lieutenant, and ever since has been teaching good people to stay alive in the face of criminal violence. His pioneering, ground-breaking work has saved countless "good guys and gals" from death on the street, and from ruin and prison in the courtroom. His contributions cannot be overestimated. I am proud to count him as a friend and a colleague. Much credit also goes to *SWAT Magazine*, for publishing this critical research.

Having addressed the distance element of the opportunity factor, we'll move next to the obstacle(s) element.

Obstacles Element

Distance and the potential running/lunging speed of the attacker are not the only elements of the opportunity factor. With contact weapon assaults, there is also the matter of obstacles.

The most obvious obstacles are physical barriers. Let's say that you are standing near a doorway fitted with a steel door. You are just outside the door, and a knife-wielding maniac some distance away in the parking lot walks toward you with a menacing glare. Perhaps a single step could put you through that doorway, and allow you to quickly slam that steel door and lock it before the opponent could reach it. Taken in a vacuum, assuming no other innocent people to whom you owed a legal or ethical duty of protection, this would certainly be the tactical thing to do. In a "back to the wall" jurisdiction that required retreat, it could be seen as legally demanded. Even in a "stand your ground" jurisdiction which did not require retreat, you can expect prosecutor, plaintiff's counsel, and even jurors to pose the question of why you didn't simply close that door and block the threat without bloodshed.

In February of 2014 in Jacksonville, Florida, the case of *State v. Michael Dunn* went to trial. Dunn, a forty-something white male, had been parked outside a convenience store when very loud rap music emanated from a sport utility vehicle next to him. Dunn asked the four young black males in the vehicle to lower the music. The driver initially complied, but passenger Jordan Davis leaned from his position in the right rear seat and turned it back up. He then engaged in a heated, profanity-laden verbal exchange with Dunn. Dunn drew a Taurus PT-99 pistol from his glove box, racked a round into the firing chamber, and proceeded to open fire. Reconstruction showed that his initial burst of three shots struck Jordan Davis with three Winchester 9mm jacketed hollow points. After a brief pause, he fired a string of four more rapid shots. In the six seconds that followed, the SUV backed out and began to drive away, and Dunn maneuvered into a position at the back of his own vehicle from which he then fired three more shots at the fleeing vehicle. This much was not in dispute.

Dunn fled the scene, but a witness noted his license tag and he was arrested the next day. Nine of his ten bullets had gone into the Dodge Durango. Jordan Davis died of his wounds, while the other three teens emerged physically unscathed. They all testified that Davis had not been armed or stepped out of the vehicle. Dunn's story, unsupported by any other testimony or evidence, was that Davis had threatened to kill him and raised what appeared to Dunn to be a shotgun, prompting Dunn to fire in self-defense. No gun was ever found.

After several days of trial and thirty hours of deliberation, the jury unanimously found him guilty of three charges of attempted murder in shooting in the direction of the fleeing teens, and one charge of firing deadly missiles into a vehicle. On the charge of murder in the first degree in the death of 17-year-old Jordan Davis, the jury hung. Their initial vote had been ten for guilty and two for not guilty on the grounds of self-defense; by the time they finally deadlocked, the vote was 9-to-3. The judge ruled a mistrial on that charge, and the prosecution announced that it would re-try Dunn on the murder charge.

This case has many ramifications relevant to this book, but the one on point to this particular discussion is that the first juror to publicly speak of the deliberations said that she was one who voted guilty, and she made it clear that she believed Dunn could have avoided the shooting by simply backing out of the parking space and moving his vehicle... in effect, creating enough distance that there would have been no opportunity factor for Jordan Davis and therefore, no deadly danger to the defendant. This, despite the fact that the jury instructions included an explanation of Florida's then blazingly controversial Stand Your Ground law, which did not require a defendant to leave a place where he had the right to be before using deadly force in otherwise reasonably perceived self-defense.

In the Dunn case, the prosecution also raised the issue that the close proximity of Davis' right rear door to the left side of Dunn's sedan acted as an obstacle to any attempt by Davis to get out of his vehicle and approach Dunn. This argument would have been weaker had there been solid evidence of Davis actually being armed with a firearm, since such a remote control weapon could quickly be deployed through an opened rear window or even blast through the safety glass of a closed window.

There are any number of obstacles which a reasonable and prudent person might recognize as capable of slowing an assailant's approach. One is as simple as uphill versus downhill. It takes longer for an assailant to travel uphill, and moving downhill he can obviously gain momentum and speed more rapidly.

An example of the former occurred in a case in which I was involved as expert witness for the defense in 2011, *Commonwealth of Tennessee v. Shawn Armstrong,* mentioned earlier here in the discussion of disparity of force in the chapter on the ability factor. Shawn, you'll recall, had been viciously beaten and flung to the ground and kicked by her larger, stronger, Army Ranger-trained husband. She lay curled in a fetal position to shield the gun in the front of her waistband so he couldn't gain control of it and turn it against her. He strode back to his car, then turned and glared at her angrily, and began to move toward her again. It was at that moment that she opened fire, killing him with a single bullet that entered his chest and lodged in his spine.

Early in the case, the Tueller Principle and the 1.5 seconds to cover 21 feet had been mentioned. I was not able to visit the shooting scene until the week of trial. The gunfight occurred in a partial clearing in the woods, and the movement path between the deceased at the moment he was hit and the spot where the defendant had pushed herself upright to a sitting position was uphill. The ground in between was "rutted" and covered with tangled plant growth. Our testing determined that an athletic, prime-of-life man such as her husband and roughly the same height and weight, might have taken more like three seconds to close the gap and "finish what he'd started."

I made that clear in my testimony. On cross-examination, the prosecutor made a big deal out of the fact that he would have taken twice as long as average Tueller Drill time to harm her again. I replied that three seconds still constituted immediate danger, and that it wasn't time for the victim's life to flash before her eyes before she was killed. The jury understood, and in less than half an hour of deliberation, they acquitted Shawn Armstrong of all charges.

The Time Element: Immediate, Imminent, Inevitable And The Robinson Hypothesis

Each case must be taken on its own merits, based upon the facts in evidence and the totality of the circumstances. No deadly force case is ever *exactly* like any other.

Let us suppose that you have been kidnapped and taken hostage by a person far stronger than you and highly skilled in unarmed combat. He has made it abundantly clear that he is going to hold you prisoner for a week, and at the end of that week, he intends to murder you. You are unarmed and have determined that you have no credible chance to overpower him without use of a deadly weapon. However, halfway through that period of your illegal imprisonment, you have noticed that each morning when he brings you a meal in the room where he keeps you captive, he turns his back on you when he sets down the food tray. You have also observed that he carries a large knife in a sheath behind his hip, and you realize that if you catch him by surprise, you can snatch that knife. You are certain that if you try to take him at knifepoint without harming him, he will unquestionably be strong enough and skillful enough to overpower and disarm you. But, if you take that knife in one smooth motion and plunge it into his heart from behind…

This, with some embellishment, is the scenario postulated by Attorney Paul H. Robinson in his excellent 1984 analysis in *Criminal Law Defenses*. Robinson's considered expert opinion is that with this set of facts, if you snatch the kidnapper's knife and fatally stab him in the back, it should be justifiable homicide. I have come to call it "Robinson's Hypothesis."

Other brilliant lawyers, Robinson's peers, have evaluated this hypothesis and come to the same conclusion. One such is Cynthia Lee, who had this to say about it in her excellent book *Murder and the Reasonable Man*:

"One way to deal with the problems caused by a strict imminence requirement is to combine the imminence and necessity elements and require the defendant to have honestly and reasonably believed that his use of force was 'immediately necessary.' This is the approach taken by the drafters of the Model Penal Code. Under the Model Penal Code, 'the use of force on or toward another person is justifiable when the actor believes that such force is *immediately necessary* for the purpose of protecting himself against the use of unlawful force by such other person on the present occasion.'" [2]

The reader will recall that my own definition of the situation that justifies use of deadly force draws from the wording of the law. "Immediate, otherwise unavoidable danger of death or grave bodily harm to the innocent." As we consider that wording, note that many states use the word "immediate" in their definition of justifiability for deadly force. Some, however, use the word "imminent."

In the parlance of the public, "words mean things." However, we must never forget that the most crafty lawyers are wordsmiths who play with definitions to win their cases. Let's look to dictionary.com's definition of "imminent":

_____

2 Lee, Cynthia, "Murder and the Reasonable Man," Pages 129-130.

im·mi·nent [im-uh-nuhnt] adjective

1. likely to occur at any moment; impending: Her death is imminent.

2. projecting or leaning forward; overhanging.

Synonyms

1. near, at hand. Imminent, Impending, Threatening all may carry the implication of menace, misfortune,disaster, but they do so in differing degrees. Imminent may portend evil: an imminent catastrophe, but also may mean simply "about to happen": The merger is imminent. Impending has a weaker sense of immediacy and threat than imminent : Real tax relief legislation is impending, but it too may be used in situations portending disaster: impending social upheaval; to dread the impending investigation. Threatening almost always suggests ominous warning and menace: a threatening sky just before the tornado struck.

So much for the plain English definition of "imminent." Now, let's look at the legal definition of the same word, from the authoritative Black's Legal Dictionary via thelawdictionary.com:

"What is **IMMINENT DANGER?**

In relation to homicide in self-defense, this term means immediate danger, such as must be Instantly met, such as cannot be guarded against It calling for the assistance of others or the protection of the law. **U. S. v. Outerbridge**,27 Fed. Cas. 390; **State v. West**, 45 La. Ann. 14, 12 South. 7; **State v. Smith**, 43Or. 109, 71 Pac. 973. Or, as otherwise defined, such an appearance of threatened and impending injury as would put a reasonable and prudent man to his instant defense. **State v. Fontenot**, 50 La. Ann. 537, 23 South. 034. 09 Am. St. Rep. 455; **Shorter v.People**, 2 N. Y. 201, 51 Am. Dec. 280.[3]

---

3   Law Dictionary: http://thelawdictionary.org/imminent-danger/#ixzz2tp77H34L

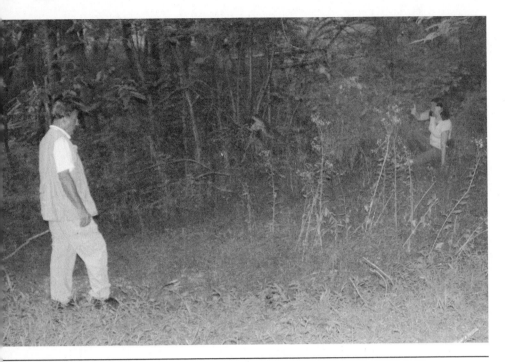

Manslaughter defendant, right, re-enacts with author in role of attacker, left, showing where she and he were when she fired the fatal shot. Charged with manslaughter in this self-defense shooting, she was acquitted at trial.

Let's analyze that. "Immediate danger, such as must be instantly met, such as cannot be guarded against it calling for the assistance of others or the protection of the law." Well, in Robinson's Hypothesis, we may still be a few days away from the arbitrary "deadline of our death" set by the murderous kidnapper, so that phrase might seem to rule out using deadly force on him today or tomorrow morning. However,"…such an *appearance* of threatened and impending injury as would put a *reasonable* and prudent man to his instant defense" found in the very next sentence appears to contradict the first, and support Robinson and Lee in their contention that deadly force by captive victim against criminal captor now meets the opportunity factor standard.

We return to plain English, via the thesaurus, which lists the following synonyms for "imminent": at hand, on the way, forthcoming, immediate, impending, inevitable, likely, looming, possible, probable, unavoidable, about to happen, approaching, brewing, close, coming, expectant, fast-approaching, following, gathering, handwriting-on-the-wall, in store, in the air, in the cards, in the offing, in the wind, in view, ineluctable, inescapable, inevasible, menacing, near, nearing, next, nigh, on its way, on the horizon, on the verge, overhanging, see it coming, threatening, to come, unescapable.

Immediate? Check! "Overhanging," that familiar definition from Black's Legal Dictionary? Synonymous, too. "Inescapable," "unavoidable," "about to happen"? Those are all there, too.

However, when I've gone through case law on this definition of "imminent," it has become apparent that in the eyes of the Courts, "imminent" is generally defined as "immediate." This explains the suggestions of Lee and the Model Penal Code that a standard of "immediately necessary" use of deadly force against danger, rather than a standard of immediacy of the deadly danger itself, is the direction in which defense counsel should go when this element becomes an issue at trial.

Pre-emptive homicide and the "Ten 'til Midnight" conundrum

What might be called "justified pre-emptive homicide" has primarily been a purview of designated police SWAT teams and elite military hostage rescue teams. A case in point occurred in the hijacking of the cargo ship *Maersk Alabama* in 2009, immortalized in the book *A Captain's Duty* and the movie "Captain Phillips." A freighter with a crew of 20 unarmed men aboard was taken over by four armed Somali pirates (yes, there is a lesson there, too). The captain was taken hostage aboard a lifeboat by three of the pirates as the fourth attempted to negotiate ransom with the US Navy.

The negotiations broke down. Captain Phillips was not necessarily in *immediate* danger of the armed pirates blowing his brains out in the next second, or even the next few seconds. But the Navy SEALS arrayed on a small boat on rolling seas knew that it was impossible for them to physically get onto the lifeboat and disarm the Somali gunmen who had threatened the execution murder of the ship's captain. And it was clear to them and to commanders aboard the Navy mother ship, the USS Bainbridge, that it was more likely than not the captain would be murdered soon.

In one of the most exemplary and astonishing displays of tactical marksmanship and orchestrated shooting in history, the SEALS opened fire simultaneously with their sniper rifles and, despite the platform of a rolling sea, instantly killed the three armed pirates and saved Captain Phillips' life.

Far from being seen as unjustified, this incident has been viewed ever since as benevolent rescue from virtually certain death. The immediate necessity to end the threat as defined by Robinson and Lee above in the Robinson Hypothesis and Attorney Lee's interpretation of the Model Penal Code, clearly prevailed over any need for the danger presented by the pirates to be measurable in mere seconds, as seen within the totality of the circumstances in the actual situation.

If you have ever talked with a victim of a seriously committed stalker, you know the maddening helpless horror they and their loved ones experience while the stalker remains at large. Rebecca Schaeffer, an up and coming young actress, was murdered by Robert Bardo in 1989 after being stalked for three years; she was 21. For every famous, murdered stalking victim such as Ms. Schaeffer or John Lennon, there are countless victims from ordinary life. It is understandable, if not excusable, when the criminal justice system seems to be doing nothing to protect them, that these victims and their loved ones think desperately of killing their stalker pre-emptively. It is a strategy that the justice system simply cannot condone nor forgive, no matter how sympathetic everyone from the public to the judge might be to the person who pulls the trigger.

In teaching Lethal Force Instructor classes, one tool I use is an old (1983) Charles Bronson movie, "Ten 'til Midnight." As entertainment, it's definitely a "B film," but as a discussion trigger for understanding lethal force law it is remarkably useful. Bronson plays a big city detective assigned to catch a particularly cunning rapist/murderer. He finds him, but the man knows how to play the system and is released. Taking the investigation personally, he stalks Bronson's daughter with obviously monstrous intent. In desperation, Bronson tries to frame him by planting false evidence…and gets caught and suspended, now shredding his own "mantle of innocence" and creating an element of malice on his own part. At the climax of the film, he barely saves his daughter from being murdered by the suspect, and chases him on foot. The killer runs into a phalanx of responding uniformed officers, who seize him. Face to face, as uniformed cops struggle to hold his arms, the killer screams at Bronson that he's going to get off on an insanity plea, come back, and take his revenge on Bronson's daughter.

Convinced after all that has occurred thus far that this is exactly what is going to happen, Bronson says coldly, "No…you…won't" -- and shoots the killer in the forehead with his Colt Detective Special.

I present this film to the class as The Facts In Evidence, and we proceed to hold "moot court" in the case of state versus Bronson's character. If there's a real judge or at least a criminal lawyer available, they take the role of judge; if not, I'm stuck with that. Prosecution and defense counsel are appointed. I've played both of those roles, against actual attorneys taking the opposite position.

Taken as it appears – Bronson's disgraced detective shooting the now-helpless stalker/rapist/murderer in cold blood to keep him from coming back for his daughter – the moot court jury has convicted more often than it acquits. Even though everyone in the room is sympathetic with the Bronson character, they do as juries generally do and apply the law as instructed…and the law does not permit individuals (whether police or private citizens) to take revenge, nor to kill to prevent *possible* killings far in the future.

The law is complicated, however, and so is the scenario of every shooting, real or fictional. Where I've been able to bring likelihood of acquittal up about equal to likelihood of conviction in the moot court case of "State v. Bronson" is when I've been in defense counsel role and changed the nature of the argument. In the film, just before Bronson kills the human monster, that man struggles with the police officers holding him and appears to break free. His hands are not clearly visible to camera or viewer, but his violent body movements are not inconsistent with trying to grab one of the officers' service handguns from its holster. With *that* possibility in the mix, reasonable doubt is created that this was a new deadly force encounter, and the Bronson character fired to keep him from killing him or other officers with a snatched gun. It's a frail reed, though, and inconsistent with Bronson's icy words, "No… you…won't." That's why, even in a moot court environment with a jury far more sympathetic to the shooter than would ever be found in a real world courtroom, conviction for murder or lesser included manslaughter results at least half the time.

The researcher will look long and hard to find a recent case where a person was acquitted for shooting to death a stalker to prevent a future crime. We recall that the standard is "reasonable fear" versus "bare fear," and the danger must be defined as imminent by the triers of the facts.

The only case of exoneration in such an instance which comes readily to this author's mind is the death of John Wesley Hardin. Hardin was the Western gunfighter who claimed

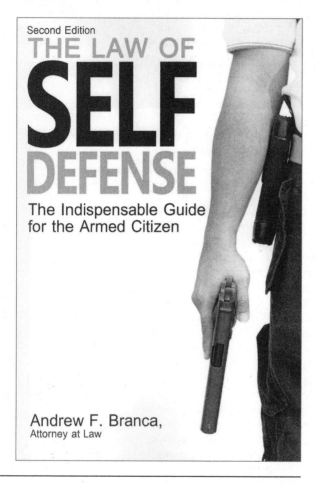

Second Edition

THE LAW OF
SELF
DEFENSE

The Indispensable Guide for the Armed Citizen

Andrew F. Branca,
Attorney at Law

Author recommends Andrew Branca's excellent book, The Law of Self Defense.

to have killed 41 men. On the night of his death, he had been threatening to kill lawman John Selman, Jr. Selman's dad, John Sr., got wind of it. He walked into the Acme Saloon in El Paso, Texas, strode up behind Hardin, and put a bullet through his head, killing him instantly. Witnesses said he shot him from behind, while Selman's defenders contended that it was a face to face gunfight. With a hole in the back of Hardin's skull, and another in his face, and little knowledge of forensic evidence yet developed in the American criminal justice community, that matter became "he said/she said." Selman was exonerated in the killing, and it was said at the time, "If he shot him from the front, he showed good marksmanship. If he shot him from behind, he showed good sense."

Selman was killed in a gunfight with US Marshal George Scarborough the following year. He had killed John Wesley Hardin in the year 1895.

The reader is reminded that it has been a very long time since 1895. Things are different now.

Opportunity factor: The bottom line

For the use of deadly force to be justified, the opponent must not only possess the power to kill or cripple, but be readily capable of employing that lethal power here and now. The fear of his doing so must be not only sincere, but reasonable, as measured by the yardstick of the reasonable person standard.

Chapter 5:
The Jeopardy Factor

In the context of this discussion, the *jeopardy* factor comes into play when your assailant utters words, and/or performs actions, which a reasonable and prudent person would construe as demonstrating an *intent to kill or cripple*.

Beware of "combat semantics" when discussing this issue. I've seen some outlines for concealed carry and self-defense courses where the "jeopardy" element is called "intent." I strongly urge the instructors I teach to get away from that terminology. When you hear someone say, "words mean things," it isn't just a hackneyed old catch-phrase. It's a truth of life, particularly in court.

Let's say the prosecutor was after your scalp, cross-examining you on the witness stand. Suppose the prosecutor (or worse, your defense lawyer on direct examination) had elicited from you a statement like, "His intent was to kill me." Actually, all he would have to do is to ask, "Did he intend to kill you?" and hear you answer in the affirmative; always remember that in legal proceedings, anything you say "yes" to is treated as if the entire statement had come out of your own mouth.

If you fell into that trap, I would expect the prosecutor to pounce. "So, you say you knew his intent! Are you telepathic? Do you have the power to read minds?" Any skilled trial advocate could make a monkey out of anyone with that.

The simple fact of life – and remember, the jury's stock in trade is the common sense garnered from their collective life experience – is that none of us can truly know the intent of another. Have you never had someone express benevolent intent to you, and then, sooner or later, stick the proverbial knife in your back?

What we all *can* reasonably and prudently determine is *manifest intent,* and that's what the jeopardy element is all about. I think the best definition of manifest intent in understanding the jeopardy factor is: *"words and/or actions which a reasonable, prudent person would construe as representing an intent to kill or cripple."*

Jeopardy is often less obvious to witnesses at the scene and the triers of the facts later, because assaultive behavior cues can be subtle. In the same sense that a dog's nose can catch scents that a human being will miss, the untrained observer who is not carefully watching your opponent can miss or fail to recognize signals which raise a red flag to you, the hopefully trained and competent armed citizen.

"Witness dynamics" are a function of human nature. Basic truth: If we are not looking for something, we are very likely not to see it. If we are not listening for something, it is very likely that we will not hear it. *And if we do not recognize or understand what we have seen or heard, it is as if we have not seen or heard it at all!*

It's true if we are the witness to the attack of A on B. And, if *we* are the "B" who is attacked by the "A," we may not see an attack coming until it is too late to defend against it.

Jeopardy is easier to show in some cases than in others. When Corporal Randy Willems was criminally charged for shooting his assailant, and he and his department were later sued over it, it was certainly helpful to me as one of his expert witnesses that his attacker had grabbed the cop by the throat with one hand and grabbed his holstered service Beretta with the other and screamed, "Give me your fuckin' gun! I'll blow your fuckin' brains out!" Enough verbalization *and* physical action to cause a reasonable, prudent person to believe that the attacker manifested intent to kill or cripple? It was certainly enough for two juries. Randy was acquitted totally in the criminal case, and he and his department won a total defense verdict in the civil lawsuit which followed.

In another case I was consulted on in California, a large, strong suspect managed to get a police officer's baton away from him. Raising it like a Neanderthal as if to club him in the head, the man announced loudly and imperiously, "I *am* going to kill you!" The officer immediately drew his service sidearm and shot the man dead. The shooting was ruled a justified homicide by the criminal justice system.

They're not all as clear as that. I remember one sad case in the Midwest where two ordinary, law-abiding, average size brothers went to a rural roadhouse to have a few drinks. One had more than a few, and was suckered into a brawl by two physically huge, immensely strong men who had a penchant for starting fights with guys they knew they could overpower, and then savagely beating them. The drunk brother agreed to "go outside," and was knocked senseless to the ground by the first punch. The other brother shouted, "He's had enough," but the two thugs then began stomping the man who was down.

With no self-defense training, knowing he stood no chance of stopping the brutal stomping with his bare hands, the victim's brother sprinted to his nearby automobile and retrieved his .380 pistol from the glove box. He ordered the men at gunpoint to leave his brother alone. One did, step-ping back and raising his hands. The other, however, leered at him and moved toward him in a menacing advance. The defender fired a warning shot, which only inflamed his op-ponent: the big man lunged at him as if to take the gun, and he fired a single shot which stopped the assailant instantly and fatally.

A reportedly anti-gun prosecutor brought him to trial. When the defense lawyer called me, I was locked into an-other case on that trial date, and referred him to Bob Houz-enga in Iowa. I had known Bob for many years. A career cop who later became a chief, he was a six-time national shooting champion and master instructor whose testimony had saved wrongly accused cops in court. He spent many hours with the lawyer, drafting his direct examination and explaining the importance of things that the attorney, and Bob, *and* the defendant when he took the stand, would have to get across to the jury.

The preparation time turned out to be wasted. When the lawyer brought Houzenga to the stand as expert witness, I've been told, he rambled through a few irrelevant questions, and then passed the witness. The prosecutor – who, if he had done his homework, must have been sweating bullets because he would have known by then that Houzenga was unimpeachable – wisely abjured from cross examination. Remember, the witness can't stand up and yell in court, "Here's what you need to know!" He or she can only answer the questions they are asked. Now there was only one chance to get the reality of the self-defense shooting across to the jury: the defendant's own testimony.

When his own lawyer gave him direct examination on the stand, defense counsel asked the defendant, "Why did you shoot him?"

The defendant answered, "He was gonna kick my ass."

And that was it.

"He was gonna kick my ass"? That's what Moe did to Larry and Curly in Three Stooges comedies. It does not sound like deadly force, and taken in a vacuum a "kicked ass" does not justify deadly force.

Convicted of the lesser included offense of manslaughter, that man spent many years in prison. Suppose instead that the defense's expert witness had been allowed to articulate the disparity of force elements – huge size and strength advantage, multiple opponents, downed and now-disabled man being stomped by the shod feet of heavy, violent men – and shown the jury why the rescuing brother had no alternative but to fire? Suppose that man had sat in that witness stand and said, as he honestly could have, "Either of those men could have killed my brother or me with their bare hands. Now both of them had him down. He was being stomped. I knew that a man on the ground would suffer much more serious injuries from a stomping than a standing man taking a kick he could roll with to lessen the impact. I couldn't face my parents and tell them I let my brother be turned into a corpse or a vegetable. I begged them to stop. One did. The other came at me, obviously about to take my gun and shoot us both. He ignored my warning shot. I knew he could overpower me and murder us both, and I fired one shot from my small caliber pistol."

Think that might have made a difference?

Dealing With Escalating Jeopardy

Many times, threats begin small and then escalate. The stalker. The "strange ranger" at work or in school. The crazy neighbor whose mission in life seems to be harassing everyone else in the neighborhood. The sort of person my friend Ron Borsch, the expert on mass murderers and how to interdict them, describes as having "**N**umerous **U**nsettling and **T**roubling **S**ymptoms." In the short term, the guy who cuts you off and gives you the finger in traffic can quickly escalate into classic and deadly "road rage."

With the latter, be the first to get on the telephone: remember that the person who first calls 9-1-1 is logged into the system as the Victim/Complainant , and the guy who calls in second has already been marked as the Suspect/Perpetrator. In the other situations described above or anything like it, you probably already know that "anything that isn't in print didn't happen"; you need to realize that goes at least double for situations such as these.

Then, there is the long term harassment/bullying/stalking situation. It is the nature of peaceable people to think, "If I call the cops, he'll only get madder and get worse. I'll just shut up and hope it all blows over." That rarely works for battered spouses, and it rarely works for victims of harassment or stalking. Often, the lack of interdiction by authorities instead emboldens the perpetrator and makes them confident that they can escalate without fear of consequences.

If it continues to escalate to the point where that individual attacks you or someone within the mantle of your protection, and forces you to apply deadly force to stop that violent attack, *you will want to have already established a paper trail determining who is who and what is what.* The entire history of modern law enforcement in this respect has been that when we get to a scene where two antagonists fought after a long period of hostility between them, we see it as illegal, voluntary mutual combat. Such mutual combat has been outlawed in the Western world at least since the principle *homicide se defendo* came into the English common law many centuries ago. The bottom line is this: *the loser goes in the meat wagon, and the winner goes in the paddy wagon.*

If there has been bad blood between you and the neighbor/relative/coworker/stalker, *and you have not reported his transgressions to the authorities,* those now-arriving authorities see it as a Hatfield-McCoy-like feud in which each party is equally culpable, and you and your defense attorneys will have a very steep uphill fight.

But if instead, the criminal justice system's own records show that you reported the other person's threats or harassment to them, perhaps repeatedly, *and they did nothing effective to stop it,* prosecutor and investigating officer alike realize that fact will come out in court, and make them appear to be ineffectual. More to the point, your reports *establish from the beginning who was the bad guy, and who was the good guy.* These factors are likely to come together to result in a determination of justifiable homicide early in the investigation, without the terrible ordeal of trial(s).

Suggested Reading

ACLDN, the Armed Citizens Legal Defense Network, has an excellent training film by unarmed combat expert Marc MacYoung titled "Recognizing and Responding to Pre-Attack Indicators." That sort of knowledge is priceless in establishing your recognition of the jeopardy factor in court, and more importantly, to recognizing the danger in time to save your life and other innocent lives in the first place. The video is available to ACLDN members via http://armedcitizensnetwork.org.

Read books on body language. Get training in it. Believe me, I've seen it work; it's valid science, not New Age yuppie BS. The single best course I've seen in recognition of assaultive behavior cues is given by Major Tania Penderakis at www.athenatraining.net. In the meantime, check out my article on recognition of assaultive behavior indicators at the *Backwoods Home* magazine website, at http://www.backwoodshome.com/articles2/ayoob87.html. It is reprinted, below, from *Backwoods Home* Issue #87:

Body Language and Threat Recognition
By Massad Ayoob

Reader mail indicates that while some *Backwoods Home* readers turn to this column for advice on putting wild game on the table or keeping four-footed poachers out of the garden, others are more interested in firearms for self-defense in lonely places. And, of course, there are readers who are concerned with family protection but don't like guns. Let's speak in particular to the latter two groups this issue. We'll get away from firearms this trip, and look at something else related to personal safety: recognition of pre-assaultive behavior cues.

People have been hurt—sometimes by strangers, sometimes by people they knew and loved—when they failed to realize that the other person was experiencing a level of hostility that was about to boil over. Being able to recognize body language associated with imminent violent action can allow you to, in the best-case scenario, disengage and leave the scene. At worst, it can give you time to activate a plan of self-defense soon enough to effectively protect yourself and those for whose safety you are responsible.

Danger Signals

The eyes, it is said, are the windows to the soul. Often, the way in which a hostile person looks at you can be a predictor of what his plans are for you.

Cops, soldiers, and mental health professionals are all too familiar with "the thousand yard stare." This is the person who seems to be not so much looking at you as through you. He may be unresponsive or inappropriately responsive in other ways.

Scowl, folded arms, weight shifting back and forth, and target stare can all be danger signals. Combat vet Zachary Rogers demonstrates.

"Target glance" can take different forms. Here, the person manifesting may be scoping out escape routes or making sure his buddy is there to back his play...

What this should tell you is that in this moment he is in an alternate reality of his own, a place where you are probably not welcome. When you see this, start "creating distance" unless you in fact are a law enforcement officer, health professional, or someone else who has a responsibility for containing and restraining this person's actions.

The opposite of the thousand yard stare is the "target stare." This is the guy who narrows his eyes and glares directly at you. The narrowing of the eyelids does for our vision what shutting down the f/stop on your camera does for the lens: it enhances depth perception. It tells you that you have become a very intense focus of his attention. If the circumstances indicate that this individual is at all hostile, the target stare is not a good sign. If you're not a cop, psyche nurse, etc., Mother Nature is telling you again to start creating distance between you and him.

There is also "target glance." Cops learned the hard way over the years that if a man casts a furtive glance in a certain direction, he may well be checking his avenues of escape: his quick look has just told the officers where he is likely to run. Is he staring at your chin? In a hostile situation, he's not admiring your Kirk Douglas chin cleft and he hasn't noticed a zit you missed this morning in the mirror. More likely, he's thinking about sucker punching you right "on the button." If his eyes go down to your crotch, he's probably not a gay guy scoping out your package...more likely, he's actively considering opening the fight with a kick to your crotch.

...and glance at your crotch may indicate that he intends to open the fight with a kick to your groin. Kevin Clark demonstrates.

A brief aside to the shooters in the audience. You know how when you see a cop, you immediately look at his holster to see what sort of sidearm he's wearing? Have you noticed that every now and then when you do that, you get a dirty look from the officer, who may step back or otherwise change his physical orientation to you? The reason is, he has been taught about pre-assaultive behavior cues, too, and he has learned to interpret a look at his holster as a "target glance" that may indicate the person is thinking about snatching his service pistol.

"Fight or Flight" Indicators

When the brain perceives that we are about to be in a strenuous physical conflict, a primitive mammalian survival reflex kicks in which prepares us to do battle or to flee. Quantified in the early 20th century as "fight or flight response" by Dr. Walter Cannon at Harvard Medical School, this phenomenon may reveal itself to another person with subtle physical manifestations...if that other person is sufficiently alert and informed to recognize what they're looking at.

When we go into a high level of "body alarm reaction," the lizard that lives in the base of our brain and controls the machinery and the thermostats decides to kick up oxygenated blood supply. The heart begins to race and the lungs begin to take in more air. Watch for rapid breathing or panting in a person who has not performed any strenuous physical activity. You may even be able to see a pulse throbbing at the neck or the temple of some individuals.

Now, let's perform a process of elimination. There is no common danger that threatens those at the scene. You have done nothing to threaten him. Neither has anyone else. He has not been exerting himself. Yet, his blood vessels are pulsing violently and he is breathing heavily. By this process of elimination, we can determine where the fight or flight thing has come from: He has already decided that he is going to fight. (Or, if you are lucky, that he is going to run.)

The adrenal system instantly releases powerful chemicals in a fight or flight state, including epinephrine ("adrenaline"). One side-effect of this is tremors, often violent ones, which will usually manifest themselves first in the non-dominant hand, almost immediately thereafter in the dominant hand, and then in the legs, particularly the knees. If you observe tremors in those locations in a situation that you perceive may turn hostile, go through that process of elimination again. Could the person be simply shivering in the cold? Do you have reason to believe he has Parkinson's disease or some other ailment of which trembling is symptomatic? If not, you know the diagnosis, and you know the first step of treatment—create distance.

The Body Language of Fight/Flight

Facial expressions and body movements can give you early warning that the person you face has gone into fighting mode. All the way back to Dr. Cannon, certain cues have been recognized as classic.

The person is likely to "quarter," that is, step back with one leg, turning his hips to something approximating a 45-degree angle. In this posture, the body is best balanced to take or deliver impact in any direction. Fighters call it the "boxer's stance." Martial artists call it the "front stance." Shooters call it the "Weaver stance." Cops are taught to stand this way, prepared immediately to react and fight, in an "interview stance."

The hands will typically be up, between hips and face, usually level with some point on the torso. The fingers may be partially closed. (The hands clenched into fists, or opening and closing into fists repeatedly, is a particularly blatant sign that the "fight" side of "fight or flight" has been internally engaged.)

The knees may flex slightly. This is the true "combat crouch." The head is likely to be slightly forward of the shoulders, and the shoulders forward of the hips. Combat trainers call this posture "nose over toes." It's what they teach their students to go into intentionally when they prepare to fight to the finish. When someone does it instinctively, it has given you what we in police work call "a clue"...

Life experience has already taught you that emotionally aroused people may not realize that their facial expression is reflecting their internal emotions outward for all to see. This happens in hostile situations too. A snarl that brings the lips back from the teeth doesn't require a professional behaviorist to interpret for you; it clearly doesn't bode well. The human is a natural carnivore, and a grimace that exposes the canine teeth is a particularly overt indication of aggressive intent.

A seemingly opposite expression can mean the same thing. Tightly clenched jaws, which may even include grinding teeth, and tightly pursed lips, can also be signs of extreme anger.

Let's go back for a moment to fight or flight basics. The heart and lungs are sending oxygenated blood through the body as fast as they can. However, if no strenuous physical activity has yet taken place, the body is now over-oxygenating, and hyperventilation can set in. Generations of medical professionals have advised hyperventilating patients to breathe into a paper bag. This causes them to inhale carbon dioxide they've just exhaled, and helps to quickly restore a normal O_2/CO_2 balance.

As it happens, people in actual fight or flight situations don't usually have access to paper bags. This includes both you, and your potential opponent.

If you are the one hyperventilating—at a high risk scene or anywhere else—I and my fellow instructors will advise you to consciously perform what has been called "combat breathing," "stress breathing," or "crisis breathing." Martial artists call it "*sanchin*" breathing." The breath is intentionally held, then slowly hissed out. It is the internalized version of the paper bag treatment. If you have been trained in the Lamaze Method of natural childbirth, you are familiar with a very similar version of stress breathing.

Sometimes, people do that automatically under stress without realizing it. If the person you are facing in a hostile situation is breathing like this, wake up and smell the coffee. Remember when we did the math before. If there's nothing else to cause stress, it is reasonable to deduce that he is planning something stressful and strenuous. One particularly common manifestation is what my mom used to call, with perhaps more justification than she knew, "blowing off steam." This is the person whose cheeks work like a bellows as he seems to intentionally hiss out a long, hard exhalation of air. It may help reduce over-oxygenation in his blood, but guess what: if he's in an uncontrollable state of rage, that building head of steam isn't going to just "blow off." There's a good chance that it's going to "blow up" instead. And you know the response. Say it with me: "Create distance..."

Look for meaningless movements. The guy who bounces up and down on the balls of his feet. The "walk that goes nowhere," that is, purposeless back and forth pacing. And, as noted before, hands which clench and unclench. (Sometimes, also, jaws that clench and unclench.) The body is subconsciously trying to burn off the excess oxygen, circulated through the bloodstream by the fight or flight response, to prevent hyperventilation. This doesn't mean the response is over with. The bottom line is, it means the fight or flight response is there.

Among Americans, nodding the head forward and back is a signal of "yes," and shaking the head from side to side is a cultural signal of "no." When you see your potential antagonist doing either of these things—and no one has asked him a yes or no question—you are experiencing another "create distance" moment. Whether he's thinking, "Yes, I knew they were going to come to take me away, and now I must attack them," or "No, I won't let them take me away this time," there's an excellent chance that what he is thinking does not bode well for you.

The folding of the arms can mean a lot of things in body language. Sometimes it just means, "I'm afraid and I'm drawing into my shell." Remember, though, that if they're showing they're afraid of you— whether or not it's a rational fear—it is the

"Blowing off steam" indicates that "fight or flight response" may have kicked in, triggered by the individual's preconceived decision to attack. Kevin Clark demonstrates.

nature of mammals in general and humans in particular to lash out at what frightens them. If the folded arms are accompanied by a tensing of the muscles, and perhaps also by a glowering facial expression or any of the other possible assaultive behavior cues, you won't be far off if you read the statement as, "I am putting on my armor, because I am preparing to fight."

Look for changes in skin color. You already know that a Caucasian who suddenly becomes "red in the face" may be displaying what is culturally recognized as the color of anger. Be aware, however, that the opposite coloration effect can mean the same thing. When the body goes into "fight or flight," vasoconstriction occurs, redirecting blood flow away from the extremities and toward the internal viscera (to "fuel the furnace" for the strenuous activity that the primal brain anticipates) and to major muscle groups. This is why frightened Caucasians tend to "turn white." However, it is also why homicidal Caucasians are sometimes seen to "turn deathly pale" before they act out their violence.

Other Signage

Street cops watch for subtle tattoos and other "subculture signals." In the gay community, a handkerchief prominently hanging out of one hip pocket or the other indicates whether you are a "top" or a "bottom." In some neighborhoods in Los Angeles, wearing red means you're with the Bloods, and wearing blue means you're with the Crips, and innocent people have found themselves dead or horribly injured for unknowingly wearing the wrong color in the wrong place.

A decade ago, I was an expert witness on the defense team for a police officer who was tried for murder after he shot and killed a man who attacked him, beat him, and tried to snatch his gun and slay him with it. A key factor in winning his acquittal was that he was able to articulate that before he was attacked, he recognized his assailant's distinctive gang tattoos and correlated that knowledge with his remembered training, which had taught him that inner-city gang members often trained themselves how to disarm and murder police officers.

Teardrops tattooed on the face mean one to five years per teardrop of hard time served in prison, for example, depending on the given subculture and locale. The tattoo "AFFA" stands for "Angels Forever, Forever Angels," and marks either a genuine member or a wannabe member of the quintessential outlaw motorcycle club, Hell's Angels. A patch—whether motorcycle club patch, or police department shoulder patch—worn upside-down on a biker's vest signifies in the outlaw subculture that the wearer has taken it from a legitimate owner he has vanquished in combat. These things are good to know if you end up fighting someone who is "wearing the sign."

Other symbols or "signage" can give you clues to where the other person is coming from. In the photos that (originally accompanied) this article, one of the role-players is wearing a cap with a logo that reads *"Pilemos Estin Ergon."* That translates from the Latin as, roughly, "War Is Work." Could it give you a clue as to the personality of the wearer, when you face him in a hostile situation?

Perspectives

Let's keep this all in perspective. What we are talking about here is taking the above cues in context with a situation which is such that hostility can be anticipated by any reasonable and prudent person. Don't forget that the guy might be

breathing heavily because he has recently exerted himself physically performing some perfectly innocent task. Always remember that the guy with the red face might simply have high blood pressure or a bad case of sunburn, or just be embarrassed, and that the person with the pale white face may come by that complexion naturally.

Let's also touch one more time on what your response should be to these "cues" we've been talking about. I cannot emphasize too strongly that "create distance" thing that has been repeated throughout this article. Any master martial artist, any role model military general, will tell you that the best battle is one you don't have to fight. The best course of action is always to avoid the conflict. The police officer, the psychiatric nurse, the professional security guard has a duty to stay at the scene and contain any violence that is threatened to those he is duty-bound to protect. For anyone else, the best thing to do is to abjure from the conflict, to back off and do everything possible to defuse the potential violence. The best fight is the one that never takes place. In many jurisdictions within the United States, the law expressly states that there is a "retreat requirement." This means that the private citizen who is assaulted is expected to retreat or at least attempt to retreat before using physi-

Clenching and unclenching fist, "quartered" stance (a/k/a "boxer's stance"), and knees flexed (not to mention facial expression) can all be pre-assault cues. Kristin Dowdy demonstrates.

cal force in self-defense. There are only two exceptions. One is an attack by a stranger in one's own home; there, under what the English Common Law called the Castle Doctrine, retreat is not required. Attacked by an intruder in one's own home, one has the right to stand his or her ground and use force immediately to repel the attack, but only equal force may be used. The other exception exists in every jurisdiction where the retreat requirement holds sway, and it says in essence, "Retreat is only demanded when it can be done with complete safety to oneself and others who are in danger."

Sometimes, the assault will come so quickly that you can't disengage, and you have no choice but to defend yourself. The law understands that. But even in that worst case scenario, being able to read the fast-developing and fast-breaking danger signals of the other person's behavior can sometimes be sufficient to buy you just enough time to react swiftly enough to defend yourself and your loved ones effectively. If things get cut that close—and they often do—the early warning of the danger signals the opponent put off can make the difference between survival and death for you and those you love. If he's going to serve up violent assault, you want to see it coming in time to return the volley more effectively than he served it, and win the match.

But if it's avoidable, recognition of pre-assaultive behavior cues may be your key to seeing it coming, in time to avoid it by breaking off contact entirely. The best advice on this doesn't come from me, or Jeff Cooper, or any of the other people who teach self-defense in violent situations. It comes from the humorous poet Ogden Nash. Nash wrote:

"When called by a panther...Don't anther."

Remember the bottom line of the jeopardy factor: it means that you, *as any reasonable person would have in the same circumstances, knowing what you knew,* concluded that your opponent was about to unlawfully kill or cripple you, or someone you had the right to protect.

We have now discussed the elements of Ability, Opportunity, and Jeopardy. When the three of them are simultaneously present, they create the situation of *immediate danger of death or grave bodily harm.*

And that, in turn, is the set of circumstances that justifies the use of lethal force.

Chapter 6:

Other Critical Concepts

To understand how the justified use of force in self-defense differs from criminal assault and homicide cases and legitimately-brought wrongful death or injury lawsuits, we need a firm grasp of some legal concepts which are not widely known among the general public. Let's start with the principle of the affirmative defense.

The Affirmative Defense

In a justified shooting in defense of self or others, the defendant would be foolish to claim that he didn't do what he did. Instead, he stipulates that he did indeed shoot his attacker, but maintains that he was justified in doing so. This is an *affirmative defense*.

The affirmative defense is a two-edged sword. I've always felt that when dealing with a two-edged sword, if the edge working for your side is the sharper of the two, you'll cut yourself free of the problem. To see why that's true with the affirmative defense, let's look at both edges of the sword, the good news and the bad news.

The good news, the righteous defendant's razor-sharp edge, is that the affirmative defense is what is known in trial strategy as a perfect defense. The website uslegal.com defines the perfect defense thus: "Perfect defense is a defense that meets all legal requirements and results the full acquittal of the accused. A defense is a denial, or answer or plea in opposition to the truth or validity of a claim by a plaintiff. For example a perfect self-defense meets all of the generally accepted legal conditions for such a claim to be valid. It is the use of force by one who accurately appraises the necessity and the amount of force to repel an attack."

Lawyers can debate interminably what does and does not constitute a perfect defense, but basically, it means this: the judge's instructions to the jury are likely to be interpretable as, "If you believe the defendant's account of the incident as a self-defense action, you must find him not guilty." Not "you may," or "you might," but – "*you **must** find him not guilty.*"

Hear the power in that! But we all know that power never comes cheaply, and here, the price is particularly high. That price is the other edge of the sword.

For all practical intents and purposes, the affirmative defense shifts the burden of proof. Normally that burden is

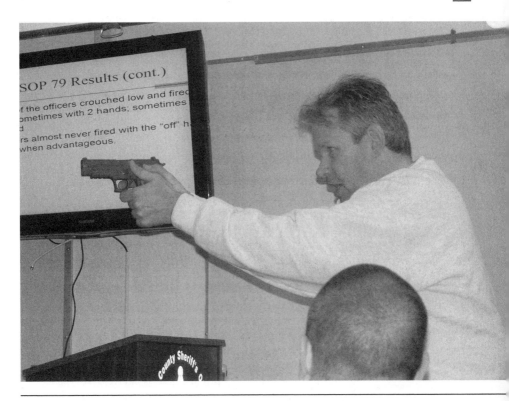

SOP 79 Results (cont.)

f the officers crouched low and fired
ometimes with 2 hands; sometimes
d
rs almost never fired with the "off" h
when advantageous.

upon the accuser, the prosecution in a criminal case or the plaintiff in a civil case. But, when the defendant has stipulated that he did the act – something much of the world will see as a "confession" – the burden falls upon him to convincingly show that he was indeed correct in having carried out that act. It needs to be proven to a preponderance of evidence standard, that is, a greater than fifty percent certainty, to the trier(s) of the facts.

Wikipedia explains, "In an affirmative defense the burden of proof is generally on the defendant to prove his allegations either by the preponderance of the evidence or clear and convincing evidence, as opposed to ordinary defenses (claim of right, alibi, infancy, necessity, and [in some jurisdictions, e.g., New York] self-defense [which is an affirmative defense at common law]), for which the defense has the burden of disproving beyond a reasonable doubt."

Wikipedia continues, "Because an affirmative defense requires an assertion of facts beyond those claimed by the plaintiff, generally the party who offers an affirmative defense bears the burden of proof. The standard of proof is typically lower than beyond a reasonable doubt. It can

Chicago street cop Bob Stasch, with well over a dozen gunfights behind him, knows when he should press the trigger, and when he shouldn't. He is demonstrating with Ring's brand dummy of the gun he prefers on duty, the SIG P220 .45 pistol.

either be proved by clear and convincing evidence or by a preponderance of the evidence."

The element of the affirmative defense's shifted burden of proof is more subtle than it appears. In his excellent book *The Law of Self-Defense*, my friend and graduate Andrew Branca writes, "While in 49 states the prosecutor must disprove self-defense beyond a reasonable doubt, in Ohio the defendant must prove he acted in self-defense by a preponderance of the evidence."[1]

So, which is correct: the definition that the affirmative defense shifts the burden of proof from accuser to defendant, or Branca's observation that the state must still carry the burden of proof beyond a reasonable doubt? The answer, I believe, is that both are correct. The law and the recommended jury instructions may indeed state that the burden of proof is upon the prosecution. However, real world jury psychology and trial tactics tell us that when the defense itself says, "Yes, the defendant killed this man," the burden is upon the defense to show that any reasonable and prudent person would have done the same, had they been in the defendant's position and known what the defendant knew. Thus, in reality, the defendant does indeed carry a burden of showing the triers of the facts that he was correct in taking the action he did.

Why do I say the defendant's side of the sword is the sharper? Because if it has been honed with the stone of knowledge and ethics, and the defendant has done the right thing, that defendant (with a good legal team!) should be able to convincingly demonstrate exactly that to those who will judge him.

The Doctrine of Necessity

The English Common Law, largely the template for law in the United States, encompasses a concept called the *doctrine of competing harms*. Some states articulate it under that terminology, but many describe it as *the doctrine of necessity*. The two are one and the same. As it applies to lawful defense of self or others, this doctrine holds that you are allowed to break the law, in the rare circumstance where following that law would cause more human injury than breaking it.

The legal section of freedictionary.com offers this definition:

"A defense asserted by a criminal or civil defendant that he or she had no choice but to break the law." This source continues, "The necessity defense has

---

1   Branca, Andrew, "The Law of Self Defense," 2013, page 14.

long been recognized as Common Law and has also been made part of most states' statutory law. Although no federal statute acknowledges the defense, the Supreme Court has recognized it as part of the common law. The rationale behind the necessity defense is that sometimes, in a particular situation, a technical breach of the law is more advantageous to society than the consequence of strict adherence to the law. The defense is often used successfully in cases that involve a Trespass on property to save a person's life or property. It also has been used, with varying degrees of success, in cases involving more complex questions.

"Almost all common-law and statutory definitions of the necessity defense include the following elements: (1) the defendant acted to avoid a significant risk of harm; (2) no adequate lawful means could have been used to escape the harm; and (3) the harm avoided was greater than that caused by breaking the law. Some jurisdictions require in addition that the harm must have been imminent and that the action taken must have been reasonably expected to avoid the imminent danger. All these elements mirror the principles on which the defense of necessity was founded: first, that the highest social value is not always achieved by blind adherence to the law; second, that it is unjust to punish those who technically violate the letter of the law when they are acting to promote or achieve a higher social value than would be served by strict adherence to the law; and third, that it is in society's best interest to promote the greatest good and to encourage people to seek to achieve the greatest good, even if doing so necessitates a technical breach of the law.

"The defense of necessity is considered a justification defense, as compared with an excuse defense such as duress. An action that is harmful but praiseworthy is justified, whereas an action that is harmful but ought to be forgiven may be excused. Rather than focusing on the actor's state of mind, as would be done with an excuse defense, the court with a necessity defense focuses on the value of the act. No court has ever accepted a defense of necessity to justify killing a person to protect property."

For a situation to exist which brings the doctrine into play, there is an indispensable ingredient. It is called an *exigent circumstance*. As applied to use of force, the exigent circumstance would be an extreme emergency in the immediate here and now which constituted a threat of injury or death to oneself or another innocent party.

If you think about it, virtually any defensive use of deadly force would fall into this category. It is simply common sense, in a world that often deals in shades of gray between pure good and pure evil. We all learn as children, "If life gives you a choice between two evils, a good person is expected to choose the lesser of the two evils." The doctrine of competing harms is simply the law's recognition of that reality. I see it as proof that the Law is wise, the Law is mature, and the Law understands the nuances of the human condition more than it sometimes appears. It is worth noting that in at least three states – Arkansas, Hawaii, and Oregon come to mind – the doctrine of competing harms is delineated in their state's law books as the "doctrine of two evils."

Some might wish to invoke the doctrine of competing harms as a defense for illegally carrying a gun. This comes up fairly frequently in situations where a convicted felon, acting for the common good, picks up a gun and shoots a violent criminal to save an innocent human life. In one case in New Hampshire, a now-law-abiding man who had a felony conviction on his record witnessed the murder of a police officer. The policeman fell, shot in the back by the cop-killer. The witness snatched the SIG .45 pistol out of the murdered lawman's holster and, as the confrontation continued, had to shoot the cop-killer to death. Technically, the witness was a felon in possession of a firearm, a felony in and of itself. However, recognizing the doctrine of competing harms, the State Attorney General's office held him harmless for the act within the totality of the circumstances, and he was not charged.

The reason the doctrine of competing harms is not often invoked on a charge of illegal carry of a weapon is that, usually, no specific competing harm exists. A few years ago, I was on the defense team of a Rhode Island man licensed to carry in that state, who had inadvertently crossed the state line into Massachusetts, where he did not have a non-resident carry permit, before he realized he was still wearing the Glock 23 pistol he routinely carried. Within hours, that technically illegal gun had saved his life: he fired a single .40 caliber bullet, which mortally wounded a man who attacked him with a knife. He was charged with manslaughter, and also with illegal carry of the firearm, a first-offense felony in that state. We explained things to the jury, which acquitted him in the shooting itself. The defense attempted to invoke the doctrine of competing harms as a defense to the gun charge. The judge would not allow it, citing case law in that state which required the competing harm – the specific danger – to have been present at the time the defendant armed himself. Her ruling was that, since he had been carrying the gun without a Massachusetts permit prior to the threat presenting itself, the doctrine could not apply. A jury that never heard the doctrine of competing harms argument found him guilty on the felony charge of illegal carry, triggering a minimum mandatory one year in jail. He would remain a felon, prohibited from owning firearms, thereafter.

(Ironically, the defendant had been eligible for a non-resident Massachusetts carry permit, and in fact the application had been on his desk for more than a year before the shooting, but sadly he had never applied. In retrospect, he never would have been charged with the offense for which he was convicted if he had simply acquired the permit for the contiguous state.)

Author learns a lot from Bill Allard, right, whom he's known for some 40 years. Bill was the one man who killed more armed robbers in gunfights on NYPD Stakeout Squad than his famous partner, Jim Cirillo. Interview with Bill can be found in archives of ProArms Podcast.

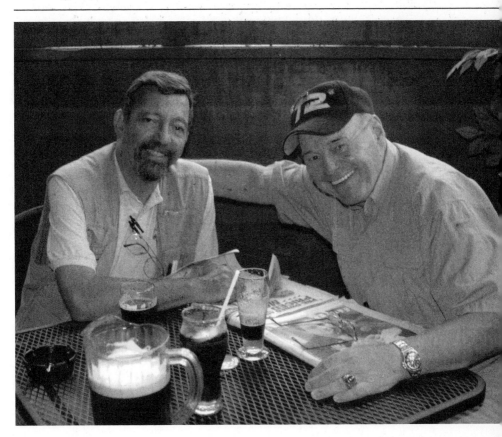

One reason I am including the doctrine of competing harms in this book is the same reason I have included it in class ever since I began training armed citizens in 1981. If it is known to the defendant and was part of the defendant's decision process at the time of the incident, if the defendant takes the stand there is an excellent chance that his attorney can bring it out during direct examination when he asks the defendant why he was armed in the first place. In a case like the one just cited, awareness of the doctrine would give jurors an excellent reason to hold the defendant harmless for the possession of the firearm.

Obviously, the best approach is to always carry the firearm *legally.*

Jury Nullification

It is not widely known that even if a jury determines that the defendant broke the law, if the jury believes the law itself is bad or stupid or wrong, the jury can still come in with a verdict of not guilty. This is known as "jury nullification." I have never heard of a case in which a judge instructed the jury that nullification was an option. Indeed, the judge's job is to instruct the jury to follow the law, not to disregard it.

An organization exists called FIJA, the Fully Informed Jury Association. Their stated purpose is to educate the general public – the jury pool – as to the fact that jurors do have the option of nullifying laws they disagree with. People often join because there are, indeed, certain laws they disagree with. Membership includes proponents of drug legalization, some who fear Draconian gun laws, etc.

While I can understand FIJA's rationale and empathize with some of their goals, I have never joined for several reasons. One is that, as this book goes to press, I have been carrying a badge for some four decades, and been certified as a police prosecutor since 1988. For me to join an organization dedicated to telling people to disregard the law would make me a hypocrite. But another reason is that it's hard for me to find a case where a person who had done the right thing *would* benefit from jury nullification, and *would not achieve* the same goal if the doctrine of competing harms was injected into the case.

Chapter 7:

Furtive Movement Shootings and Other Widely Misunderstood Events

The dynamics of violent encounters are, in legalese, "beyond the ken of the jury." That's an Old English phrase still in common legal use, and it describes matters that the average layman in the jury pool could not be expected to know without explanation by court-approved experts. Indeed, these things are seldom if ever discussed in law school.

If you keep or carry a firearm for defensive purposes, you are a potential victim of an unjust accusation based on legitimate actions that will need expert testimony so the jury can properly and fairly interpret the evidence to determine the facts. It will be hugely helpful in court – and to your decision-making ability at the danger scene itself – for the law-abiding armed citizen to understand these things beforehand. We'll look first at the "furtive movement shooting."

Furtive Movement Shootings

A furtive movement is a physical action which provokes suspicion. It often evinces stealth or secrecy, but not always. It can encompass a great many things. We're talking about a very narrow, specific subset here. In a furtive movement *shooting,* the individual who was shot has made a movement *consistent with reaching for a weapon, but **not** reasonably consistent with anything else within the totality of the circumstances.*

A man's hand reaching to the hip or the pocket, in and of itself, is obviously not enough to warrant whipping out a gun and shooting him. As the courts say, the situation has to be judged by *the totality of the circumstances.* I teach my students to assess the furtive movement as satisfying only one prong of the ability/opportunity/jeopardy test, the *ability* element: however, *the opportunity and jeopardy elements must be separately present.*

If those other elements are present, the furtive movement may create the ability element by giving the potential victim prudent reason to believe that the suspect is armed with a deadly weapon. Let's say you've just had a fender-bender auto accident. The driver of the other vehicle comes boiling out of his car and approaches you rapidly, screaming, "You SOB, I'll blow your brains out," and reaches under his clothes as if going for a gun.

Well, his obvious threat to shoot you in the head creates the element of jeopardy. Since your vehicles were close enough to make contact and he is now coming toward you, he is obviously within gunshot range: the opportunity element is clearly present. Within the totality of the circumstances, his movement consistent with going for a weapon and not reasonably consistent with anything else, now completes the triad with the element of ability.

True, you have not yet seen the gun. However, a part of the dynamics of violent encounters is understanding how rapidly an opponent can deploy a concealed weapon. Once the hand is on the hidden gun or knife, it can be brought to bear in a fraction of a second. It's true of knife or gun. Years ago, I filmed it with legendary blade master Mike Janich for the Paladin Press training film on knives and knife fighting, "Masters of Defense." Starting with my hands empty and in front of me, I was able to reach to a start signal, draw my concealed training knife, and stop the time by striking an electronic timer in front of me with that knife. The impact stopped the timer at under one half of one second. With a real knife instead of a training drone, and a human abdomen instead of an electronic timer as the target, that would have produced an eviscerating, life-threatening wound. And, be assured, there are lots of people out there with faster hands than mine.

Decades ago, I spoke in defense of a police officer charged with manslaughter for shooting a suspect who, as the cop and his partner were arresting him for illegal concealed carry, went for his gun. The suspect's gun, stolen and fully loaded, was in evidence; it was found on his person, still with its barrel barely inside his waistband. This was consistent with him just starting to clear it from its hiding place to draw and shoot the cops when the police bullet short-circuited his central nervous system and killed him instantly.

Incredibly, one of the prosecution's theories was that it couldn't be justifiable because the patrolman had not yet seen the suspect's gun coming clear when he fired. When asked at the scene what he observed, the cop said he saw the man's upper right arm coming forward, consistent with a cross-draw; the dead man's gun had been butt-forward in the left side of his waistband, and he had been reaching with his dominant right hand. A detective from his own police department testified that the cop was wrong to fire, because he should have waited to see the other man's gun.

When I was asked about that on the witness stand after being called in the officer's defense, my answer was, "If you wait to see the gun, you're going to see what comes out of it." And then I demonstrated for the jury in the courtroom. They understood…and they acquitted the officer on all counts.

I never considered that particular case to be a furtive movement shooting, simply because the man who was killed *did* have a gun, and the officer knew it! That's why he was making the arrest. However, the prosecution painted it as a furtive movement shooting, so we had to address it as such to defeat the unsubstantiated allegation of a bad judgment shooting.

In years past, when something like this happened and the man who was shot *didn't* have a gun, it was common for the prosecutor to think something like this: "Let's see…you say you shot him because you thought he had a gun. But you were wrong. I'll consider that to be bad judgment. What do my old law school notes say? It looks like 'bad judgment plus death equals manslaughter.' That's it, then; I'll charge you with manslaughter." And that ain't just theory, folks; it was happening in court. Such things led, in the old days, to the practice of officers carrying "throwdown guns" or "alibi guns."

Elsewhere in this book, we discuss why planting a weapon on the man you've shot when his actions put you in reasonable fear for your life is a hugely bad idea. The advice came from a time when legal principles of deadly force were not so well established as they are now.

One of my mentors was the great Border Patrol gunfighting trainer Bill Jordan; he wrote the foreword to my first book, *Fundamentals of Police Impact Weapons*, in 1978. I had read and re-read his classic book on gunfighting, *No Second Place Winner*. It remains one of the timeless classics on the topic. In *No Second Place Winner*, Bill Jordan wrote:

"Let us suppose that an officer is checking freight trains at night. He receives urgent information that a man had just shot and killed two policemen in the adjoining town and was believed to have caught and be riding the freight our officer is about to check. The killer is described as 'medium height and weight, wearing a brown hat, khaki pants and shirt, and believed to be heavily armed and of course, obviously dangerous.' As the train pulls into the yard and stops, a man, answering that description in externals, steps from between two box cars. Anticipating the possibility of trouble, our officer has his gun in

*one hand and his flashlight in the other. Flashing the light on the
suspect he says, 'I am an officer. Don't move!' Then, instead of
obeying the order, the suspect reaches for his hip pocket. What
would YOU do? Well, so did our hypothetical officer! But, sup-
posing further, when he goes over to examine the remains, he
finds that it was all a mistake. This man wasn't armed. Instead,
he had a bad cold and had selected a particularly unfortunate
time to decide he needed a handkerchief to blow his nose.
Although completely sincere in his conviction that his life was
in danger and despite the fact that HAD this been the man the
officer believed him to be, his wife would in all probability by
now be a widow if he had waited to see what came out of that
hip pocket, our officer is in a bad spot. That's where the alibi
gun came in. It was a small, inexpensive gun of the 'Owl Head'
or 'Saturday Night Harrison' persuasion, was fully loaded and
would shoot, had no fingerprints on it and all in all was a very
comforting thing to have around for the 'suspect' to hold until
the coroner got there! If this looks like an unethical action to
you, it is suggested that you go back and again put yourself in
the officer's spot. Then do a little honest soul searching before
adopting a 'holier than thou' attitude.*

*"Well, alibi guns are no longer needed and are a thing of
the past, so I am told."*[1]

For all but historical purposes, Bill's last sentence above
is the operative lesson of the entire passage. *"…alibi guns
are no longer needed."*

Things have changed since Bill's time on the job, working
mainly in violent areas during the second and third quarters
of the 20th century. As is explained in the chapter on "myths"
where we talk about "drop guns" and "throwdown weapons"
and why they're a spectacularly bad idea, it has been decades
since anyone could expect to get away with such a ploy. The
state of forensic evidence gathering and analysis today has
advanced beyond the wildest dreams of, say, an investigator
in the 1950s. But, more to the point, there is a better understanding of these things now in the legal arena.

By the late 1960s and 1970s, police defense teams were
winning these cases. Such great police defense lawyers as
George Franscell in Los Angeles pointed out to judges and
juries that the law had never demanded that the assailant's
gun be loaded instead of empty, for example, or even there
at all. All the law had ever demanded was that the opponent's actions be such that a reasonable and prudent person

1   Jordan, Bill, "No Second Place Winner," pages 15-16, published by Police Bookshelf, PO
Box 122, Concord, NH 03302, copyright 1965 by Bill Jordan

would believe him to be armed with a deadly weapon. If opportunity and jeopardy were separately present, that created a situation of immediate danger of death or great bodily harm which warranted recourse to a lethal response.

Remember the words of great police trainers like Chief Jeff Chudwin, and great police defense lawyers such as Laura Scarry: "You don't have to be right, you have to be *reasonable.*"

Fleeing Felon Shootings

Some people believe that they can shoot any fleeing felony suspect. They are absolutely wrong! On the other end of the spectrum, some people believe that the shooting of any fleeing felon is forbidden, since he is not at that moment attempting to kill or cripple anyone, so the shooting is no longer righteous defense of self or other innocent persons. Those people are not quite so wrong, but they are technically incorrect. For the private citizen, a very rare confluence of circumstances can occur which may justify the use of deadly force on a fleeing felon.

Let me make one thing clear: if your concealed carry instructor has told you, "Don't shoot fleeing felons, period," I'm not disrespecting him or her in any way. Concealed carry courses tend to be short, and have a great deal of ground to cover. This writer has the luxury of forty-hour courses for armed citizens, which allow greater detail, and treatment of situations which are less likely to occur, but still possible.

Another point to clarify: suppose an armed robber is running away, and you shout at him to halt. It's not the smartest thing to do, but it is legal under the principles of citizen's arrest, which exist in the black letter law of most states. He pivots, his back still to you, but swinging his gun in your direction. You fire, and your instantly fatal bullet strikes him "in the back," that is, behind the lateral midline of his body. Was that a fleeing felon shooting?

Some will say so, but in fact, it was straight up self-defense! He was trying to kill you; you fired to stop him from killing you, not to stop him from getting away; and at the moment he swung a gun in your direction with obviously construable intent to use deadly force, the "fleeing felon" argument just became moot. At that moment, your opponent has become the aggressor in a new, life-threatening assault upon you, while you are acting within the law.

The pivotal US Supreme Court decision on this matter is found in *Tennessee v. Garner,* decided in the mid-1980s.[2] It

---

2 *Tennessee V. Garner*, 471 U.S. 1 (1985),471 U.S. 1, Appeal From The United States Court Of Appeals For The Sixth Circuit, No. 83-1035.

is recommended as useful reading for anyone who keeps or carries a gun, if only because it is one of the very few cases in which the highest court in the land has addressed the use of lethal force. However, for purposes of this discussion, it is also a cornerstone case on the use of deadly force against fleeing felony suspects, and the take-away lesson from this important decision seems to be, *deadly force will only be justified if, within the totality of the circumstances, the suspect's continued freedom constitutes a clear and present danger to innocent human life and limb.* That determination is made through the prism of the reasonable person doctrine.

There are other key standards in this complicated area of deadly force law. What makes the fleeing felon a felon in the first place? He has committed a crime punishable by a year or more in prison. There are a great many offenses in that category which are not worthy of capital punishment or deadly force response by even the victim. For a fleeing felon shooting to be justified, it would have to involve a *heinous felony against the person.* In other words, a particularly atrocious crime that involves death or great bodily harm to an innocent human being. A "crime against the person" involves actual or threatened serious physical harm, not theft of what the SCOTUS itself has called "mere property." For example, armed robbery is a very serious felony, but is not normally considered a heinous felony against the person. The victim of an armed robbery can certainly shoot the robber *while still in danger,* for the simple reason that he or she is not firing the gun to save the valuables being stolen, they are firing to save themselves and others from the explicit danger of being killed that made it an *armed* robbery in the first place. Once the offender has broken off from his deadly threat and is fleeing, that danger of being killed no longer exists, and few jurisdictions will look kindly on him being shot down as he runs away; at that point, society and the minions of the law may see shooting him as an act of revenge, or a killing undertaken to recover "mere property." Legal definitions as to exactly what is a heinous felony against the person vary state to state, but will generally encompass murder, attempted murder, arson of occupied buildings, stranger kidnapping, and violent sexual assault.

Notice that there are qualifier terms hanging on most of those definitions. Juries can take days to determine what is murder and what is manslaughter; you, the person with the gun, are expected to make that determination in an instant. Prosecutor A may define him shooting at you and missing

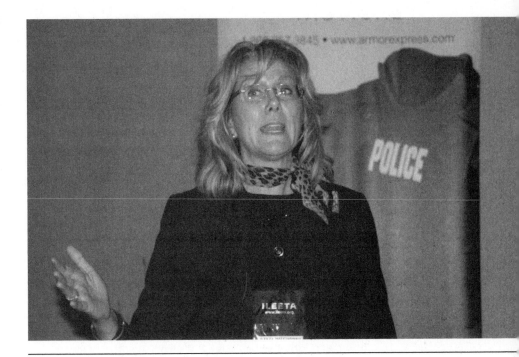

as attempted murder, but Prosecutor B may consider it only aggravated assault – a serious felony, but one not usually seen as a *heinous* felony. A non-custodial divorced parent driving away with his own child may be seen by the custodial parent as a kidnapper, but very likely won't be seen that way by the courts; hooded drug cartel members kidnapping a witness against them are a different story entirely. The man who burns down an unoccupied barn he has no right to destroy is indeed a felonious arsonist, but not in the heinous felony class of the person who deliberately sets fire to an orphanage full of children. A chauvinist boss pats his employee on the buttocks; in the strict letter of the law, he may be technically guilty of simple sexual assault, but as much as his employee might want to shoot him at the moment, the law clearly does not allow that. A true rapist, on the other hand, is a heinous felon by every standard, and "bought and paid for."

The shooter has to be certain that this fleeing person *is* the one who committed the heinous felony in question! For all practical intents and purposes, that means you've seen him do it.

Deadly force must always be a last resort. If the totality of the circumstances is such that the fleeing felon's capture is obviously imminent, killing him to stop him now would

Experienced police defense lawyers like Laura Scarry teach the fine points of what is and is not justifiable in the eyes of the law.

not be a great idea. But if the totality of those circumstances indicated that he would remain at large indefinitely to commit more heinous crimes if not immediately stopped, the balance now tilts toward justifiability.

By that same "last resort" criterion, all other means of capture should either be obviously impossible or impractical, or have actually been tried and have failed.

Another element comes in, not from law or case law, but from common sense. Suppose that within the totality of the circumstances you realize that if you shoot this fleeing felon now, after he has already committed his crime and perhaps thrown his weapon away, it will look to all the witnesses as if *he* is a helpless victim running for his life, and *you* are the cold-blooded murderer who shot him in the back? Nature is warning you that if you pull the trigger, you will be plunging yourself and your loved ones into a long legal nightmare. If you take your finger off the trigger without firing, no one has grounds to blame you. Remember, for the private citizen, a *duty* to kill never arises, only the *right* do to so. Again… common sense.

Reviewing the above, you can see why it is so rare for those six criteria to be simultaneously present. Heinous felony against the person…known for certain to have been

Being filmed for "Personal Defense TV" Season 7 on Sportsman Channel, Rich Nance in role of bad guy spins away as Ayoob is still firing, and bad guy takes Airsoft hits in back while still a clear danger to good guy.

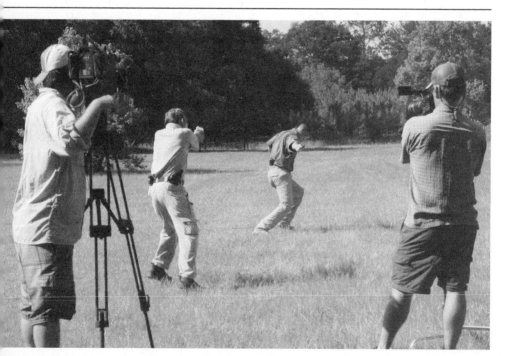

committed by THIS individual…who is likely to remain at large to do it again if he is not stopped right here, right now…in a situation where you are clearly the Good Guy and he is clearly the Bad Guy…with no other reasonable way to stop him…and, overriding everything, a situation in which his continued freedom presents a clear and present danger to innocent human life and limb.

Remember that this book does not give legal advice, it merely offers practical advice. The bottom line of practical advice on the use of deadly force against a fleeing felon is this:

*If there is the **slightest** reasonable doubt, **Don't Shoot!***

"Shot in the back"

Bullets in the back don't always involve fleeing felons. Again and again, the shooter says, "He was coming at me with a weapon, I fired, and I stopped shooting when he spun and fell." All well and good…total conformance with the rules of engagement. But the lead investigator says, "You're lying, because the autopsy shows that one or more of your bullets *hit him in the back.*"

Is the shooter lying? Very probably not. What is happening here is a demonstrable action/reaction paradigm that is not taught in law school and often not taught in professional homicide investigation seminars.

Back in the 1970s, my friend and colleague John Farnam did tests which proved that the *average* person – not just a shooting champion – can fire four shots in one second from a double action only handgun with a long trigger stroke for each shot, and five shots in one second from a semiautomatic pistol with a short-reset trigger. World champions can shoot roughly twice as fast. Two men I've learned a lot from and shot with often, whom I'm proud to call my friends, are named Rob Leatham and Jerry Miculek. Jerry is, almost indisputably, the finest double-action revolver shooter who has ever lived, and he is on record and on video firing eight shots in one second from an eight-shot Smith & Wesson heavy-frame revolver…and getting all hits. Decades ago, at the first Single Stack National Championships, I saw Rob pump six shots from a Springfield Armory 1911 .45 automatic into a fast-turning target in what couldn't have been much more than one-half of one second. Hold all those times in your mind for a moment.

We've just looked at it from the defender's side. Now, let's examine it from the attacker's side. He is lunging at his victim, probably not the first time he's done something like that, and now something unexpected happens: the victim comes up with a gun! Instinct tells him to turn away from the danger, and what we know now about human reaction time shows he can start that turn in a quarter of one second, or even less. As a rule of thumb, a human being can pivot his torso a quarter turn in, oh, a quarter of a second. That's 90 degrees, and if his side was angled toward you, the defender – something common in the "body language" of human-on-human assault – the lateral midline of his body has passed your gunsights in 0.25 of one second. The human can do a half-turn, 180 degrees, in half a second. That means that even when the bad guy is square-on when you started shooting, he can have his *back* square to you in 0.50 of one second.

The third thing we have to factor in is the shooter's reaction time to the unanticipated change of events when the attacker suddenly turned away. Reaction time to *anticipated stimulus* runs plus/minus a quarter of a second. But the shooter firing in self-defense does not anticipate a sudden break-off of the assailant's attack; after all, if he or she thought the attacker was going to suddenly stop attacking, he or she would not have fired at all.

This brings us into another range of human reaction: reaction to *unanticipated* stimulus. The brain has to cognitively analyze this change of events, and respond accordingly through the OODA Loop defined long ago by Col. John Boyd, the famed master trainer of USAF fighter pilots. OODA stands for Observe, Orient, Decide, Act. The defender must OBSERVE that the assailant is turning away. He or she must cognitively ORIENT to this change of events, and figure out what it means, which in this case is, "I may not have to shoot anymore." He or she must DECIDE to change actions. Finally, he or she must ACT, and physically carry out the new game plan, which in this case is to stop pulling the trigger.

Reacting to *unanticipated stimulus* therefore takes far longer, and in the meantime, the original justified action – in this case, firing as fast as one can to stop the threat – is still taking place. By the time the finger comes off the trigger, several shots may have been fired.

During this time, the attacker's body has been turning, bringing his back toward the incoming gunfire. Thus, it becomes perfectly understandable how defensively-fired shots could enter behind lateral midline.

The first case of this kind in which I was involved as an expert witness was *Florida v. Mary Menucci Hopkin*, mentioned elsewhere in this book, back in the 1980s. It involved a battered woman who shot the homicidal common-law husband who smashed his way through the door of her mobile home and came at her, after already having once tried to kill her and left her for dead. She fired three shots from her double action revolver as fast as she could, and stopped shooting when she realized he had turned away and broken off the attack. Her first shot entered the front of his torso, the second from the side, and the third in the back. The "shot in the back" element was one cornerstone of the prosecution's case against her.

Her defense lawyer, Mark Seiden, led me through an explanation very much like what I've just described above. It got the point across. Mary was acquitted of all charges by the jury.

This turning and shooting factor was later quantified in peer-reviewed literature by Dr. Bill Lewinski, head of the Force Science Institute, and still later rediscovered and quantified by Dr. Martin Fackler and one of his associates at the International Wound Ballistics Association, in the 1990s. I documented it on film in 2001 for ALI-ABA in a CLE (Continuing Legal Education for attorneys) training film on management of deadly force cases. ALI is the American Law Institute, the "blue chip provider" of CLE training material, and ABA is the American Bar Association. It remains in the archives of ALI-ABA in their CLE-TV series. It was documented on film again in 2012, including live fire demonstrations on turning targets, for "Personal Defense TV" on the Sportsman Channel, available in their archives as well.

I have had occasion to demonstrate this in court in other cases, most recently at this writing in *West Virginia v. Jonathan Ferrell* in 2012. The first case I know of in which it was pivotal to the defense was the aforementioned *Florida v. Hopkin*, but it's hard for me to believe that I was the first one to figure that out; if you know of any previous case where this was proven earlier, please let me know, in care of the publisher of this book.

The bottom line is simple, yet comes from something complicated. That bottom line is that things which seem impossible or wrong at first glance, can be recognized as not only possible but absolutely right when analyzed scientifically and professionally, in context and detail.

It is something all too many in the legal profession haven't grasped – the prosecutors who bring cases which shouldn't have been brought, and the defense lawyers who don't know how to explain to the jury how those things happened.

And the good people who fired the shots, and didn't understand how to explain what happened, to those who held their lives and futures in their hands as they judged them for those acts.

Chapter 8:

Castle Doctrine and Stand Your Ground Laws

Cato Institute's 2012 "Stand Your Ground Symposium," still archived at their website. Here, Cato's Tim Lynch moderates...

As this book is written, the concepts of Stand Your Ground and the separate and distinct Castle Doctrine have become widely confused and blurred in the public eye. The following is reprinted from a handout that accompanied this writer's CLE training lecture for the attorneys attending the 2012 Firearms Law Symposium sponsored by the Texas Bar Association.

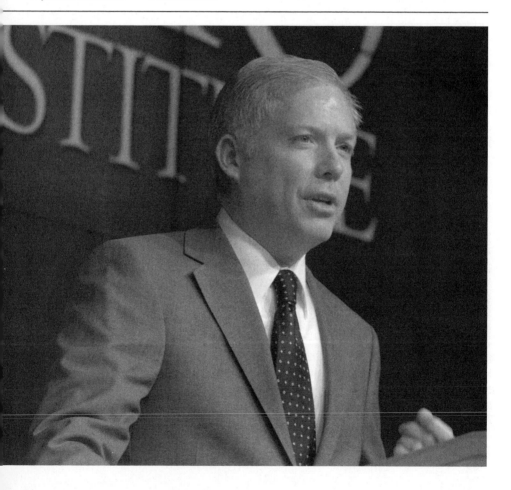

Stand Your Ground and Castle Doctrine Issues Today

Presented by Massad Ayoob,
Texas Bar Association Firearms Law Symposium
September, 2012

In a nation that has become a sound-bite society – with CNN Headline News almost as popular as regular CNN, and *USA Today* our second-most widely-read newspaper – we have a public and therefore a jury pool that is increasingly vulnerable to misinformed simple answers to complicated questions. This has certainly been true in recent years, with print and electronic media having disseminated false perceptions about such topics as Castle Doctrine and Stand Your Ground laws.

We are told on editorial pages that with these laws in place, anyone can kill anyone and get away with it by claiming "I was in fear for my life." We are told that this allows criminals to commit murder and get away with it by uttering the magic words, "It was self-defense." We are told that with these laws rivers of blood will run in the streets, that both malicious and negligent shootings will go unredressed in the civil courts, and that homicides will rise and already are rising as a direct result.

The facts, however, show otherwise.

When Terms Get Confused

Castle Doctrine derives from the ancient principle in the English Common Law which held that the individual's home is his castle; attacked there, he need not retreat, and even the king could not enter the cottage of the most humble peasant without a warrant. While the latter element touches on Fourth Amendment issues not on point to the topic of the moment, "a man's home is his castle" is so well established that it has long since entered daily American idiom.

The doctrine speaks to home and curtilage: the house or apartment itself, and attached or adjacent buildings; actual definitions of "curtilage" may vary in case law state by state. Normally, however, it will not extend to the front lawn, the sidewalk, or the far boundaries of one's farm or ranch.

Castle Doctrine issues can be murky. In one famous case in New England in the mid-1970s, *Commonwealth of Massachusetts v. Roberta Shaffer,* a state Supreme Court held that a woman who shot her common law husband when he attacked her in their home was not covered because the home was his too, and therefore her invocation of the Castle Doctrine was not applicable. In 2012, however, in *State of Nebraska v. Darrel White*, the Nebraska State Supreme Court upheld a man's right to, without retreat, kill the roommate who violently attacked him in the abode they both shared.

Stand Your Ground (SYG) laws are geared to confrontations which occur outside the home, since they would be redundant to the Castle Doctrine which already makes it clear that the individual need not retreat before using defensive deadly force against a home invader. SYG protects your client ONLY if –

- *He was not the aggressor, or if he was, has attempted to break off hostilities before the second party's attack on him now necessitates your client's use of deadly force.*
- *He was in a place where he had a right to be.*
- *He was not committing a crime at the time.*

... historian Clayton Cramer explains the development of Castle Doctrine and SYG principles over the centuries...

Since the passage of the relevant Texas law authored by State Senator Jeff Wentworth, R-San Antonio, retreat has not been required before resorting to deadly force if the latter is necessary. However, even prior, retreat has NEVER been demanded UNLESS IT COULD BE ACCOMPLISHED WITH COMPLETE SAFETY TO ONESELF AND OTHERS. This is true in Texas, and has long been true in the rest of the country as well, including the so called "retreat states."

It is imperative that your client know the difference. As you know, self-defense is an affirmative defense which shifts the burden of proof. In most jurisdictions, for a self-defense plea to prevail, the defense will have to convince the triers of the facts to a preponderance of evidence standard that the shooting was indeed justified. This burden, vastly higher than merely creating an element of reasonable doubt as to his guilt, is far more easily met if the defendant takes the stand. After all, you are stipulating that he shot the deceased: the issue is why he did so. Was his purpose malicious, or justifiable? You can say whatever you

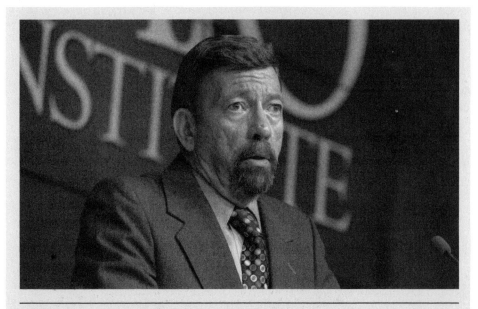

want in opening statement, but by the time you're ready to close, you have to introduce testimony or evidence to back up any assertions you make at opening. If your client doesn't take the stand, who ELSE can testify as to what his purpose was when he pulled the trigger?

...Ayoob speaks in favor of Stand Your Ground laws...

Since there is therefore a high likelihood that your client will take the stand, it is important for you to have schooled him as to the difference between Castle Doctrine and Stand Your Ground. Suppose your client was attacked by a knife-wielding mugger in a public park, and instead of attempting to retreat, drew his legally-carried gun and shot the assailant dead. During cross examination, opposing counsel may ask him, "Mr. Defendant, what do you believe justified you using a gun on him without at least attempting to just run away without bloodshed?" If your client makes the mistake of answering "Castle Doctrine," opposing counsel has your man in a very disadvantaged position.

I would expect the opposing lawyer to hand him a copy of Black's Legal Dictionary and have your client read the definition of Castle Doctrine to the jury. Then, your opposite number will pounce. "So, Mr. Defendant, it's the home that's the castle. But this shooting took place in a park. Are you telling this jury you consider the park to be your castle grounds? Who was it, exactly, who made you the king of all the rest of us?"

This is why it's important for anyone who carries a gun to know the difference between Castle Doctrine and Stand Your Ground.

Immunity to Prosecution

Since late in the first quarter of 2012, when a shooting in Sanford, Florida, captured the headlines, that state's law is the one that has received the most popular discussion. Passed in 2005, this law not only clarified Castle Doctrine in the Sunshine State, and rescinded the previous retreat requirement, but also provided for a presumption of innocence element. The defendant can request a hearing (in this case, more of a mini-trial) in which a judge who determines the act to have, more likely than not, been justified, may dismiss the case.

Immunity to Lawsuit

...and prosecutor Steve Jantzen speaks against them.

Texas, like Florida, has a provision in its law that if the shooting has been determined to have been justified, the shooter should be immune to civil lawsuit. It is reasonable to assume that an allegation of negligence by the plaintiff may, if credibly

presented, bypass this protection, since by definition there can be no justifiable accident. In one case now proceeding through the civil system in Florida, the State's Attorney has chosen not to pursue the matter of a young man who killed a burglar who was menacing him and his mother. However, that prosecutor's office has not yet issued a Memorandum of Closure declaring this use of deadly force to have been justified. At this point the lawsuit is still alive and well and progressing toward trial... since it has not, by definition, been "determined" to have been justified.

In Tyler, Texas, in February of 2007, rancher Terry Graham came home to catch a drug-addicted long-time felon and burglar leaving Graham's freshly looted house. When the homeowner challenged him, the burglar gunned his getaway car at Graham with his left hand on the steering wheel and his right hand reaching into a bag of stolen guns, when Graham fired a single shot. This shot killed the assailant, and undoubtedly saved Graham's life and perhaps the lives of two other people who were with the homeowner.

I spoke for him in front of the grand jury convened by a fair District Attorney, Matt Bingham. They no-billed. The family of the deceased sued. Attorney Tracy Crawford called Albert Rodriguez and me as experts for the defense at trial in July of 2009. The jury found entirely for defendant Terry Graham. By then, however, Mr. Graham had amassed substantial legal fees and been placed under tremendous stress for nearly two and a half years.

It was to prevent such obvious injustices that the Texas state legislature passed its law creating civil liability immunity for justified use of deadly physical force, authored by Texas State Senator Jeff Wentworth (R-San Antonio). However, that law did not go into effect until September of 2007, some seven months after Mr. Graham had to fire in what was later clearly shown to be legitimate self-defense. Tracy Crawford and many other Texas attorneys felt that if the law had been in place at the time of the Graham incident, much unnecessary grief might have been saved.

While the Castle Doctrine and SYG principles are mature, long-established concepts in the law, the civil immunity provisions in Texas and Florida law are fairly recent. They have not been tested all the way up through the appellate process. In Texas, it remains less than perfectly clear as to what "deems" the use of fatal force justifiable for purposes of civil immunity.

SYG Myths

Will an increase in justifiable homicides in states with SYG laws mean that more lives are being lost? **Not necessarily.** Historian Clayton Cramer noted that when *Time* magazine did a story on every death by gunfire for one week in America, and returned a year later to follow up on the outcomes, a significant number of those fatal shootings which had originally been implied to be criminal homicides turned out to be justified self-defense incidents.

Cramer cited one study in which justifiable homicides by armed citizens had increased three-fold – *but so had justified officer-involved shootings in the same region.* The change in law as it affected citizens certainly didn't change anything from the police side. Cramer considers it logical to conclude that, within the studied population, violent activity

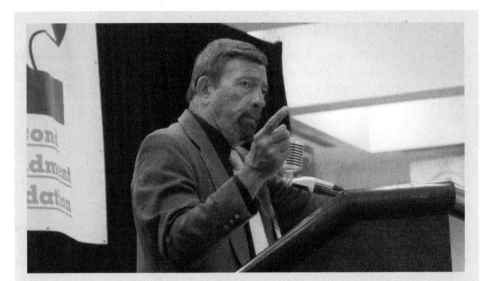

Author lectures on Stand Your Ground and Castle Doctrine issues at Gun Rights Policy Conference, September 2013, Houston.

by criminals warranting defensive use of deadly force had simply increased.

The recent Texas A&M University study on homicides as related to SYG laws notes, "This indicates that, in addition, we look at justifiable homicide, which is a separate classification available in the Supplemental Homicide Reports. One concern with these data is underreporting; Kleck (1988) estimates that only one-fifth of legally justified homicides are classified that way by police." Many shootings which previously had to go to trial to determine justifiability – at the expense of many tax dollars, and much human suffering by the wrongly accused and their families – are now simply found justifiable earlier. Far from being A Bad Thing, early determination of justifiability reduces the cost in public treasure and private trauma, and better serves Justice in both respects.

Will criminals kill people and get away with it by claiming self-defense? **Obviously not**, as witness the jury's recent verdict in *Texas v. Raul Rodriguez*. Skilled prosecutors have been winning convictions against murderers who falsely claimed self-defense for as long as there have been murder trials. One need look no farther than the 2012 conviction for murder of Raul Rodriguez, the Houston area man who went to a loud neighbor's house with a video camera and a gun, and as the prosecutor told the jury in her opening statement, used every "CHL (Concealed Handgun License) buzzword" in an incident that escalated until he had shot three men, killing one. Despite his on-camera statements of "I am standing my ground" and "I am in fear of my life," the Houston jury saw it as a malicious set-up. Mr. Rodriguez is now serving a long prison sentence.

Will the families of men killed in SYG self-defense shootings be denied civil justice because of the civil immunity clauses? **No.** A finding of self-defense at the hearing level means that justifiability has already been proven to a preponderance of evidence. Wrongful killings are exempt from immunity, a fact obvious to anyone who reads actual laws instead of newspaper headlines or the catch-phrases created by people with agendas.

Master attorney Alan Gura has won multiple landmark cases for gun owners civil rights. Here, he is speaking at Gun Rights Policy Conference.

Will SYG laws mean that cops will slough off investigations of homicides as soon as the shooter claims self-defense? **No,** and with 38 years of carrying a badge this speaker takes personal offense at that false allegation. "The death of a citizen" is a top-tier priority for law enforcement and the prosecutorial bar alike, and it is a gross insult to both to suggest that either entity would cut corners in the investigation of any homicide.

The conscientious police and prosecutors of America well know that their duty is as much to exonerate the innocent as to punish the guilty. The recent, thoroughly-considered changes in the law from Texas to Florida to other parts of the country simply reinforce the principles of justified use of lethal force for the protection of the innocent from violent criminal assaults, principles older than American jurisprudence itself.

The bottom line is simple: sometimes, criminals are so violent that there is no way to stop them but with deadly force. It happens for cops, it happens for security professionals, and it happens with armed citizens. It is good to see responsible entities of the legal profession presenting both sides of this matter to those trial advocates who will take these cases to court, and I thank the Texas State Bar Association for the opportunity to have addressed all of you today.

Chapter 9:
Debunking Myths of Armed Self-Defense

In April of 2014, the expert testimony of my friend and colleague Bob Smith in Spokane helped win acquittal for Gail Gerlach, who was charged with manslaughter. Gerlach had shot a man who, while stealing his car, had pointed a metallic object at him which appeared to be a gun, and Gerlach had fired one shot, killing the man, who turned out to have been holding shiny keys in the dimly lit vehicle. In the anti-gun Spokane newspaper, internet comments indicated that many people had the clueless idea that Gerlach had shot the man – in the back – to stop the thief from stealing his car. One idiot wrote in defense of doing such, "That 'inert property' as you call it represents a significant part of a man's life. Stealing it is the same as stealing a part of his life. Part of my life is far more important than all of a thief's life."

Analyze that statement. The world revolves around this speaker so much that a bit of his life spent earning an expensive object is worth "all of (another man's) life." Never forget that, in this country, human life is seen by the courts as having a higher value than what those courts call "mere property," even if you're shooting the most incorrigible lifelong thief to keep him from stealing the Hope Diamond. A principle of our law is also that the evil man has the same rights as a good man. Here we have yet another case of a person dangerously confusing "how he thinks things ought to be" with "how things actually are."

As a rule of thumb, American law does not justify the use of deadly force to protect what the courts have called "mere property." In the rare jurisdiction that does appear to allow this, ask yourself how the following words would resonate with a jury when uttered by plaintiff's counsel in closing argument: "Ladies and gentlemen, the defendant has admitted that he killed the deceased over property. How much difference is there in your hearts between the man who kills another to steal that man's property, and one who kills another to maintain possession of his own? Either way, he ended a human life for mere property!"

Why was Gerlach acquitted in this shooting? Because Bob Smith and the rest of the defense team were able to show the jury that he had not shot the man "for stealing his car" at all. As the car thief drove away, he turned in the front seat toward Gerlach and raised a metallic object and pointing it at him. In the prevailing light conditions, it looked like a gun – and Gerlach fired one shot from his 9mm pistol *to keep the car thief from shooting him!* Since the man was aiming backward at him over his shoulder, the defensively-fired bullet necessarily entered the offender's body behind the lateral midline. At that point, the man stopped pointing the metallic object at him, so Gerlach stopped shooting. It turned out that this object, which Gerlach reasonably presumed to be a gun, was a key holder that resembled one.

Gerlach's belief had been reasonable, and that allowed for the acquittal. It was not a case of a man being acquitted of a homicide charge for shooting "to save mere property."

Let's look at some other common myths which often suffuse discussion of armed citizens' justified use of force.

The "Drag the Corpse Inside and Plant a Knife in His Hand" Myth

The oldest and, sadly, most enduring myth out there is "when you shoot the bad guy on your porch, drag his body inside and put a knife in his hand before you call the police." If I've learned anything in three and a half decades of defending shooters in court, it's that The Truth is their strongest defense, and compromising that truth will kill their case and bring a verdict against them.

The time when someone could actually get away with altering evidence such as this is long gone, destroyed by modern forensic investigation techniques. When a body is moved, something called Locard's Principle comes into play, the principle of "transfer." Evidence from the body – clothing fibers, hair, blood, even skin cells and DNA – will transfer to the surface over which the body is dragged. Simultaneously, dirt or sand or carpet fibers, etc. from the surface will transfer to the body and the clothing of the deceased. The person trying to "cover his tracks" can get on his knees with a bucket of cleanser and scrub the floor "until the cows come home," but he won't get all the evidence off the scene. Much of it will be microscopic: the person who tried to change the evidence won't have a microscope, but the CSI (Crime Scene Investigation) crew most certainly *will*. The floor can be scrubbed until the naked eye sees no bloodstains, but the investigative technicians need only put down some Luminol, turn on the special lamp, and what their eye could not see before will now glow clearly.

Fingerprint experts are aware of "use patterns," the way human hands grasp certain objects. These fingerprint patterns are distinctly different from what the latent prints look like when a knife or other object is pressed into a dead man's hand. The difference shows up, to them, like a giant red flag.

In short, you could not expect to get away with this stupid "strategy" in this day and age.

Once you were discovered, what criminal charges would you have left yourself open for? Well, let's count...

- *Alteration of evidence is a crime in and of itself, sometimes coming under the umbrella of an Obstruction of Justice charge. You may as well plead, because if you've done something this stupid, you're prima facie guilty of that crime.*

- *Manslaughter is now very much on the table of possible indictments, because what you've done is something the general public, the jury pool from which the Grand Jury is drawn, associates with someone who panicked, shot someone they shouldn't have shot, and is now trying to cover up their guilt.*

- *Premeditated murder is another possible charge, on the theory that "alteration of evidence may be construed as an indication of prior planning of a crime."*

- *Perjury, lying under oath, is a felony in most jurisdictions, and is implicit in the incredibly stupid "alter the evidence" meme.*

The "Shoot and Scoot" Myth

It's not uncommon to hear, "If you have to shoot someone in self-defense, look both ways for witnesses and if you don't see any, just leave. That way you save all the hassle." I'm told there's a fellow on one of the gun-related Internet boards who claims he's a lawyer (interestingly, without giving his real name) when he posts that stupid advice.

Think about it: The prisons are full of people who looked around for witnesses, and didn't see any until they appeared to testify against them at trial. When an innocent person who did the right thing takes this terrible advice, they fall into an ancient trap called "flight equals guilt." It's the assumption that the cause for leaving the scene was "consciousness of guilt." In the classic US Supreme Court case *Illinois v. Wardlow,* SCOTUS upheld the actions of police who chased a man, caught him, and found inculpatory evidence upon search. They had chased him solely because he ran when he saw them coming. The majority opinion stated, "Headlong flight–wherever it occurs–is the consummate act of evasion: it is not necessarily indicative of wrongdoing, but it is certainly suggestive of such."[1]

Suppose you are a careful driver, and one night a drunken pedestrian lunges in front of your car faster than it was humanly possible to stop. You remain at the scene and call 9-1-1. You can expect responding and investigating authorities to be sympathetic to you; after all, you went through something horrible that wasn't your fault. But suppose that instead of staying and calling in, you fled the scene. That turns it into "hit and run," and you can expect neither sympathy nor mercy when the weight of the criminal justice system comes down on you full force, soon to be followed by a massive civil suit.

The exact same effect kicks in on the person who leaves the scene without calling the authorities after having had to use a gun in defense of self or others. I've told my students for decades that after their gun comes out, they're in a race to the telephone. The first participant to call in the incident is generally perceived by the justice system as the "Victim/Complainant." The participant who is NOT the first to call in becomes, by default, the "Suspect." Many thugs have been going through the revolving doors of the criminal justice machine since they were juvenile offenders, and know how things work; they'll ditch their weapon, call 9-1-1, and claim that you assaulted them with a gun for no good reason. Your subsequent claim of self-defense will ring hollow in a world where cops and prosecutors alike expect the victim to be the first caller.

Failing to call in immediately, and instead leaving the scene, is the single most common mistake I've seen armed citizens make after they've otherwise properly used their gun to lawfully manage a dangerous incident instigated by a criminal. Once the "flight equals guilt" factor kicks in, you and your attorney will have a very steep uphill fight to prove your innocence.

The "I Can Shoot Anyone I Find in My House" Myth

Yes, there's a legal doctrine that says, "Your home is your castle," but that doesn't include an execution chamber. In

---

1   *Illinois v. Wardlow* (98-1036) 528 U.S. 119 (2000) 183 Ill. 2d 306, 701 N. E. 2d 484.

virtually every state, the fine print of the law and case law requires that there be a reasonably perceived threat within the totality of the circumstances.

There are any number of situations where you might come home to find someone there whom you do not immediately recognize, even if you live alone. Most people have a key to their home out to *someone:* a landlord, a cleaning lady, a relative, a friend who comes by to feed the cat when they're gone. Perhaps another member of the family has called a plumber or electrician without bothering to notify you. We see case after case of the trusted person with the key coming unexpectedly to that house when they experience something traumatic at their own home and can't think of anyplace else to go, or the guest who already has a key and arrives unexpectedly early. Such things can make for particularly ugly tragedies if the home defender doesn't take that possibility into consideration when they see an unexpected figure in the shadows.

The "I Was in Fear for My Life" Myth

Opponents of Stand Your Ground laws claimed that they allowed anyone to kill anyone and get away with it by claiming they were in fear for their life. It was blatantly false, but it was claimed so many times in so many newspapers and on so many television programs that some gun owners came to believe it. *It's simply not true.* As written in Florida at the time of this writing, for example, a successful Stand Your Ground defense requires the shooter to prove that, more likely than not, he or she did indeed fire in self-defense.

Earlier, we mentioned that one Raul Rodriguez strapped on a pistol, shouldered a camcorder, and marched to a nearby home where a neighbor he disliked was holding an outdoor party that was louder than Mr. Rodriguez liked. Walking onto the other man's property and ostentatiously complaining (all the while recording), he started and escalated an argument. When people became angry, and frightened by his gun, he said loudly for the benefit of the camera, "I am in fear of my life" and "I will stand my ground." The situation ended when Rodriguez shot and killed the neighbor he despised, and wounded two other persons present. Charged with murder, he claimed self-defense.

It did him no good. In her opening statement, the prosecutor contemptuously noted that Rodriguez had "used every CHL (concealed handgun license) buzzword in the book." The state presented a damning witness who testified that prior to the shooting, Rodriguez had told her he could kill anyone he wanted and get away with it by uttering the magic words "I was in fear for my life."

There are no magic words, and Raul Rodriguez was convicted of murder and given a long prison sentence.

The "In My State I Can't be Sued for a Self-Defense Shooting" Myth

That's a huge oversimplification. The old saying still pretty much holds true: "anyone can file suit against anyone for anything." As noted elsewhere in the Castle Doctrine/Stand Your Ground chapter, the civil suit preemption provisions found under the umbrella of some SYG laws at most provide for the judge to throw out the case if it has already been determined to be an act of self-defense. However, merely not being criminally charged may not be enough. That's because the decision not to charge may have been motivated by the prosecuting authority's assessment that it could not gain a conviction by proving the act to have been criminal, beyond a reasonable doubt; for a lawsuit, the plaintiff need only meet the much lower standard of preponderance of evidence. The same is true if the defendant in the lawsuit has been tried and acquitted in criminal court. These things fall well short of a "determination" that it was self-defense.

In the states that do have protection against civil suit if the shooting has been ruled to be in self-defense, the question is, who makes that ruling? A ruling by the judge to the effect that the court has determined the act to have been in self-defense may do it. A memorandum of closure by the prosecuting authority specifically stating that their investigation has determined the act to have been in legitimate defense of self or others may do it. The mere fact that the case was not prosecuted, or even a trial that resulted in acquittal in criminal court, may not be enough.

And if the plaintiff's theory of the case is that the incident occurred by accident or through negligence, the protection against lawsuit will most likely be bypassed also.

The defendant's belief that the shooting was justified carries little weight in and of itself.

The "I'm Having a Heart Attack, Call an Ambulance" Myth

The recommendation that the shooter should pretend to be having a heart attack has been propounded widely, sometimes by people who should have been expected to know better. The theory is that the police will stop questioning the shooter for fear of civil liability and rush him to the hospital, where emergency room doctors and nurses won't let an interrogator near them. What's wrong with that theory?

Lots of things.

1. *The hospital examination will show that you're not having a heart attack. At best, you are now seen as the panicky sort who exaggerates and overreacts – not at all the profile of the responsible person who effectively and properly managed an emergency. Or, worse, you are recognized as a liar at a time when your credibility will probably be more important than at any other time in your life.*

2. *In many jurisdictions, the act of making false pretenses to emergency services personnel (police, fire, emergency medical services) is a crime in and of itself.*

3. *Those who judge you will learn that you tied up limited emergency rescue resources that a real heart attack or trauma victim might have needed in a true life-or-death situation. Why? For the shady purpose of misleading and delaying law enforcement investigation of an act for which you are responsible. What sort of impression do you think that will make on judge and/or jury?*

4. *Finally, you're going to get a big ambulance/ER bill for no good reason, since you could have forestalled questioning simply by asking for an attorney.*

The "Warning Shots Are a Good Idea" Myth

You know a myth is widespread when it emanates from the White House. In 2013 while campaigning for a ban on so-called "assault rifles," Vice-President Joseph Biden told the public he had advised his wife that if there was a home invasion, she was to take a double barrel shotgun and fire both barrels upwards. One can only imagine how the Secret Service Vice-Presidential detail felt when they heard that. I can tell you that across the nation lawyers, cops, and gun-wise people rolled their eyes and shook their heads.

The fact is, warning shots have long been prohibited by most American police departments. This is for several reasons:

5. *What goes up, must come down. The stereotyped warning shot is fired skyward. Shooting live ammunition into the sky is a practice normally associated with Third World countries where respect for human life is not as great as in the United States. There are many cases on record where such bullets "fell from the sky" and killed innocent people. In one New England case, a man carelessly fired a warning shot upward in the state's largest city; the bullet struck and killed an innocent bystander who was on the upper porch of a tenement building.*

6. *To fire the warning shot safely, the shooter would have to aim it into something that could safely absorb the projectile. This would force the shooter to take his eyes off of the potentially dangerous criminal opponent he was trying to intimidate – always a poor idea tactically.*

7. *What appears to be a safe place to plant the warning bullet, may not be. I know a police officer who, trying to break up a riot, fired a warning shot from his 12 gauge shotgun downward from the upper floor walkway of a hotel into what appeared in the dark to be a soft patch of earth. It was, instead, darkened pavement. Double-ought buckshot pellets caromed off the hard surface, one striking a young woman in the eye.*

8. *Suppose the person who caused you to fire the warning shot runs around a corner. Another gunshot rings out; someone else has shot the man, in a moment when deadly force was not warranted. The bullet goes through and through, fatally, and is not recovered. The man who wrongfully shot him claims that he fired the warning shot, and it was your bullet that caused the wrongful death. It's your word against his...unless you can say, "Officer, you'll find the bullet from MY gun in the friendly oak tree right over there." But it would have been*

better in these circumstances if you had not fired at all.

9. *Warning shots can lead to misunderstandings with deadly unintended consequences. Years ago in the Great Lakes area, two police officers were searching opposite ends of a commercial greenhouse where a burglar alarm had just gone off. One confronted the burglar, who ran. The officer raised his arm skyward for the traditional silver screen warning shot. As is often the case, the blast just made the suspect run faster. On the other end of the building, the brother officer heard the shot and shouted to his partner, asking if he was all right. But the powerful handgun had gone off so close to the first officer's unprotected ear that his ears were ringing, and he didn't hear the shout. The second officer then saw the suspect running. Concluding that the man must have killed the partner who didn't answer, that second officer shot and killed a man who was guilty only of burglary and running from the police.*

10. *A single gunshot sounds to earwitnesses (and, depending on the circumstances, even eyewitnesses) as if you tried to kill a man you were only trying to warn. Did you yell the standard movie line, "Stop or I'll shoot"? It could sound to an earwitness as if you threatened to kill a man for not obeying you, and then tried to do exactly that. Don't make threats you don't have a right to carry out, and as will be noted elsewhere in this book, the confluence of circumstances that warrants the shooting of a fleeing felon is extremely rare. (Remember that there are usually more earwitnesses than eyewitnesses; sound generally travels farther than line of sight, especially in the dark. Remember the infamous case of Kitty Genovese, who was murdered as 38 New York witnesses supposedly watched and did nothing. A study of the incident shows that only two of those witnesses actually saw the knife go into her body. However, more than 38 apparently heard her scream, "He stabbed me!")*

11. Even if there are no witnesses and the man claims you shot at him and missed, evidence will show that you did fire your gun. If he claims you attempted to murder him, it's his word against yours.

12. Murphy's law is immutable: if your weapon is going to jam, expect it to jam on the warning shot, and leave you helpless when the opponent comes up on you with his gun.

13. The firing of a gun even in the "general direction" of another person is an act of deadly force. If deadly force was warranted, well, "warning shot, hell!" You would have shot directly at him. The warning shot can tell judge and jury that the very fact that you didn't aim the shot at him is a tacit admission that even by your own lights, you knew deadly force was not justified at the time you fired the shot.

14. If the man turns on you in the next moment and you do have to shoot him or die, you've wasted precious ammunition. With the still-popular five-shot revolver, you've just thrown away 20% of your potentially life-saving firepower. In one case in the Philippines, a man went berserk in a crowded open-air market and began stabbing and slashing people with a knife in each hand. In a nearby home, an off-duty Filipino police officer heard the screams, grabbed his six-shot service revolver (with no spare ammunition), and ran to the scene. When he confronted the madman, the latter turned on him. The officer fired three warning shots into the air, sending half of all he had to protect himself and the public into the stratosphere. He turned and ran, trying to shoot over his shoulder, and missed with his last three shots. He tripped and fell, and the pursuing knife-wielder literally ripped him apart. Responding officers shot and killed the madman, but their off-duty brother was already dead by then.

A subset of the warning shot is what I've come to call the "chaser shot." This is the sort of warning shot that sends the message, "and keep running and don't come back!" This too can backfire in multiple ways. I worked on one case where a retired physician was attacked by a burglar, and fired a shot at him and missed. The criminal turned and ran. In the grip of fear, untrained, the physician fired a "chaser shot"; he didn't intend for it to hit the suspect, but it did. The criminal ran a considerable distance and then collapsed, dying, from the wound. The doctor was charged with manslaughter. His lawyer was able to keep him out of jail, but it took a lot of legal fees to do that. I consulted in another where a man was attacked by multiple people in a driveway. He shot and killed his primary assailant, and then drove away. As he did so, he raised his .38 and fired one shot over the heads of the attacker's accomplices to keep them from running toward his vehicle and dragging him out. The bullet went harmlessly over their heads and buried itself in a roof. The jury acquitted him entirely on the homicide charge, understanding that it was self-defense, but due to an obscure law in that state intended to combat drive-by shootings, convicted him on the lesser included charge of firing a gun from a moving vehicle. It was a felony level conviction, and he ended up serving prison time for it.

It is clear why most law enforcement agencies forbid warning shots, and why most private sector instructors including this writer recommend against firing them. For many years, however, I have taught Ayoob's Law of Necessary Hypocrisy, which holds this: "If I have told you, 'Do not do this, it is incredibly stupid,' and you have replied, 'Well, I might be in some situation you haven't foreseen where I may feel a need to do it anyway,' I want you to know the *least* incredibly stupid way of doing the incredibly stupid thing." That applies to things like trying to do a building search alone, for example. Applied to the warning shot, if I felt some unique set of circumstances fit the doctrine of competing harms and compelled me to fire a warning shot, I would shout "Final warning!" (*not* "Stop or I'll shoot"), and would take care to fire the bullet into something that could safely and retrievably absorb the projectile. Safely, for all the reasons stated above, and retrievably because if someone else was doing some shooting, I'd want to be able to prove that my warning shot wasn't the one that caused death or crippling injury.

But, clearly, the take-away lesson is **DON'T FIRE WARNING SHOTS!**

The "Make Sure Your Opponent is Dead" Myth

This is the theory which says that if you ever have to shoot someone, make sure he's dead before you call the police. It's born in the public fear of liars and lawyers and of a legal system most people don't fully understand. It's the old "dead men tell no tales" theory. If he's dead, he can't lie, right?

There is a great deal wrong with that sort of thinking. We shoot to stop, not to kill; if he drops his weapon and ceases hostility after a minor wound, he has been stopped. Hell, if you shoot at him and *miss* and he throws his weapon away and screams, "I give up," your right to shoot any more has just come to a screeching halt.

Can he lie? Sure. But just as smart homicide detectives and forensic pathologists can truly reconstruct events from their examination of the scene and the silent dead, a cunning and unscrupulous lawyer can craft a "theory of the case" around a criminal's corpse better than he could from the testimony of a wounded member of the underworld.

Why? Because Mark Twain was absolutely right when he said that the best thing about telling the truth was that it's easy to remember. If it was me and not fate determining whether or not my opponent died from my gunfire, I'd rather he survive. Not only because it spares his innocent family grief, but because the decades have shown me that the criminal himself can usually be caught in his lies. Caught by good detectives, and caught by your attorney. If he's dead, though, a crafty attorney who has put his ethics in his wallet can come up with any BS theory he wants, and be much harder to trip up than a live criminal. On the other hand, if your opponent has survived to give false testimony as to what happened, skilled questioning by everyone from police detectives to your defense lawyer can reveal him for the lying SOB he is.

Finally, the "make sure he's dead" meme implies that you can look at an opponent who's now out of the fight, *hors de combat*, and execute him to keep him from lying about you. There's a word for that: Murder.

Anyone who thinks he can do that, I'd rather not be reading one of my books. I'd rather he take his eyes off this page, instead, and go look in a mirror, and ask himself what kind of human being he has become.

Given the advanced state of evidence analysis and homicide investigation today, I can tell you what kind of person he is *going* to become: a convicted murderer, spending his life in prison.

The "You'll Never Have to Take the Stand" Myth

This is one that actually comes from the lawyers. It's no big secret that the great majority of people who are charged with criminal offenses are in fact guilty, either of the crime with which they are charged or at least, some lesser included offense. These people become the mainstream, meat-and-potatoes clientele of defense lawyers. If guilty men get on the stand under oath, one of two things will happen during competent cross-examination by skilled prosecutors: they will tell the truth and absolutely convict themselves, or they will lie and get caught in the lie, and still convict themselves. If they choose the latter path, the defense attorney is in the line of fire for an accusation that he suborned their client's perjury: a low-level felony in and of itself in certain jurisdictions, and certainly grounds for the attorney to be disbarred. Therefore, it's not surprising that they advise their clients not to take the stand.

This is a classic example of why the strategies defense lawyers employ, to guard the Constitutional rights of their often-guilty clients, do not work for the innocent person who has been falsely accused. If it was indeed self-defense, you'll be employing the affirmative defense discussed at length elsewhere in this book. You'll be stipulating that you did indeed fire the shot(s) that killed the deceased, but that you acted correctly in doing so.

The prosecution has the burden of establishing *mens rea*, literally "the guilty mind." They have to show that you either intended to commit a crime, or acted with negligence so gross that it rose to a culpable standard. Your only defense against that is your "mind-set": what was in your mind when you took that action. *Why did you do it?*

If you *don't* go on the witness stand to testify to why you did it, *who else on earth* **can?**

Oh, sure, your attorney can state in opening argument that you did it in lawful defense of self or other innocent parties…but whatever your lawyer says has to be backed up by facts, evidence, and testimony. The key testimony will be yours.

I've had a few cases where we simply couldn't put the defendant on the stand. In one, the defendant's doctor flatly told the lawyer that if he went on the stand, he'd win the case but lose the patient, because the defendant's heart condition was so precarious the physician didn't think he would survive the stress of the experience. Fortunately, the evidence in favor of self-defense was so strong that the attorney – Jeff Weiner, who wrote the foreword for this book – was able to make it clear to judge and prosecution alike before trial. The result was a withhold of adjudication, meaning essentially that if the defendant kept his nose clean for a certain period of time, the charge would go away. He did and it did, and the client was a free man who soon had his concealed carry permit back.

Another was a battered woman so beaten down throughout her life, we knew she'd be putty in the hands of an alpha male lawyer cross-examining her. Mark Seiden tried the case brilliantly without putting her on the stand, and the evidence and testimony of other witnesses was so strong that the jury "got it." They acquitted her on all charges after about two hours of deliberation.

Those were exceptions, in my experience. The "keep the defendant off the stand" strategy is used primarily for guilty clients. One of what I whimsically call "Ayoob's Laws" is this one: "If you hire a guilty man's lawyer who gives you a guilty man's defense, you can expect a guilty man's verdict."

Think about it. Why would your attorney tell you not to take the stand?

Perhaps he thinks you're guilty, like so many of the rest of his clients. If you are truly innocent, do you really want your life in the hands of someone who thinks you're guilty?

Maybe he thinks you're so stupid that you can be easily led down the primrose path in cross-examination by opposing counsel. Maybe he thinks you're too weak to withstand cross examination. Maybe he thinks you're a lunatic gun nut who will say something stupid on the witness stand and turn the jury against you.

Whatever his rationale, I can only tell you this: If I was the defendant in a righteous shooting case that had turned into a false accusation, and my lawyer told me, "Don't worry, you'll never have to take the stand," I know what I would do.

I would ask that lawyer, "How much do I owe you for your time so far?" I would then write a check for that amount, put it on his or her desk, and say, "You're fired."

Because that lawyer will have just told me that he or she has no clue how to deliver an affirmative defense for a person who has used a weapon in honest defense of self or other innocents.

Chapter 10:

State of Florida v. George Zimmerman: **A Case Study for Armed Citizens**

On a dark, rainy, unseasonably cold February night in 2012 in Sanford, Florida, George Zimmerman was driving to the supermarket when he saw an unfamiliar figure skulking around people's windows in a housing development not far from his own home. As elected captain of the neighborhood watch, Zimmerman called police dispatch to report it. The dispatcher asked for the exact location, and Zimmerman obligingly got out of his car to look for a street sign. The man he'd seen, who by now had disappeared from his view, suddenly emerged from the darkness to confront him, and without warning delivered a powerful punch to his face. Zimmerman staggered backward and fell, with the assailant on top of him, raining blows in a mixed martial arts "ground and pound" fashion. He grabbed Zimmerman's head and banged it on the sidewalk – and then spotted the licensed, concealed 9mm pistol holstered inside Zimmerman's waistband and reached for it, saying, "You're going to die tonight." Zimmerman stated that he was able to slap the other man's hand away, draw, and fire one shot himself.

The single Sellier & Bellot 115 grain jacketed hollow point bullet had found the heart of 17-year-old Trayvon Martin, killing him. Seasoned police investigators, despite their initial professional skepticism, quickly determined that all the physical evidence exactly fit Zimmerman's account of the incident. He was not arrested, and the prosecutorial authority, the State's Attorney's Office, did not even see a need to bring this clear-cut self-defense shooting in front of a grand jury. However, the understandably grieving parents of the slain teen hired a lawyer, who in turn reached out to a public relations firm with powerful connections in the mass media. Soon, the "murder of little Trayvon" had become a national, even worldwide *cause celebre,* with such celebrities as CNN's Nancy Grace leading the lynch mob that howled for the head of George Zimmerman. The case passed from the hands of the highly-respected State's Attorney who had jurisdiction and into the purview of appointed

Special Prosecutor Angela Corey. Rather than put it before a grand jury, she indicted him for murder on her own authority under an offer of information.

The trial began on June 10 and ended with a verdict of total acquittal on July 13, 2013. His life ruined, George Zimmerman remained perhaps "the most hated man in America," thanks to the unrelenting mass media attack on him that continued with little abatement. The Zimmerman case was clear cut proof that the mantra "a good shoot is a good shoot" is a myth born of wishful thinking.

The day the verdict came in, I began a twenty-part series analyzing the case and the issues at trial in my blog at *Backwoods Home Magazine*, a publication I've served as firearms editor since the mid-1990s. (www.backwoodshome.com/blogs/massadayoob.) It is reprinted here with the publication's permission, edited only to remove some electronic links which are no longer available. It begins with my blog post of 7/13/14.

The Zimmerman verdict, part 1

Minutes ago as I write this, justice has triumphed in a courtroom in Sanford, Florida. I wish to congratulate six brave, honest, intelligent jurors. And two fine defense lawyers. And the honest cops and witnesses who testified, and the many who contributed to the defense fund for a wrongfully accused armed citizen.

Several blog followers have asked me why I haven't written here (or spoken anywhere) on this, the most important armed citizen case of our time. The answer is this:

I did write on it once, on Friday, March 23, 2012. The following day, I received a phone call from Craig Sonner, George Zimmerman's original legal counsel, to retain me on the case as an expert witness for the defense.

The weeks wore on. Attorney and client parted ways. I was subsequently contacted by Mark O'Mara, the new defense lawyer. Late in May of 2012, I met with him in his office, along with his co-counsel Don West. I also attended the bail hearing in which Zimmerman's bond was revoked. During the hearing, TV cameras swept the courtroom. Some folks saw that, recognized me, and apparently assumed I was involved with the case.

In fact, I don't take expert witness cases until I've seen all the evidence, and the prosecution was extremely slow in providing that. I wound up not being involved. However, having been retained by one of the defendant's lawyers and consulted with another, I felt bound by confidentiality and did not think it would be professional to comment directly on the matter from then on.

I've been biting my tongue ever since, because there was much that I wanted to say.

The verdict is now in, and I'm gonna smooth those teethmarks off my tongue, and in the next few entries here will discuss some elements of the Zimmerman case which have been widely and profoundly misunderstood.

In the meantime, to get the commentary and analysis of the case that most of the mainstream media denied you, go to the excellent day by day writing of Andrew Branca, an attorney who specializes in this sort of case, at www.legalinsurrection.com.

Your commentary is more than welcome here.

Zimmerman verdict, part 2: The "unarmed teen"

It seems that the verdict of a sworn jury in our criminal justice system means little to the haters, who are still screaming that George Zimmerman killed "an unarmed seventeen-year-old." Given that seventeen is old enough to enlist in the Marine Corps and to be tried as an adult – the *Gainesville Sun* recently headlined that a "sixteen-year-old man" was to be charged with murder in the selfsame Florida criminal justice system – the age issue doesn't hold a lot of water when seen through a clear glass.

"Unarmed?" Actually, NO. The history of adjudicating deadly force actions shows that Trayvon Martin was "armed" two or three times over.

First, the haters (like the prosecution) assiduously ignored George Zimmerman's statement that while Martin was "ground-and-pounding" him, Martin saw Zimmerman's gun in its now exposed holster, told Zimmerman that he was going to die tonight, and reached for his victim's pistol.

If I'm your criminal attacker, you don't have to wait for me to shoot you before you can shoot me to defend your life, and you don't even need to wait until the gun is in my hand. If I announce my intent to murder you and reach for a gun, I'm bought and paid for right there. *And it doesn't matter whether the gun I'm reaching for is in my holster, or yours.* That's why every year in America, when thugs try to grab a policeman's gun and are shot, the shootings are ruled justifiable.

Even before Martin's reach for Zimmerman's still-holstered pistol, the circumstances that were proven to the satisfaction of the jury showed that Zimmerman was justified in shooting his attacker. Remember when defense attorney

Don West said in the defense's opening statement that Martin was armed with the sidewalk? That sounded ludicrous to lay people, and I would have phrased it differently myself, but professionals understood exactly what he was talking about.

The operative principle at law is called "disparity of force." It means that while your opponent(s) may not be armed with a deadly weapon per se, their physical advantage over you is so great that if their ostensibly unarmed assault continues, you are likely to die or suffer grave bodily harm. That disparity of force may take the form of a much larger and stronger assailant, a male attacking a female, force of numbers, able-bodied attacking the handicapped, skilled fighter attacking the unskilled, or – in this case – position of disadvantage.

Security camera photo from convenience store Trayvon Martin went to shortly before his death. Note that Martin, right, is markedly taller than clerk at left, known to be 5' 10" tall.

Position of disadvantage means that the opponent has full range and freedom of movement, and you don't. You're seat-belted behind your steering wheel while he rains punches onto your skull through the open window…or you are down and helpless in a martial arts "mount" while your opponent pounds you at will.

Finally, we have the clearly proven element of Martin smashing Zimmerman's head into the sidewalk. If I picked up a chunk of concrete or cement and tried to smash your skull with it, you would certainly realize that you were about to die or be horribly brain-damaged if you didn't stop me. It would be what the statutes call "a deadly weapon, to wit a bludgeon." *There just isn't a whole hell of a lot of difference between cement being smashed into head, and head being smashed into cement.*

Clearly, Trayvon Martin possessed the power to kill or cripple Zimmerman. That is why, under law, Zimmerman was justified in defending himself with a *per se* deadly weapon.

The jury got it. Too bad the haters didn't understand…or didn't want to understand.

Zimmerman verdict, part 3: "Who started it?"

Welcome to the new commentators here, many of whom seem to feel that Zimmerman started the encounter, a concept that concerns many of our regulars as well. Whenever there's a fight, no matter the degree of consequences, the first question is always "who started it?"

Zimmerman took the first action, calling police when he observed Martin. He said that he was concerned because the man in the hoodie appeared to be wandering slowly and aimlessly in heavy rain. This is more consistent with what might be called "casing the joint" than with someone in a hurry to get somewhere dry. He didn't mention Martin's skin color until expressly asked about it by the call center operator.

The evidence indicates that Zimmerman didn't get out of his car until the operator asked where the suspicious person was, and where the police should meet Zimmerman, the complainant. Taking that as a request for information, Zimmerman obligingly got out of the car to gather the intelligence that seemed to have been implicitly requested of him. He was, after all, the elected (not self-appointed) captain of Neighborhood Watch, and his function as Eyes and Ears of the Police had been drilled into him and the other Watch members through the Police Department itself. When the call-taker asked if he was following the man, Zimmerman replied in the affirmative. He was then told, "We don't need you to do that."

The evidence indicates that he stopped following Martin at that moment. His former rapid breathing returned to normal and wind noise from his phone stopped, consistent with his testimony that he stopped following and had lost sight of Martin. The dispatcher did not "order" him to stop following, and later admitted in court that he had no authority to do so. Nonetheless, it was clear that Zimmerman was simply following Martin to keep him in sight and report his whereabouts, not "pursuing" with any intent to "confront."

Put together the timelines of the calls – hard evidence – and the testimony of the prosecution's "star witness" Rachel Jeantel. When Zimmerman lost sight of Martin, the latter was a very short distance from home. Yet in the four minutes thereafter, he had to have left that location and gone toward Zimmerman's. Even Jeantel admits that the first words of the confrontation she heard were from Martin, before the phone went dead.

Keeping an eye on someone from a distance is not against the law. Leaving the safety and mobility of your vehicle when suspicious unknown people are around may not be the best tactical move, but is no evidence of wrongdoing or intent to confront.

Who struck the first blow? Virtually all the evidence supports Zimmerman's account; no evidence contradicts it, and no evidence supports the theory that Zimmerman assaulted Martin first, in any way. If as some conjecture Zimmerman had drawn the gun at the first, why did he wait until his scalp had been split open on the sidewalk and his nose smashed before he pulled the trigger? And if Martin really believed he was in danger from the man watching him, why didn't he simply call the police from the phone he was already speaking on?

Within the totality of the circumstances presented in court by the prosecution itself, it would seem that saying "Zimmerman started it" is like saying that a woman was raped "because she asked for it."

It's about evidence, not about "what-ifs." The simple fact is, no matter what some want to believe and no matter how much the brainwashers of the media have twisted the facts, there is no solid evidence to support any theory other than that Martin didn't like being watched, attacked Zimmerman violently, and was shot in self-defense by the man whose head he had been smashing against the sidewalk with potentially lethal effect.

There are more issues, of course, and we'll explore them here shortly.

Zimmerman verdict, part 4: The stand your ground element

Few elements of this case have been more widely misunderstood than the "stand your ground" (SYG) element. Quite simply, Florida's SYG law, statute **776.012**, simply rescinded a previous requirement that one had to retreat if possible before using deadly force in self-defense. This did not particularly change the rules of engagement. The previous law had demanded retreat only if it could be accomplished in complete safety to oneself and other innocent people present. It is hard to imagine a situation in which one WOULD kill another person if they could have simply walked away unscathed.

The evidence showed incontrovertibly that Zimmerman, straddled by his attacker in the MMA mount and being savagely beaten while supine, could not possibly have retreated or otherwise escaped at the time he pulled the trigger. His wise lawyers knew that from the beginning, Craig Sonner when I spoke with him in March of 2012, and Mark O'Mara and Don West when I discussed it with them a couple of months later.

The media is largely either confused or deceptive about this, and so I'm afraid are many lawyers, including the Attorney General of the United States, who has called for an end to SYG laws. Florida Governor Rick Scott empanelled a blue-ribbon committee to study the law last year, which included some vociferous anti-gunners. Nonetheless, their collective recommendation was to **leave SYG in place**. The Governor now stands up in defense of it as well.

Stevie Wonder has announced that he won't perform in Florida until SYG is done away with. Stevie Wonder, through no fault of his own, is blind. He has my sympathy for that.

But the other opponents of SYG seem to be willfully blind, and for that, there is no excuse.

Zimmerman verdict, part 5: The gun stuff

The firearms and ballistics evidence in this case was very important, one reason why the Kel-Tec PF9 9mm death weapon was first and foremost in the minds of journalists reporting on Eric Holder's recent decision to have all evidence in this case held pending Federal investigation (again). One of the area newspapers reported in March that the death weapon was found with a spent casing still in the chamber. This would have been consistent with someone's hand grabbing the gun and retarding the slide mechanism at the moment of the shot, and I surmised as much in the one blog entry I made on it at that time, prior to being contacted by the then-defense team and confidentiality issues kicking in from then on.

It turned out that this was not the case. The officers who recovered the evidence unloaded the death weapon. The spent casing from the one shot fired in the incident was recovered from the ground on which it had ejected, and another live round was ejected from the firing chamber after the officer removed the magazine. All eight cartridges, the gun's full capacity, were accounted for. The pistol had functioned normally, as designed.

Prosecutor John Guy, in his dramatic opening statement, made a big deal out of the fact that Zimmerman carried the Kel-Tec with a live round in the chamber, as if this implied malice and a man looking to kill someone. Over in CNN Headline News Land, Nancy Grace took up the same cry. Zimmerman's after-the-assault attackers even made a big deal out of the fact that he had a pistol with no dedicated manual safety. Ms. Grace claimed that he carried it with the safety off, and when a friend of Zimmerman's was on her show and told her the gun HAD NO safety catch per se, she yelled at him that he was wrong, she knew all about Kel-Tec PF9s, and implied that Zimmerman must have flicked the safety off beforehand. (Premeditation, don't cha know?)

Of course, the PF9 pistol DOESN'T have a safety catch. Ms. Grace apparently Googled "Kel-Tec PF9" and mistook the slide lock lever for a safety lever. Did any of you folks ever hear her apologize to Zimmerman's friend, who was right when she was wrong? Let me know, 'cause I must have missed it if she did.

For perspective, very few American police officers carry guns with manual safety levers. The most popular police pistols don't have them, including the Glock and the SIG, the two most widely used. The Smith & Wesson Military & Police has an *optional* ambidextrous thumb safety, but most police departments order those guns without that feature, and the same is true for the majority of defensive pistols bought these days by America's armed citizens. The old style service revolver didn't come with a safety either.

Like those revolvers, semiautomatics such as the Kel-Tec are normally carried ready to fire with a simple pull of the trigger, i.e., with a round chambered.

Another element I warned O'Mara and West about back in second quarter 2012 was that they could expect the prosecution to attribute malice to Zimmerman for loading with hollow points. Such ammunition is standard in virtually every police department in our nation, and is the overwhelming (and logical) choice of armed citizens. The expanding bullet is less likely to ricochet, and it is more likely to stop inside the body of the offender instead of passing through to strike an unseen bystander. It also, historically, stops gunfights faster, saving the lives endangered by the attacker who had to be shot. Finally, for that latter reason, it reduces the number of wounds the offender must suffer before he stops forcing good people to shoot him. Except for the ricochet factor, all of those elements were present in the Zimmerman>Martin shooting. The prosecution didn't harp on this as much as I expected, but prosecutor Richard Mantei did bring it up: *http://statelymcdanielmanor.word-press.com/2013/07/09/george-zimmerman-hollow-points-and-reality/*.

Fortunately, the defense covered this superbly. They did so with the testimony of material witness Mark Osterman, the Federal Air Marshal who trained Zimmerman, and told him to get a double action only pistol with no manual safety and carry it with a round in the chamber. His personal knowledge carried more weight than any outside expert could ever have brought to the game, but defense expert Dennis Root did a good job of batting clean-up and filling in other points. Together, they tanked the bogus allegations of the prosecution in this case insofar as guns, ammunition, and malice or premeditation that could be ascribed to either.

The take-away is not to avoid such unmeritorious courtroom attacks by carrying a .25 auto with an empty chamber. The take-away is, be able to logically explain your choice of gun and method of carry. The defense did exactly this, to their credit.

This case, of course, was about much more than guns, and we'll continue with that in the next entry.

Zimmerman verdict, part 6: "What if" versus "What is"

Much of this case came down to speculation versus fact. We saw it in the trial, we saw it in the prosecution's case, we see it even in comments on this blog. In the spring of 2012, in the question/answer session that followed the CATO Institute "Stand Your Ground Symposium", a sincere young man who happened to be African-American asked me if SYG protection would have been in effect for Trayvon Martin if he had been violently attacked by George Zimmerman, and had killed Zimmerman in self-defense. My answer was "Yes, of course." And I would give the same answer now.

The only problem with that hypothetical is, there is nothing to substantiate it, and there is a large body of facts in evidence to support the jury's verdict that Zimmerman was not guilty of murder, or any lesser included offense. A large body of collective evidence showing that it was Martin who attacked Zimmerman, and not vice-versa.

"*What if* Zimmerman hadn't gotten out of his car, and just driven on to his destination, the Target store?" Well, certainly, the confrontation would not have occurred. But that pales in comparison to *what if* Trayvon Martin had not attacked him and smashed his head into the sidewalk? In following a strange man who was looking into windows in a community riven by burglaries and even a home invasion, Zimmerman never broke the law. Indeed, had it not ended in death, most would have appreciated him taking notice and calling the authorities...as people had done earlier, when the head of the homeowner's association in that community had chased down and captured a burglary suspect.

"What if Zimmerman had avoided any danger by not getting involved at all?" Well, if the **nineteen firefighters killed** last month in Arizona hadn't "gotten involved," they wouldn't have died either. Does that make them responsible for their own deaths? Review the **case of Kitty Genovese** and then get back to me with your "Don't get involved" argument. But take a long look in the mirror, first, and ask yourself how long you'd want to live with looking in the mirror at the face of someone who "didn't get involved" enough to pick up a phone to help Kitty Genovese, and didn't do what a reasonable and prudent person would construe the voice of authority on that phone asked you to do.

"What if Zimmerman hadn't carried that evil gun?" Well, with Zimmerman having his head smashed against the sidewalk and being unable to escape, Trayvon Martin would probably have stood trial for the murder of George Zimmerman. The evidence and testimony are consistent with Zimmerman's account of what happened. So is something the jury never learned of during trial: the lie detector test (voice stress analysis) which Zimmerman passed shortly after the shooting, and which confirmed that he was telling the truth. He also passed the "bullshit detector test" of not one but two veteran police officers who expertly and vigorously interrogated him, without defense counsel present.

"What if it turned out that Zimmerman had made the first confrontation and pulled his gun on Martin, causing Martin to jump him and beat him in self-defense?" That WOULD have been justifiable for Martin…but there is ABSOLUTELY NO EVIDENCE TO INDICATE THAT IT DID HAPPEN. Stop and think: would a man hungry to kill, with a loaded gun already in his hand, have taken the savage beating Zimmerman did, for at least 40 seconds, before firing?

"What if" is not the standard of the law, nor the standard of logic. "WHAT IS" remains the standard for both. The evidence, not a hypothetical "theory of the case," is what counts in every aspect of the real world…the real world of the courts, and the real world of the streets.

A duly empanelled jury determined the truth from the facts in evidence and the testimony presented. Even the testimony of the *prosecution's* witnesses overwhelmingly favored the defense.

And that was only the evidence the jury was allowed to see. There was much more evidence which was confirmatory to Zimmerman's account of a clear-cut self-defense shooting. We'll get to that soon in this space…and why the jury was not allowed to see it.

Zimmerman verdict, part 7: Why the jury didn't learn about Trayvon Martin

The discovery materials which the defense finally received from the prosecution after a long and arduous fight revealed Trayvon Martin to be deeply into drugs, and a young man who reveled in street fighting, and more. (Didn't seem to have much respect for women, either.) None of that was allowed in.

The reason tracks to something found in the **Federal Rules of Evidence in the Rule 404** series, particularly Rule 404(b). Among other things, it means that prior bad acts of the person you harmed, IF THEY WERE NOT KNOWN TO YOU AT THE TIME YOU HARMED HIM, cannot be used by you to defend inflicting that harm. This is because, being unknown to you, they had no part in your decision to act as you did, and it is that act and that decision for which you are being judged at trial.

Some courts have disagreed with that. The Massachusetts State Supreme Court in two precedent cases, and the Arizona State Supreme Court in one, have ruled that if the deceased had attacked people previously a manner similar to how the defendant described being attacked by him, the jury SHOULD be allowed to know. (There was reference in the discovery materials to Martin having punched out a school bus driver.) There is no such precedent in Florida that I know of. State Supreme Court decisions from other jurisdictions do not bind on other states, but can be used as persuasive argument during a pre-trial *motion in limine* to allow such evidence.

Back in 1984, I was on the defense team as an expert witness called by two of the finest attorneys I've ever worked with, the great Roy Black and the brilliant Mark Seiden. Mark and I later served two years together as co-vice chairs of the forensic evidence committee of the National Association of Criminal Defense Attorneys, and Roy's courtroom accomplishments are legend. It would be worth your time to read Roy's autobiography "Black's Law." In the 1984 trial, Roy and Mark defended Miami Police Officer Luis Alvarez against Manslaughter charges in the shooting death of one Nevell "Snake" Johnson. (There were interesting parallels between that case and Zimmerman's. An officer of Hispanic descent had shot a 20-year-old black man who was reaching for a gun as that officer and another attempted to arrest him. The shooting triggered a race riot. A scapegoat was needed. Janet Reno, then State's Attorney there, indicted the cop.)

In that case, the state had portrayed the late Mr. Johnson as a perfect specimen of innocent young manhood, and this is what opened the door for the judge to consider the 40-page memorandum of law that Black and his team put before the bench. The judge set aside 404(b) to allow the defense to rebut that characterization, and the jury got to hear an elderly black woman describe the terror she had experienced when Nevell Johnson had made her the victim of an armed robbery. To make a long story short, Alvarez was acquitted. (Which triggered another race riot, but that's another story.)

The lead prosecutor in *Zimmerman,* Bernie de la Rionda, was too smart to open that door. I understand why Judge Nelson did not allow evidence of prior bad acts by Trayvon Martin to go in front of the jury. Interestingly, though – at the very end of the trial, when it was too late for the defense to do much of anything about it – second seat prosecutor John Guy made the state's final argument to the jury, a soliloquy rife with references to Martin, who was much taller than the man he attacked, as a "child." "Child" was also used in this respect by New York City Mayor Michael Bloomberg after the verdict, and was Martin family lawyer Ben Crump's refrain from the beginning.

Yet the Trayvon Martin who emerged from the state's reluctantly-provided evidence, the evidence the jury didn't see, was something else entirely. (Discovery available *here*.)

If Guy, Bloomberg, or Crump had ever met 17-year-old Trayvon Martin in life, and called him a helpless "child" to his face, I strongly suspect Martin would have kicked them in the balls.

Zimmerman verdict, part 8: The quantity of injury argument

Professionals in the justice system knew that the prosecution was desperately scraping the bottom of the barrel when they tried to make it look as if George Zimmerman wasn't justified in shooting Trayvon Martin because Martin hadn't hurt him badly enough yet.

Anyone smart enough to pass a bar exam and research the laws of self-defense and use of force, would know that you don't have to sustain a gunshot wound before you shoot the criminal gunman pointing his weapon at you. Similarly, you don't have to let the guy fracture your skull or spill your brains onto the sidewalk before you are justified in stopping him with lethal force.

Photos taken immediately after the shooting, along with eyewitness testimony, confirm that Zimmerman's nose was smashed into a swollen mess, and there was blood all over the back of his head from the lacerations there. Whether or not the physician's assistant who saw him later could confirm that the nose was broken, the evidence supports not only the violent sucker punch to Zimmerman's face that he said began the encounter, but also his contention of his head being smashed against the hard surface of the sidewalk. It doesn't much matter whether your opponent is banging a chunk of hard sidewalk into your head, or banging your head into that part of the sidewalk. Either way, profound or fatal brain injury is the likely result if it continues.

Why wasn't he killed or knocked unconscious by the first few such strikes? The neck muscles are among the strongest in the body. A few months after birth, they become involuntary muscles which hold your head up without having to think about it. When you instinctively resist the hands that are smashing your head into the pavement, those muscles help you mitigate the force to some degree. But with each blow of the back of your head against that unforgiving surface, you become less and less able to resist. Soon, the inevitable happens, and fatal or crippling brain damage ensues.

From what the evidence shows us, deadly force was indeed warranted at the time Zimmerman pulled the trigger and fired the single shot of the encounter. The lay jurors, even the one who couldn't quite distinguish between homicide and murder when she talked about it on TV Wednesday, understood that.

The argument that Zimmerman didn't sustain enough injury to warrant using deadly force in self-defense is simply a false argument. An argument so blatantly bogus that the knowledgeable observer can't help but wonder what motivated the lawyers who raised it in the first place.

Zimmerman verdict, part 9: The propaganda factor

Can someone spoon-feed BS to the media and sucker them into believing it? Well, TV newscasters in California were pranked after the recent crash of a Korean airliner in San Francisco. They dutifully read on the air from their Teleprompter that the plane's crew was named Sum Ting Wong, Wee Tu Lo, Ho Lee Fuk, and Bang Ting Ow.

Something similar happened in the Zimmerman case. The family of the deceased, understandably filled with grief and anger that their unarmed son had been shot to death by a man never arrested for it, hired Attorney Benjamin Crump. Crump in turn brought in a high-powered public relations firm associated with left wing political causes, as reported by the Washington Post. *http://articles. washingtonpost.com/2012-04-12/ lifestyle/35450681_1_trayvon-martin-story-george-zimmerman-unarmed-teenager.*

The story fed to the press would outrage anyone...and, predictably, it outraged everyone. The family provided a picture of Trayvon at age 12 or 13, which the media ran with the ugliest picture of Zimmerman they could find. The meme of a huge armed adult "stalking" a "helpless child" was born fully grown, to a Godzilla-like size. It loomed over America unopposed. The investigating officers and the State's Attorney's Office knew that the evidence showed something else: Zimmerman attacked by Martin, who towered over him, beat him to the ground, clearly smacked his head into the concrete, and might have even gone for his gun. But cops and good lawyers don't try their cases in the press, and no voice rose loud enough with the facts to drown out the roar of the fantasy.

MURDERED in Cold BLOOD
Trayvon Martin

16 YEAR OLD ACADEMIC SCHOLAR was MURDERED - EXECUTED in cold blood. Trayvon Martin had dreams of being an aviation mechanic. However, the 16-year-old Black teen is dead, the murderer George Zimmerman has not been charged or arrested. The parents Tracy Martin and Sybrina Fulton stated " We're not getting any closure, any answers, it's very disturbing. As a Father I'm hurt..."

Child killer of Trayvon Martin
WANTED DEAD or ALIVE

GEORGE ZIMMERMAN

GEORGE ZIMMERMAN

BLACK POWER MOVEMENT- TOPS The Ordinary Peopl
Society and NEW BLACK PANTHER PARTY For Information Contac
National Education Minister **James J Evans Muhammad 904 613-0729**
Email:jamesteacher@att.net or Minister Mikhail S. Muhammad Chairman **Southern Region New Black Panther Party** Call 904-705- 8556 Email: mikhail45@live.com
designed By JEM

We can only imagine Zimmerman's own emotional turmoil at that time. Like many Americans in their twenties, he was not yet fixed on a career and far from his peak earning years: the cost of hiring attorneys must have been terribly intimidating. He did not stay in touch with his original attorney, Craig Sonner – who, I thought, had an excellent grasp of the case and would have done very well for him – and Sonner and his co-counsel had nothing to work with. By the time Zimmerman had retained Mark O'Mara, the false perception had become a national reality. While O'Mara did an excellent job of trying to get the truth to the public, it was too late: his voice was simply drowned out by the media's "all Trayvon, all the time" crusade against his client.

The egregious editing of the dispatch tape by one major network, and the false report by another claiming that Zimmerman's clearly visible, well-documented head

abcNEWS **EXCLUSIVE**

injuries were non-existent, will be taught as warnings in journalism school for evermore. I expect that legal settlements by those networks in the suits brought by Zimmerman will be huge.

One function of the grand jury is to reassure the public that a case has been investigated and the evidence evaluated. The State's Attorney of jurisdiction, Norm Wolfinger, had a reputation for being both tough and fair, and had already scheduled this matter to go before the grand jury in the next session, when he stepped away from the case, apparently at the request of Governor Rick Scott, who appointed Angela Corey as special prosecutor. It was necessary to show an outraged public that their anger had found receptive ears.

When Ms. Corey announced that she would bypass the grand jury, it was clear to any criminal justice professional that she was going to indict him on her own, via an offer of information. There is generally one reason why a chief prosecutor will take a case away from a grand jury: the prosecutor wants an indictment and doesn't think a grand jury that has heard the evidence will deliver one.

At this point, the die was cast. The show trial was inevitable, and America had experienced a triumph of propaganda that would have been worthy of Joseph Goebbels or Josef Stalin. Even today, after the opportunity to watch three weeks of intensive trial broadcast live minute by minute which brought much of the truth to light, a majority of Americans seem to be ignorant of the facts and still convinced that a self-appointed vigilante racially profiled a black child and murdered him. Never mind that the facts in evidence clearly showed otherwise.

When that TV station in California realized they had been pranked on the "Sum Ting Wong" broadcast, they admitted it and apologized. The mass media, sadly, has not done the same in the Zimmerman matter.

Zimmerman verdict, part 10: The semantics

Anyone who has trained with me in the last few years has heard me talk about what I call "combat semantics." Smart debaters know that many words in our language have multiple shades of meaning, and they'll often try to tell people that one of those words meant "B" when you used it, when in fact you really meant "A". We saw this in more ways than one in the Zimmerman case.

At a bail hearing in April of 2012, George Zimmerman told the family of the deceased Trayvon Martin that he was "sorry." The next morning, newspapers all over the country ran headlines like "Killer Apologizes."

We all speak English here. You apologize for having done something wrong. When you say "I'm sorry" in any number of contexts, such as this one, you're probably trying to convey, "I'm sad for your loss, and I feel compassion for you, and I wish this bad thing had never happened." But another connotation of "sorry" is "I apologize," and "apologize" in turn carries the connotation of guilt. At the risk of cliché, "Self-defense is never having to say you're sorry."

Another example – already discussed earlier in this blog series, in one of the commentary sections – is "pursue" versus "follow." It is clear from the evidence that for a brief period of time, Zimmerman followed Martin – indeed, he answered "Yeah" when the dispatcher asked him if he was following the other person. Those who wanted to pillory Zimmerman turned that into an imperfect synonym: "He pursued him!"

To "pursue" carries the connotation of intent to seize and control. A police pursuit is intended to end with the laying on of hands which takes the pursued into custody. Pursuit of wild game implies the intent to turn the animal into a carcass that will be butchered and devoured. Even "pursuit of happiness" implies that when you succeed, you will possess that happiness. There is absolutely nothing in evidence to indicate that Zimmerman ever did, or even ever intended to, lay hands on Martin and take control of him. But this simple choice of words – by those who indeed did "pursue" Zimmerman in their way – helped to convince much of a nation that Zimmerman's actions were not what the evidence now shows them to be.

"Combat semantics" is a debater's game. Trial lawyers, if you think about it, are debaters playing for much higher stakes than the high school Debate Society.

And clearly, many of those who were out to hang Zimmerman were, uh, master debaters.

Zimmerman verdict, part 11: Rating the lawyers (Defense)

Watching the Zimmerman trial in 2013 was like watching the OJ Simpson trial in 1995: while the general public got a hell of an education on how these things work thanks to live TV trial coverage, those "in the business" were assessing the skills and strategies of the key players.

The face of the defense was that of a two-man team, Mark O'Mara and Don West. The general consensus was that they did a helluva good job, and that O'Mara was the best lawyer in the courtroom during that trial. Some criticized him for not being harsher on some witnesses; I respectfully disagree. When the jurors finally tell their stories in full detail, I think you'll find that his gentility scored big points with them. The jury figures out early in the trial that the lawyers are the Alphas and the witnesses are the Betas in the cross-examination dialogue...they tend to identify more with the "ordinary people" witnesses than with the "power-figure" lawyers...and they consciously or subconsciously resent those who bully the witnesses called by the opposing side. O'Mara got his points across without brutalizing anyone called by the state.

Don West was co-counsel in the truest sense of the term: he was O'Mara's partner in the battle, not his sidekick. West's long career in criminal defense practice has made him a master of caselaw and rules of evidence. But he also knows how to handle witnesses. Those who wanted a conviction complained that he was hard on Rachel Jeantel, the inarticulately angry young woman who had been speaking on cell phone with Trayvon Martin just before the fight in which he was shot. I must profoundly disagree. He could have gone MUCH harder... and come across as a bully. He came across, instead, as the avuncular older man who just couldn't get what she was saying, and let the jury come to their own conclusion that she was confessing to multiple lies.

West got a lot of crap about the "knock-knock" joke he used early in the defense's opening statement, and clueless talking heads will mention that for as long as the case is discussed. The lightweights also said that he spent too much time on details of the defense case in that opening. But for as long as people like me teach Continuing Legal Education courses on trial tactics in self-defense cases, West will be better remembered for laying out the defense's key elements in detail at the beginning of trial, so that each time one of the state's witnesses spouted BS from the stand, the jury had the defense's theory of the case to compare it to, and could recognize the BS when they heard it.

Of course, when you rate the players, you have to look at both teams...and we'll discuss the other team next. (Spoiler alert: they were more skilled than the trial made them appear.)

Zimmerman verdict, part 12: Rating the lawyers (Prosecution)

While there were two lawyers at the defense table, there were three at the State's: Bernie de la Rionda, John Guy, and Richard Mantei. With about a hundred lawyers to pick from, knowing her office would be in the spotlight, State's Attorney Angela Corey wouldn't have put anyone on the team she thought would make her look bad.

Mantei was third chair, and the lowest guy on the totem pole gets the scut work in any organization. For instance, he was the one they sent in to argue that the state had proven its case when it hadn't during the argument for judgment of acquittal. Perhaps the two senior guys didn't want to be on film forever BS-ing the judge. I suspect Mantei is a good prosecutor when he actually has a case.

The lead prosecutor in the courtroom was de la Rionda. He's the only one of the three I've seen live in a courtroom, and I can tell you that he knows the law and presents himself with articulate confidence. De la Rionda is said to have an extraordinarily high conviction rate. Why he accepted a case like this, as close as he is to retirement age, I cannot understand. His frustration was obvious throughout the Zimmerman trial; I can't imagine a man with his skill and experience being so abrasive in front of a jury for any other reason.

In second seat was Guy, by far the best orator on that prosecution team. My students have heard me warn them about attorneys who seem to have majored in drama and minored in law, and Guy certainly fit that mold in *Zimmerman*. Remember his "Fucking punks" opening, and his breathless assertion that the defendant killed the deceased "because he wanted to"? If he is as good a prosecutor as I hope he was when he really had a case, he may be disgusted enough after this trial to quit. If so, he'll have a future in theater. I would suggest something Shakespearean, because the *Zimmerman* case gave him experience in things that were "full of sound and fury, signifying nothing."

I've seen other cases, more than one in Florida, where assistant prosecutors flatly refused to argue a case for conviction when the evidence showed the defendant wasn't guilty. That didn't happen here. Perhaps they truly believed Zimmerman was guilty, though it's hard for me to believe that, given the evidence they must have studied at great length. On the other hand, they worked for Angela Corey, who does not have a public history of treating kindly those employees who go against her wishes.

I've seen many people on many a forum and blog call these prosecutors incompetent. I don't think they were. They simply had no case. If you hired the greatest chefs in the world to cook for you, and you stocked the larder with feces, the best you could hope for them to put on the table would be a big, steaming pile of shit. And in the end, through no lack of argumentation skills on their end, that's how these three prosecutors' case ended up.

Now, forevermore among their peers, they're stuck with the blemish of this case, and the accusations of withholding evidence which have come along with it, and which don't seem to have been fully resolved at this writing. When retirement comes to each, I doubt that any will consider trying this case to have been their best career move.

Before you blame the team, blame the coach who sent them into a game that never should have been played. We'll discuss their coach later.

Zimmerman verdict, part 13: Angela Corey

In the last installment, I said that it was the coach who sent the prosecution team in to try to win a game that never should have been played. The police had determined they didn't have probable cause. The highly respected state's attorney who had responsibility for the case, Norman Wolfinger, apparently agreed. When the plaintiff-orchestrated *cause celebre* created public outcry, Wolfinger scheduled the matter for the grand jury. But Florida Governor Rick Scott turned it over to Angela Corey, the state's attorney for the Jacksonville area, to act as special prosecutor.

Some have blamed Scott for this. I can't, at least not at this time. "The perception is the reality," it's said, and when the people who elected them cry out for a deeper investigation, those in charge have a duty to act. This is, in part, what the grand jury is for. While I think it should have been left in Wolfinger's capable hands, I can understand Scott's decision. His choice of Ms. Corey, however, is open to question in hindsight.

I gave Ms. Corey the benefit of the doubt as I watched this case unfold. I had hoped she would simply present the evidence to the grand jury. When she didn't, instead indicting on her own, it was inescapably obvious why: she had to have known that the grand jury would refuse to indict, once they had seen the evidence.

The job of the defense is to be a zealous advocate for the defendant. The prosecutor's role is different. She is supposed to be the minister of justice, every bit as responsible for exonerating the innocent as for aggressively prosecuting the guilty. It is an egregious breach of prosecutorial ethics to, for example, prosecute for Murder a man who the evidence shows is telling the truth about acting in self-defense. And of course, there is the very serious breach of both rules and ethics encompassed in withholding evidence from the defense, a matter which in this case is still hanging in the air.

The right is unhappy with the special prosecutor. National Review had this to say about Ms. Corey: *http://nationalreview.com/article/353633/angela-coreys-checkered-past-ian-tuttle/page/0/1*. The left apparently isn't too thrilled with her either, as seen in the Daily Beast, here: *http://www.thedailybeast.com/articles/2013/07/19/angela-corey-s-overzealous-prosecution-of-marissa-alexander.html* . Her fellow attorneys seem, for the most part, to be aghast at how she has handled the Zimmerman case, as seen here in law professor Jonathan Turley's blog: *http://jonathanturley.org/2013/07/18/zimmerman-prosecutors-angela-corey-under-fire-for-public-comments-and-allegedly-threatening-action-against-harvard-law-professor/*.

The most damning moment for Ms. Corey in this case was her commentary to the press after the acquittal. A prosecutor should respect the system, and the jury's verdict. The man she assigned to spearhead the state's case, Bernie de la Rionda, obviously understood that. One journalist asked both of them to describe the defendant and the deceased in a single word.

De la Rionda chose the words "lucky" for defendant George Zimmerman, and "victim" for the deceased Trayvon Martin. He knew how to straddle the line. Despite Zimmerman's ordeal, a lot of people think anyone who is facing life in prison and gets set free is "lucky." And "victim" *is* the term that is generally and automatically used for someone who is killed.

But Corey described the young man who was shown by the evidence as the one who started the fatal battle as "prey," and the man the jury had just found Not Guilty of Murder as "murderer."

The difference is profound. It doesn't just show her to be a bad loser, it shows her to be utterly contemptuous of the jury, and the system she is sworn to serve. Her answer was simply egregious.

There are those who believe that Ms. Corey took the case and tried to destroy Zimmerman's life because, in the cases mentioned in the links above, she had lost voter support in the African-American community and thought that prosecuting Zimmerman would be a good political move. If one accepts that, it begs the question, "How did that work for ya, Ms. Corey?"

What some call "the next Trayvon Martin case" – a white guy who wound up shooting a black teen in Jacksonville after an argument that began with the latter and his friends playing loud music in an adjacent vehicle – falls into Ms. Corey's jurisdiction. The **Florida Civil Rights Association has called for the case to be taken out of Angela Corey's hands**, because they think after the Zimmerman case, she doesn't have enough credibility to prosecute this one.

Zimmerman verdict, part 14: The judge

Of all the key figures in the courtroom during the Zimmerman trial, I found Judge Debra Nelson the most enigmatic.

Some of Zimmerman's advocates called her the fourth prosecutor. It's true that she granted more approaches to the bench to the prosecution than to the defense, and those who kept count said she sustained far more objections from the prosecution than from the defense. Her insistent questioning of the defendant himself as to whether he chose not to testify is something I haven't seen before in more than 40 years in the criminal justice system.

I would have liked it if she had allowed prior bad acts by the late Trayvon Martin to come in to the jury. At the same time, as **I've explained earlier in this blog series** , she was well within judicial prerogative to make the decision to keep that material out.

The trial lasted a month, and it's been more than a month since the jury delivered a verdict. I'm still waiting to hear how she will rule on the requests the defense made for sanctions against the prosecution for the prosecution's failure to provide discovery material – evidence – in a timely manner.

But, hey: did you watch Judge Nelson when the jury verdict was read? Is it my imagination, or was she wearing a very slight smile, a smile as inscrutable as the Mona Lisa's?

Zimmerman verdict, part 15: Talk at the scene, talk on the stand?

Many advise people involved in shootings to say nothing to the police. I'm not among them. I've seen too many cases where declining to speak is heard as "I ain't sayin' nuttin' 'til my mouthpiece gets here," and only the bad guy's side of the story gets told or assumed. I do recommend that people caught up in these things tell the responding officers the nature of the attack on them which forced them to fire, and indicate that they'll sign a complaint on the perpetrator. I also recommend pointing out evidence and witnesses, because both tend to disappear otherwise. From there on, I strongly suggest that they advise the police that they'll fully cooperate after they've spoken with counsel.

Zimmerman did otherwise, answering all questions that night and in the time that followed, and he prevailed at trial. He convinced the investigators that he was telling the truth about being a victim, not a murderer. He even passed a lie detector test (voice stress analysis) administered by the police shortly after the shooting. When defense lawyer Mark O'Mara got lead investigator Chris Serino to say that he believed Zimmerman was telling the truth, it was crushingly powerful for his client. Even though the judge ordered the jury to disregard that statement the next morning in court, it was a bell that simply could not be unrung. It turned out that his having done a videotaped walk-through of the scene was also critical to his acquittal: it allowed the jury to see the complicated layout of the scene, all the more important since Judge Nelson denied the defense's request to have the jury visit that scene.

I also advise my students to expect to take the stand on their own behalf after a self-defense shooting. Since both sides are going to stipulate as to who shot who, it's going to come down to why you shot him…and, in the last analysis, that's something the defendant can answer better than anyone else. Sometimes, *only* the defendant can really answer that question.

Why didn't Zimmerman take the stand? When I talked to Mark O'Mara a year before the trial, I got the impression he was expecting Zimmerman to testify; that Zimmerman *wanted* to testify; and that O'Mara thought his client would handle it well. After the trial was over, O'Mara confirmed that Zimmerman wanted to take the stand.

I personally think he would have done well. He certainly did when he was talking to the cops. If he's as articulate as his brother Robert, he would have done fine. Shortly after the acquittal, Robert Zimmerman went into the lion's den in an interview by hostile Piers Morgan on CNN, and the young man absolutely handed Morgan's pompous, prejudiced ass back to him on a silver platter.

Only Zimmerman and his defense lawyers can tell you why he didn't take the stand, but I can give you an educated guess: *He didn't have to.* The state's case had imploded even before the defense began theirs, with virtually every prosecution witness turning into a defense witness. *Zimmerman's walk-through* **at the scene, when everything was fresh in his mind,** *was already in to the jury…and it was* **the best evidence.** There was simply nothing important enough to add.

I will continue to recommend that people involved in these confusing, high-stress incidents not submit themselves to detailed questioning and re-enactment in the immediate aftermath. That said, it worked for George Zimmerman. I will continue to warn my students that they can expect to take the stand to explain why they shot their attacker…but in this case, George Zimmerman had already done that very well during police interrogation, and had nothing to gain by repeating himself.

Zimmerman verdict, part 16: The impact on the black community

When propagandizing media made this case out to be something other than what the evidence showed it was, a hoax had been played on the whole country. It was a particularly cruel hoax on the African-American community.

Look at it this way. Suppose the mass media – whether through gullibility or complicity – had told a false story of a cancer victim being horribly wronged. Any of us would have been outraged and hurt…but genuine cancer survivors would have been put through more unnecessary pain by the story than anyone else. Basically, that's what happened here.

Look back to the days of slavery. Fast forward to the Emancipation Proclamation, and another century forward to the time of Martin Luther King when the desegregation finally became law. Another half century since, and African-Americans are still disproportionately burdened by poverty and crime.

Is it any wonder that this group felt more pain from what their country, from the White House on down, seemed to tell them was a threatening, potentially homicidal slap in their face?

A few days after the Zimmerman acquittal, I attended a meeting at an African-American church in the deep South, sponsored by the local chapter of the NAACP and focusing on Stand Your Ground Laws. The discussion panel included the local police chief, undersheriff, chief prosecutor, and public defender. It became apparent that many of the mostly black attendees believed what the media had told them: that SYG laws had allowed a racist vigilante to murder a helpless young black man and get away with it. The professionals explained how things worked. The audience understood. Before long, talk from the almost entirely African-American audience had turned toward black-on-black crime, their real concern. While in the distant past their community had been preyed upon by the Klan and suffered lynchings, they understood that past was buried, and their real concern was present crime from within their own community.

In the weeks that followed, I was a guest on Tracey and Friends, an African-American-centric radio show headquartered in Ohio. If you have a couple of hours, listen to it here: *http://www.blogtalkradio.com/traceyandfriends/2013/07/31/ hump-day-with-tracey-jeff-and-sticks.mp3*
You'll get a better understanding of how bitter people are when they're singled out as suspects for their color, and followed suspiciously for that reason, and why some are angry enough about it to think that Trayvon Martin was right to physically confront and assault the man he perceived to be following him. I did another interview with an old friend and stalwart of the gun owners' civil rights movement, Kenn Blanchard, on his podcast *Black Man With A Gun*.

We have recently celebrated the memory of Martin Luther King, the march on Washington, and the "I have a dream" speech. It reminds us all that Dr. King made it clear that the civil rights movement was about healing, not about wounding.

The way the media – and, yes, the criminal justice system – distorted this case did a disservice to all of us. The facts in evidence clearly showed that it had nothing to do with race, and making it look as if it did plunged a knife into our consciousness as Americans.

But the way they made it look, often comparing it to the lynching of Emmett Till, the media twisted that knife into our African-American citizens with particular cruelty.

Zimmerman verdict, part 17: The cops

In the first installment of this series, I mentioned that the cops were among those to thank for justice having been done in this case. Let's look at that.

Every commentator has noted that it was the police witnesses called by the state – civilian dispatcher and community watch coordinator and evidence technicians, as well as the responding and investigating officers – who cut the legs out from under the prosecution's weak case before it could ever get to its feet. Fewer commentators have spoken of the price paid by many of those honest members of the criminal justice system.

Sanford Police Chief Bill Lee, a highly respected CLEO (chief law enforcement officer) resisted powerful demands from elected officials to file a case even though he knew there was nothing there. He did his duty and did the right thing. He was fired for that.

Detective Chris Serino was the lead detective in the case. He took a lot of heat for not wanting to file a case because he knew he didn't have probable cause. He wound up as a patrolman back in uniform.

Doris Singleton was in the role of investigator on the night of the shooting. She handled things competently. She comforted Zimmerman when she saw he was emotionally devastated by having had to end a young man's life. And she was at the rank of patrol officer at the time she testified almost a year and a half later.

Ben Kruidbos, IT director in the office of the special prosecutor, realized that the office had failed in its duty to turn over full discovery material to the defense. He fulfilled the office's duty and got that information to Zimmerman's defense team. As soon as the trial was over, special prosecutor Angela Corey fired him for doing what she should have done.

Norman Wolfinger, the designated State's Attorney (chief prosecutor) for the district, apparently realized that there was no probable cause to arrest Zimmerman but nonetheless scheduled the case for the next session of the grand jury. This is a normal procedure. It wasn't enough to placate the media-fueled lynch mob, and the case was basically taken away from him by the governor and given to special prosecutor Angela Corey. Wolfinger retired shortly thereafter. He may have been due for retirement anyway, but it was a lousy note on which to end a long and stellar career as one of Florida's most respected prosecutors.

The next time some tells says "Never talk to the police, they're your enemy," remember each and every one of those honest members of the criminal justice system who stood up, told the truth, and did their duty. The next time someone tells you that the police are the mindless minions of the Gestapo/Leviathan/The Zionist Occupation Government/The Man (pick one as suits the given agenda), remember the ones who were severely and unmeritoriously punished for having fulfilled their oath and hewed to the truth. And remember the role they all played in getting that truth across to the jury, and helping to acquit an innocent man who, by every objective analysis of the evidence, was wrongly accused.

Interviewed later about his firing, Chief Lee wistfully told the reporter that at least, at the end of the day, he had kept his integrity.

That's more than some involved in the prosecution can say.

Zimmerman verdict, part 18: Aftershocks

There was no winner of the fight that dark, rainy night in Sanford. Only degrees of losing.

When the President and the galaxy of movie stars extended their condolences to the Martin family after the verdict, we heard from them no sympathy for the defendant and his family. George Zimmerman's life has been horribly and irreparably changed. We learn that a divorce is in progress, something not uncommon after traumas like what he and his family were put through. His loved ones at various times have been in hiding, subjected to the same death threats as George Zimmerman. The guy gets a warning for speeding in Texas and a ticket for 15 MPH over in Florida, and each time it's national news. When I heard of the latter on CNN radio, they thought it important enough to announce it ahead of the suicide of Ariel Castro, a genuine monster of our time, which occurred in the same news period.

Trayvon Martin's family has suffered the loss of a seventeen-year-old, his life wasted twice over. He threw it away himself on that February night – dealing drugs, planning beatings, and negotiating to illegally buy guns according to his own digital records, his liver damaged already at seventeen by his drug abuse according to the autopsy – when he suffered a sudden, acute, and fatal failure of his victim selection process.

His father had supposedly put an association with the Crips street gang behind him and was gainfully employed as a truck driver, and his mother was a government employee with a Masters degree. The dad loved him enough to take him in when the mom had enough tough love for him to kick him out, and the stepmother for most of his life (who was, for the most part, excluded from the media narrative) loved him too. Supervision and intervention did not come in time to save Trayvon Martin from his own violent tendencies.

The second waste of his life is being witnessed now. His mom is on the talk circuit calling for an end to Stand Your Ground laws, which any honest and competent legal analyst could tell her had nothing to do with her son's death. It would do much more good, and perhaps save the lives of young men across the spectrum of the color lines, to hear this woman speak of the importance of seeing what's in your son's cell phone and on his Facebook page before homicide investigators have to do it.

Will there be a civil suit? Very probably. I would expect plaintiff's counsel to wait to file it until there's some money there. I predict substantial settlements of George Zimmerman's lawsuits against the networks whose minions deliberately libeled him, whether or not he ever signs a lucrative book contract, but as soon as deep pockets are there I expect to see vultures circling. Perhaps a Florida Statute **776.032** hearing will ward that off, if it takes place in front of a judge with the courage to do the right thing. Time will tell.

The much bally-hooed Federal investigation under Eric Holder, to see if Zimmerman violated Martin's civil rights? Inconveniently for both the media and the Administration, that has already been done by a horde of specially-assigned FBI agents, all of whom reported absolutely no indication of racism or malice on Zimmerman's part. If you'll forgive vernacular, "they got nothin'." But of course, that was true of the case Angela Corey brought against him, and it didn't stop that travesty from taking place.

Zimmerman verdict, part 19: Lessons

There was much for us all to learn from this case. For anyone who came in late, let me refer you here *http:// www.backwoodshome.com/articles2/ayoob143.html* for a summary. It ends with one such lesson. Let's pick up from there.

In this society, the person who moves toward danger in any respect is seen as "having gone looking for trouble," and widely blamed accordingly if it does not end well. I've explained earlier why I don't think anything Zimmerman did within the totality of the circumstances was the proximate cause of the death, but there's a reason for the saying "It's not about fault, it's about blame."

When you're on trial, you aren't the player, you're the stakes. The players are your lawyers, and you want the best. Zimmerman had that, and it saved him. The evidence dealt them a powerful hand of cards. I think their two highest cards were Ace of Experts Dr. Vincent DiMaio, Jr. and Ace of Eyewitnesses John Good. The master forensic pathologist tied it all together and proved from the hard evidence what Good, the closest eyewitness, testified: it was Martin on top brutally beating Zimmerman until the shot. I did a murder case with Dr. DiMaio in Texas years ago, also resulting in an acquittal, and DiMaio was extraordinary there, too.

If anyone still has the fantasy that you'll always be treated as a hero after a clean shoot, this case teaches us the reality. It's often an ordeal of lies, misunderstandings, and false accusations…and, as seen here, your family will go through that ordeal with you.

It's not something you want to face alone. Kudos to those who donated to Zimmerman's legal defense fund: you helped enormously to do justice. O'Mara establishing a website to show the actual evidence *(www.GZlegalcase. com)* was powerful and effective, and I think we'll see other defense lawyers modeling on this strategy in the future. One useful ally would be the Armed Citizens Legal Defense Network, which I'm involved with and have seen do good work. *(http://armedcitizensnetwork.net)* . Mark O'Mara consulted with ACLDN head Marty Hayes on the case, and appears to have put some of his advice to good use. Hayes' excellent analysis is found here: *http:// www.armedcitizensnetwork.net/images/stories/Net- work_2013-08.pdf* .

Don't believe everything you see in the papers or on TV when the news in question is a self-defense act. For decades as an expert witness in these cases, I'd get back to the hotel after testifying, watch the news report on the day's events in court, and wonder what the hell trial the reporter was watching. We saw that classically here. The honest reporting was more in the blogosphere than in the mainstream media.

The gun prohibition subculture in this country is power- ful, abetted heavily by the MSM, and you can expect them to seize on incidents like this and demonize the shooter. Zimmerman has become the poster person for this venom- ous trend. Even those who grudgingly accept the verdict still mutter aloud, "If Zimmerman hadn't had a gun, Tray- von Martin would still be alive."

That's probably true, but the final lesson is the flip side, which those commentators sometimes blindly and some- times studiously ignore: If George Zimmerman hadn't been carrying a gun routinely on a night he wasn't expecting trouble, he would probably be dead.

Zimmerman verdict, part 20: ...And into the future

Today is two months exactly since the day of the Zim- merman verdict, which I started blogging on that same day. Two months, and twenty entries, are nice round numbers to end upon. That's right at twice as long as the trial took, including the week of jury selection.

The strangeness continues, with the prosecution's medi- cal examiner **Dr. Shiping Bao being fired for his egregious performance in this case, and suing for a hundred million dollars over that.**

The divorce proceeding of Mr. and Mrs. George Zimmer- man grows weirder. A key player in the case has decided that **he doesn't want to play anymore**, and **has a new gig.**

The story will continue. It's been about twenty years since the O.J. Simpson trial, and *he's* still in the news. But I won't discuss that case until I've walked a mile in O.J.'s blood-stained, "ugly-ass" Bruno Magli shoes.

There will be books. Damn near everyone associated with the Simpson case eventually wrote one. I'll be inter- ested in hearing from the *Zimmerman* prosecutors, and from the defense lawyers, and from the judge (from whom

I'm still waiting to hear a ruling as to the allegations of the prosecution withholding evidence from the defense). I'll be particularly interested to read George Zimmerman's own account. Earlier in this blog, I mentioned that he had reportedly wanted to testify, that I thought he handled himself well talking to the investigators, and would have done well on the witness stand if he was as articulate as his brother Robert, who tore Piers Morgan a new one on CNN. Robert Zimmerman later sent a tweet in which he said he thought his brother George would have been more articulate than he.

There already *are* books. *"Florida v. Zimmerman: Uncovering the Malicious Prosecution of my Son, George"* by the defendant's father, Robert Zimmerman, Sr., and *"Defending Our Friend: the Most Hated Man In America"* by Mark Osterman, the close friend who trained him with a gun and testified so well on his behalf, are available. The co-author of the latter was Sondra Osterman, who also helped show Zimmerman's human face when she testified at trial. I've mentioned in this series that when the mainstream media dismally failed to tell the truth, the blogosphere picked up the ball they dropped. A classic example of that was the work of **Conservative Treehouse**, the "Treepers" who told the truth about the case in all its dimensions. The best digest I've seen of that good work is *"If I had a Son: Race, Guns, and the Railroading of George Zimmerman"* by Jack Cashill. There is also good reading on the topic to be found in "*The Lynching of George Zimmerman"* by Hunter Billings III. Those are just the ones I've read; there are more.

The titles of the dad's book and that of the friends show that they're obviously advocates for one side. The Cashill and Billings books clearly have advocacy in them, but that doesn't distract from the truth if the advocates are on the side of that truth, and the evidence showed that these advocates were.

I hope another book on the trial will be forthcoming from my friend and former student Andrew Branca. His reporting from right there in the courtroom was, I think, the gold standard for commentary on the trial as it unfolded. It can be found day by day for the trial, which went from June 10 to July 13, 2013, at *www.legalinsurrection.com*. When you go there, budget yourself some time to read the huge volume of commentary on each day's blog. Legal Insurrection draws an audience very heavily populated by lawyers and other criminal justice professionals, and there is gold in their assessment of the strategy and execution of the tactics seen in this trial. Branca is a lawyer who specializes in self-defense (get his excellent book on *that* topic at ***www.lawofselfdefense.com).*** His commentary and that of the readers will *sound* like advocacy for Zimmerman, but if you read it carefully, you'll see that he and most of the commentators are really advocating for law and reality…which just happened to favor Zimmerman.

This nationally divisive case brought out tribalism at a disturbingly high level. Black versus white. Anti-gun versus pro-gun. I for one didn't come from that angle. As an advocate for armed citizens, it's as important to me to step on the ones who screw up as to celebrate the many more who save innocent lives. The history of it is, any community that does not police itself will be policed from outside. If I thought Zimmerman had done wrong, I would have said so.

Had I been going with tribes, I would have sided with special prosecutor Angela Corey. We have a lot in common. We've both made our careers in the justice system, we've both prosecuted, and we both have Arabic-American ancestry. Sorry, homegirl, I just can't side with you on this one. My career has taught me to go with the evidence to find out who's on the side of the angels, and in this case, Angela, you were on the wrong side. Simple as that.

When John Guy did his dramatic opening statement for the prosecution, he ended with his now-famous line, "We are confident that at the end of this trial you will know in your head, in your heart, in your stomach that George Zimmerman did not shoot Trayvon Martin because he had to. He shot him for the worst of all reasons, because he wanted to."

Under the prosecutorial duty to be a minister of justice, this writer believes that Ms. Corey should have simply brought the evidence before a grand jury and given them the option to indict. Instead, she bypassed that key element of the criminal justice system and set the stage for a cruel show trial. I suspect that historians will write of it more as, "Angela Corey did not put George Zimmerman and his family through this ordeal because she had to. She did it for the worst of all possible reasons…because she wanted to."

Previously published on *Backwoods Home Magazine's* blog by Massad Ayoob at ***www.backwoodshome.com***

Backwoods Home Magazine
P.O. Box 712, Gold Beach, OR 97444
1-800-835-2418

Chapter 11:

Case Study: *State of Arizona v. Larry Hickey*

The Larry Hickey case was a classic in terms of teaching points for law-abiding armed citizens who carry guns. Having testified in his second trial, I can tell you that the following account is spot on. It was written by Gila Hayes of the Armed Citizens Legal Defense Network, which came to his aid and earned kudos from the extraordinary able team of public defenders who carried him through both trials. It is reprinted here with ACLDN's permission. –Mas Ayoob

Analysis of the Larry Hickey Case
by Gila Hayes

Western states like Arizona are generally friendly to ideas of firearms and self- defense, but we may forget that any state can harbor a city in which the population leans toward liberal social politics and buys in to the flawed theory of gun control for public safety. Anti-self-defense attitudes, cloaked in good intentions, can intrude when a self-defense shooting entails factors that are not always clear cut, such as when one man shoots several unarmed assailants and must argue disparity of force as justification for his actions. This is at the heart of an ordeal that ran from late November 2008 through May 2010, in Tucson, Arizona.

Larry Hickey, his wife and young son lived on a cul-de-sac in a modest Tucson neighborhood. Across the street lived three adults – two 30-something sisters and the 26-year old boyfriend of one – along with the women's two children. The households were only peripherally acquainted through limited contact between Hickey's seven-year-old son and the two boys, ages 4 and 11, living in the house across the street. Mr. and Mrs. Hickey both had demanding jobs, Mrs. Hickey working shift work in the telemetry room in a local hospital, and Mr. Hickey employed by the Union Pacific Railroad, a job that took him away from home for several days at a time. At 37 years of age, Hickey's previous employment history included work as a safety trainer for a big chain store and a stint as a corrections officer in a high-risk facility where he dealt with violent behavior.

Hickey owned guns and had a concealed carry permit, having carried a defensive pistol for 14 years. For ten years, he'd been an avid student of defensive weaponcraft. He took classes from local instructors, as well as a number of courses from James Yeager of Tactical Response in Camden, TN. He became one of Yeager's instructors, and he also taught pre-deployment military personnel about foreign weaponry for a local firm, C&T Enterprises. At the time he ran into trouble, his day job with the Union Pacific Railroad was in temporary hiatus, as he had just been furloughed pending an uptick in economic conditions.

The Incident

On Monday, November 17, 2008, day fades into night as the Hickey family returns home from a bicycle ride. Trying out a headlamp he had just mounted on his new bicycle, Larry Hickey remains in the street in front of their home, riding for a little longer while his wife goes into their garage and brings the trashcans to the street for collection. He pedals over to his wife and they stand near the trash-cans discussing the dinner menu, how to dispose of some bulky trash and the other minutiae of daily living. The sisters who live across the street are sitting in their garage smoking with the doors open, and one calls out aggressively to Mrs. Hickey, then jumps up and barges across the street to confront her.

On the 15th, the women had argued – not in person, but by cell phone texts that included nasty name-calling. Mrs. Hickey filed a police report alleging harassment and threats. When the enraged woman rushes up, Hickey gets between the two women to protect his wife. He will later testify that he says, "Hey, no one has to get hurt over this…could you please go back to your side of the street?" though he has to raise his voice to be heard over the woman.

As an older woman who lives nearby drives past, she sees the other sister stride across the street and join the fray in Hickey's driveway. This neighbor will later testify that the second woman approached with fist raised, and another woman, also driving home on the street, will testify to simi-lar aspects of the fight.

The woman flicks a lit cigarette at Mrs. Hickey and then darts around the garbage cans toward her, saying "I'm going to kill you, bitch," according to Hickey's testimony in court.

Hickey pushes his bike away and tries to intercede as he sees one of the neighbor women with a raised fist rushing toward where he thinks his wife stands. He moves between them, trying to intercept her, and the sisters begin hitting him. Blows from both sisters rain down on the crown of his head and his arms as he blocks their fists. Hickey ducks down, and while blocking the blows with his arms, he tries unsuccessfully to activate a remote control to open the garage door so the couple can run to safety. The front door to the Hickeys' home is securely locked, limiting their options.

From his experience and training as a corrections officer, Hickey knows about force options for various situations, and in court will describe his control of the sisters as using "soft hands."

Nearly two years later, pondering his decisions that night, Hickey wonders if the fight could have been aborted had he initially used more decisive physical force. "I was just trying to block the blows and keep them pushed away from me. I did not want to hit anybody," he says now. "Looking back, I wish I had been more forceful in trying to discourage them from attacking us. It almost seemed like the fact that I wasn't hitting them emboldened them. It made them attack more. They claimed that I struck them numerous times. They claimed that I grabbed their hair and beat their faces in but there was no physical evidence of it, no black eyes, no swollen or split lips, nothing."

Hickey manages to grab the first woman by her arms and push her away. Her feet become tangled and she falls. He pushes away the second woman who is also hitting him and she falls as well. "I got them pushed away and we were trying to get back up the driveway and they were just up like a shot; there was no time at all and they were back and attacking us again," Hickey recalls.

As the neighbor women renew their attack, screaming at Hickey and hitting him with their fists, Hickey hears the sound of running feet and glass breaking in the street. Through the narrowed field of tunnel vision, Hickey senses only a flash of movement and then feels a staggering impact to the side of his head.

Loud voices and Hickey's struggle to fend off the women have drawn the attention of the boyfriend who had recently returned home from work, removed his dress shirt, and poured a glass of wine in the house across the street. Hearing the fracas, this man ran across the street, dropping the wine glass en route, and jumped into the fight, slugging Hickey hard on the left temple. That blow changes Hickey's decision to try to get through the beating by just blocking the blows. When the other man nails his temple, Hickey's vision blurs to white, his legs buckle, and he staggers back, nearly passing out. In court, Hickey will testify that when "the new attacker showed up, then it went from scary to terrifying, just like that the whole dynamic just changed in a split second."

Hickey's mind flashes back to a video clip his CCW instructor showed, in which a Texas police constable is attacked, disarmed and shot by three smaller assailants during a drug investigation (see < Lunsford murder > Set as hyperlink in layout version: *http://www.policeone.com/policeonetv/videos/1736783-reality-training-lunsford-incident/*). While this flashes through his mind, Hickey simultaneously tries to confirm the location of his wife and son to be sure they are not endangered.

The mind can process a lot of things at one time, Hickey later comments, and his mind is racing as he falls backward from the blow to his temple. Trying to shake off the onset of unconsciousness from the impact, Hickey draws his Glock 19 from a Blade-Tech IWB holster. From the retention shooting position, he fires three shots at the attackers pressing up against him, hitting the male in the abdomen and hand, and striking one of the women in the lower leg.

As his attackers back away, Hickey desperately scans the area as he has been taught, to avoid being blindsided by another attacker. Hickey describes tunnel vision like looking down the tube of the paper towel roll, and he tries to break it up. The man who hit Hickey's temple and one of the women return to their home; the other woman screams loudly that she has been shot. At the same time, Hickey fears that his wife and son may not be safe. It turns out that the 7-year-old boy has opened the front door, and probably witnessed the final portion of the fight. Mrs. Hickey sends him back inside.

THE IMMEDIATE AFTERMATH

While trying to dial his cell phone to summon medical aid and police assistance, Hickey goes into his garage and grabs his trauma kit, then closes the garage door behind him as he rushes to the woman's side. He has already removed the magazine from his Glock, shucked the live round out of the chamber, and placed the gun and magazine on his yard's retaining wall.

In the darkness, Hickey cannot see the screaming woman's wound, but he applies a compression bandage where the woman is holding her leg and ankle. Finding blood, he also applies a tourniquet higher up on the leg to stop the blood loss. As he is tending to the woman who a moment earlier was hitting him, he looks up and sees that neighbors have circled around, drawn by the gunshots and screams. Many have dialed their own 9-1-1 emergency calls.

As a female neighbor takes over tending the bleeding woman, an off-duty male police officer draws Hickey away and sits him down. This neighbor ascertains the location of Hickey's gun and in answer to his inquiries, Hickey says, "I shot." Feeling the blood and sweat running down him, Hickey asks, "Am I bleeding?" But the neighbor tells him, "Don't say anything; just hang tight." When police arrive, the neighbor calls out that he has the shooter, and turns Hickey over to responding officers. Worried that he had not taken time to put on gloves before treating the woman's wounds, Hickey asks if he can wash his hands, but the request is denied. He will not be allowed to wash them for several hours, not until after he is taken to the police station and photographed.

Hickey relates that the first officer on the scene took him to the patrol car and cuffed him. As he is escorted to the patrol car, he is taken past the injured woman lying on the ground. As the officer escorting him asks, "What happened? Did they come across the street?" Hickey responds, "Yes, they ran over here and attacked us." Not part of a formal interview, those words are forever lost, and appear nowhere in the police reports from that night.

After Hickey sits for some time in the police cruiser, an officer returns and tells him that he is going to take him to the station, where detectives will interview him. While waiting in the car, Hickey thought about the case of Harold Fish, the AZ schoolteacher who was imprisoned after a self-defense shooting. He'd read that as Fish's memories cleared, he gave statements that contained minor variations, leading the prosecution to accuse him of lying. Worried that he, too, may say the wrong thing, Hickey invokes his right to have an attorney present during questioning when an officer later approaches him and asks if he would like to make a statement. "I was very, very brief," Hickey relates. "I said, 'Other than the fact that these people ran over and attacked us, I would rather wait to give a full statement until I have a lawyer present,' or something to that effect."

All three attackers recite versions of the incident that differ from the one told by Mrs. Hickey, which will be different from the report eventually given by Larry Hickey when he describes the incident to his attorneys and legal defense team. All but one of the uninvolved witnesses tell similar stories, but most of their recollections begin after the shots were fired, and contribute little to explaining what precipitated the shooting.

"As far as the State was concerned, I was completely silent because there was no record of me making those brief statements. I just said, 'They ran over and attacked us,' and I didn't get into any detail beyond that. I was trying to put the responding officers on notice about who was really the aggressors, but it didn't get noticed," he says. To this day, Hickey refuses to believe overlooking his statements was intentional, surmising, "They just got lost in the whole shuffle."

Hickey estimates that he had been handcuffed in the back of the patrol car for about half an hour when the arresting officer transported him to the police substation. "What do I need to do to press charges against these people?" Larry asks, and later he asks the same question of officers at the jail. There, he is told that he must put that question to his lawyer. In the car riding to the substation, the officer explains that Hickey will meet with detectives at the station, but once there, he is placed in an interview room, where he remains for five or six hours. His only human contact comes when he asks for water and a bathroom break.

Eventually, the arresting officer returns and announces that he needs to take Larry to the jail for booking. "What for?" Hickey asks, and the officer responds that he thinks the charge is aggravated assault.

"Well, don't the detectives want to talk to me?" Hickey asks.

"I guess they got all they needed," the officer responds.

The end result? Larry Hickey never made a statement to police about what happened in his driveway the night of November 17, 2008. His assailants gave plenty of other statements and though they were at odds with the physical evidence, the State prosecuted Hickey for aggravated assault. "I'm sure it was nothing malicious, but I don't know. There were hard questions that just were not asked," Hickey muses.

Later, when Hickey reviewed transcripts from the grand jury hearing at which he was indicted, he was surprised to read statements from the lead detective that did not concur with physical evidence from the shooting scene about which he must surely have known. In this case, the defendant was not allowed to testify to the grand jury, and Hickey found it unnerving to read the unrefuted allegations against him. "When I read this, I thought, but the evidence was in my driveway, not in the middle of the street! This is kind of a big deal! They're saying I ran out into the middle of the street and we got into mutual combat. That is different from them running 100-plus feet across a street to attack us in our driveway. I said we attempted to retreat and were forced to use deadly force to defend ourselves. That is a big difference."

71 Days In Jail

After waiting for hours to speak with detectives, Hickey was booked and placed in a cell. He told the medical technician taking down his information during booking that he was hit in the head. Most of the marks from the fight were hidden by Hickey's hair, landing as they had on the crown of his head. The blow to his temple left some swelling and Hickey had headaches for about a week after the attack. Later when Hickey reported headaches, the jail doctor made a simple examination of eyes and reflexes, telling him that his symptoms were consistent with a concussion and telling him to watch out for warning signs of complications. He gave him Ibuprofen for the pain.

When the case went to trial, asking the jail doctor to testify was deemed too risky, because when Hickey's attorney interviewed him, his attitude so worried the lawyer that he would not risk calling him to the witness stand. "This guy had some sort of an agenda. In my view, his attitude was that everyone lies in the jail so they just give them stuff to shut them up," said the attorney. Although Hickey could have hired a different doctor to testify to the different types of concussions and compare those with Hickey's symptoms, Hickey's lawyer feared that doing so would not end well, since the prosecutor would wonder why Hickey chose not to bring in the jail doctor, and would probably call that doctor on behalf of the prosecution.

On November 18, Hickey attended his arraignment by videoconference. During the hearing, one of the women who attacked him repeated her story that he went crazy and shot them, and so bail was set at $200,000. With no attorney beyond a public defender who was present to advise all of the prisoners that day, Hickey was charged with a half dozen charges of aggravated assault with a deadly weapon, two for each of the three attackers.

On the outside, Hickey's mother took charge. "I'll tell you who rallied everybody together," Hickey declares. "It is my mother, Callie Anderson. She is quite a fighter. She left no stone unturned. I probably wouldn't be in the position I am in today if it wasn't for her. It is kind of difficult to work on your case when you have to do it with leg irons on during a once-a-week visit with a lawyer!"

Within 24 hours, Mrs. Anderson obtained an attorney for her son. "I tell him I'd like to make a statement," Hickey recalls. "Obviously, these guys [police investigators] aren't seeing what really happened." This lawyer called the detective sergeant, leaving a voice mail message asking to set up a meeting in which Hickey will make a full statement. The call was never returned. The lawyer also represented Hickey at a bail reduction hearing and the cash bail was cut in half to $100,000.

Two weeks later, during another videoconference from the jail, Hickey spoke with Pima County assistant public defender Matthew Messmer, and was immediately impressed. About ten years out of law school, Messmer impressed Hickey as someone with "fire in his belly," who would fight for Hickey's freedom. "He is really switched on. You could just see the spark when you talked to him," Hickey remembers. He was so impressed by Messmer from their videoconference that he immediately told his family he wanted Messmer to represent him.

During his initial meeting with Messmer, Hickey remembers drawing a little map, diagramming the incident step by step. "Messmer said, 'OK, well, I'll get back to you,'" Hickey recalls. "This was before any statements or any photos had started trickling in," Hickey explains. "I think I saw him a week later and he had started getting reports and photos showing where the evidence was located. I met with him and he said, 'Well, the evidence is starting to come in and you know what? You're telling the truth!'"

"And I said, 'I know,'" Hickey concludes quietly.

Matthew Messmer explains: "I really like my job, and I don't care who the person is, I have a job to do and I fight for everyone the same, but there was something about Larry's case. From the first time I saw him on that videoconference, nothing changed about his story, it was always exactly as he said. It was very easy to work on Larry's case just because he is such a polite person. He was honest from day one; nothing in his story ever changed."

"When we got the police reports," Messmer continues, "we compared the evidence that they had with what Larry had, and everything matched up to what the real evidence was. They [the assailants] were all lying. There were different stories, and I remember seeing that this was not all in the middle of the street the way they said. This was all on the edge of the Hickey property." His voices rises as he adds, "This did not happen on the street! It was all on the Hickey property! It just bewildered us that no one was seeing that besides our team!" he exclaims.

Still, Messmer was frank with Hickey, outlining the challenges they faced defending his shooting. "I told him from Day One, 'I believe you, but we are going to have to figure out how to get over this hurdle, because there are a lot of people out there that do not believe you can use a gun even if you are being attacked,'" the public defender explains.

Raising Bail

As the Thanksgiving, Christmas and New Year holidays passed, Hickey remained in jail while his family scrambled to raise $100,000 for bail. With a collapsing housing market, there was little equity in the family's homes against which to borrow, so Mrs. Anderson arranged private loans. She also reached out to Hickey's peers – fellow gun owners who communicate on James Yeager's Tactical Response forum, Get Off The X. "People would offer $1,000 saying, 'Just send it back when you're done,' and even those who put $5 in my mother's hands helped," Hickey relates. "One individual put us over the top at the very end. He sent my mother a cashier's check for $20,000," he says, awe evident in his voice. "It is humbling, and brings emotion out of me."

In late November, Armed Citizens' Network member William Aprill telephoned Network President Marty Hayes to ask if he had heard about the Larry Hickey incident. "Mr. Aprill has a lot of contact with the folks from the training business, Tactical Response, and he related this incident to me," Hayes recalls. "He wanted to make us aware of this and see if we could help. Unfortunately, Mr. Hickey had not joined the Network, though, interestingly, Tactical Response, which he teaches for, is one of our affiliated training schools to which we give complimentary memberships in exchange for their help promoting Network membership. So I felt a little bit of moral responsibility to see what I could do to help Larry Hickey in his defense."

Hayes called James Yeager, president of Tactical Response, who confirmed the report. He referred Hayes to Get Off the X on which details and updates in Hickey's case were being discussed. Topics included both short-term and long-term worries – concerns about obtaining the best possible legal defense for Hickey and the more immediate need of raising bail to get him out of jail.

Hayes points out that, "Typically, with $100,000 bail, they could raise $10,000 cash, pay a bondsman and get him released, but the prosecutor requested a cash bail. I guess he thought Larry was a dangerous guy he couldn't see running loose in the streets of Tucson so they imposed that restriction," Hayes surmises. "Owing to that it took two or three months to raise money to get Larry released. They had to bring in $100,000 in cash and hand it over to the court. For most people, it is pretty difficult to raise that kind of cash. But they got some loans and worked hard at it and eventually came in with $100,000 cash."

Since it was not appropriate to draw funds from the Network members' legal defense foundation to help a non-member, Hayes turned his efforts to raising funds elsewhere. "Larry needed to raise some serious money, so I got involved in that fundraising, not realizing that later I would be as intrinsically involved in the case as I was," he recalls. "I went out to both my students at The Firearms Academy of Seattle and the membership of the Armed Citizens' Legal Defense Network and I explained through email that I was convinced this was a legitimate case of self-defense and that this guy was one of us, an armed citizen, and, in fact, he was an instructor. Now he was being railroaded by the system and he *was* going to be found guilty unless we did something. I don't know how much money was raised but it was a considerable amount," he notes.

Hayes continues, "In the meantime, the discussion was going on between contributors to the fundraiser about whether this money should be used for bail money or for his legal defense. It was a cordial discussion, but nonetheless there were passionate arguments on both sides. I fell in with the camp that funds raised should be legal defense money not bail money, and I think everybody pretty much agreed with that, and so Larry sat in jail for a few months because the money we had raised was not going to bail him out of jail, it was to fight the legal claim."

Though Hickey had complete confidence in his public defender, Hayes was deeply concerned whether a public defender's office could put on an adequate defense for such a complicated case. "Usually a public defender would not have enough resources for this kind of case," he explains. "They needed an investigator hot on the trail of this situation, talking to all of the witnesses, getting photographs of the wounds, etcetera, and they didn't have one. This happens all the time. Because many times public defenders don't have the resources to do their own investigation, they may rely on the prosecution's investigation," Hayes continues. "When the train is going down the tracks toward a conviction, the prosecution doesn't always look at all the evidence. They only look at the evidence that tends to help convict the person, as opposed to possibly showing that he was justified."

In the end, some of the money raised was used to put on a mock trial for Hickey's attorneys to test defense strategies before going to court. Additional expenditures covered travel expenses of expert witnesses for the trial, including instructors under whom Hickey had trained and Hayes, who gave testimony to explain the ballistic evidence including bullet trajectories and the retention position from which Hickey fired, to prove the extremely close proximity of Hickey's attackers at the moment that he drew and fired. This testimony stood in stark contrast to the testimony of Hickey's assailants. Hayes advised on the case pro bono, accepting only travel expenses, freely contributing his time and expertise.

Hickey Set Free

On January 27, 2009 Hickey was bailed out of jail. Within a week, he went to work full time for a friend who owns a manufacturing business in Tucson, and was later called back to his regular job at the railroad. Under his bail conditions, Hickey was prohibited from coming within a five-mile radius of his assailants (and thus needed to avoid his own home), so the family moved into a spare room offered by one of Hickey's friends, a retired law enforcement officer who lives on the other side of town.

As the public defender's office was ramping up to defend Hickey in court, a second public defender, Matt Rosenbluth, joined the team, owing to the seriousness of the charges. Hickey calls both "stellar lawyers," and praises the efforts of their support staff as well.

Because the Public Defender's office so rarely deals with self-defense cases, Hickey became immediately immersed in forwarding information from all his prior training, as well as researching principles including justifiable use of deadly force to defend against a mob attack and other disparity of force issues. "I had a completely legitimate self-defense claim owing to disparity of force but we all know that is the toughest thing to show," he recalls.

Wisely, the defense team reached out to a leading expert on the subject, internationally renowned Massad Ayoob, who advised on Hickey's case along with Hayes. Neither Ayoob nor Hayes is sure who went to work on the case first, though both remember that in May of 2009, while Ayoob was teaching at Hayes' school, The Firearms Academy of Seattle, both men participated in a phone conference with Hickey and his lawyers.

"After the phone conference, Massad was on board to serve as an expert to explain the issues to the jury," Hayes says. "A problem arose early after he accepted this case, when Massad discovered he had another trial scheduled for the same time, a previous commitment that he couldn't back out of, so I was basically the pinch hitter. I substituted for Mas and got involved early on as the expert to go down and testify in court," Hayes recounts, adding that during the preparatory phases Ayoob continued to offer advice though he was not able to participate in the trial.

Instead, Hayes testified, focusing primarily on ballistic evidence. "My role was to look at the ballistic evidence and see if I could make sense of it by comparing it to Larry's account of the incident versus the other people's account," Hayes explains. "When I studied the evidence, I was convinced that Larry's account was absolutely consistent with the evidence and that the other accounts were not."

Hayes continues, "My testimony was to counter some of the claims made by the people who had the altercation with Larry. Their first claim was that after Larry shot two people, he turned his gun toward the third and as she was running away, he fired a shot at her. I thought that was pretty ludicrous, based on what I had heard. It just didn't make sense to me. I got all the discovery including the photographs, looked through it and determined there were three shots fired and those three bullets struck two of the people. There was no way Larry fired at a third person as she was running away," he says.

Character Assassination

In addition to the struggle to match up limited evidence with all the different stories being told, Attorney Messmer faced several more hurdles. The first was prejudice about men fighting women. Messmer admits, "Even in our own office, we were very divided. A lot of people couldn't get over the fact that Larry shot one female. That [reaction] just dumbfounded us: the aggressor coming toward you doesn't have anything to do with gender," he exclaims. "What we knew from talking to Marty [Hayes] and Ayoob was that this is a disparity of force situation. Being able to convince the jury that this was a disparity of force situation was really the key. We had to make them see that these people were acting in concert and that they were one force. I think it was always hard for some people to grasp that concept."

In addition, the defense team needed to counter the picture that Hickey's accusers painted of him as a crazed gun nut. Initially, hoping to discourage prosecution, the defense team disclosed all the information they had about firearms classes he had completed. "From day one we wanted to avoid trial, so we disclosed all of Larry's training, that he's an instructor who has taught all these people, he has been training all these years, and he knows when it is proper and when it is not. We disclosed all that to the prosecutor," Messmer stresses.

They learned early on that they would have to take care to explain how Hickey's training led to tactical decisions he made during the attack. In an effort to find the best strategies for Hickey's defense, Messmer, Rosenbluth and their team hired a Phoenix firm that puts on mock trials in which attorneys practice their presentations and watch the reactions of a test jury to their arguments. "The practice jury said that Larry had too much training and he should have known better. So how much we were going to get into [his training] was always very difficult to figure out because it was absolutely important to show Larry as this person that isn't just out there with a gun and doesn't know how to handle it."

Even if the defense had chosen to give only cursory mention to Hickey's training, the prosecutor would have forced their hand at trial. He harped endlessly on the various shooting classes Hickey had completed. "It worked to our advantage in both trials because we disclosed all that to the prosecutor from Day One," Messmer states. "In trial, the prosecutor went overboard with that and he really disgusted the jury because he wasted their time," Messmer explains, relating how, like a broken record, the prosecutor asked each expert and material witness about each class Hickey had completed, what it covered, challenging why a private citizen would need that knowledge.

Messmer believes the jury eventually thought, "Get to the point. We know that!" He adds, "It made the prosecution look bad because Larry was getting training and doing his job and they were attacking him for that. It blew up on them in the first trial, and they went back to it and it blew again in the second trial. We knew they were going to bring it up, but it actually helped us out."

Hard Evidence

Having prepared to confront these and other issues, on September 30, 2009, Larry Hickey, represented by Matthew Messmer and Michael Rosenbluth, went to trial in the Superior Court of the State of Arizona in and for the County of Pima, defending his case before Judge Teresa Godoy. On the other side of the aisle sat the deputy county attorney, Daniel Nicolini.

On the third day of the first trial, Network President Marty Hayes presented ballistic evidence, identifying the most likely bullet trajectories and explaining how that proved that Hickey's attackers were right on top of him when he fired from the retention position. Using a Crimson Trace aiming laser on a plastic molding of a gun, he demonstrated how the bullets traveled at trajectories that would have made the wounds only if the attackers were extremely close.

These wounds, he testified, were consistent with shooting a handgun from what is sometimes called a retention position. He gave the history of the technique and then explained that it exists for use in circumstances under which it is impossible to bring the gun to eye level and use the sights to take aim.

Messmer clarified that the shooting method would be for use "...when the attacker is right on top of you?" and Hayes concurred, "Absolutely, yes."

"...In close proximity?" Messmer pressed. "Yes," Hayes averred.

Hayes later explains that the court recognized his expertise because, "In order to be considered an expert or give expert testimony and expert opinion in court, the court requires that the individual have gained a knowledge of the specific discipline you are testifying to considerably beyond the average layman's knowledge of that discipline and that is done through formal training, formal education or simply hands-on experience. Because I've had all three, I met the criteria of a ballistics expert very easily and the judge allowed me to give that testimony."

Still, Nicolini challenged Hayes' testimony, asking if he was a forensic pathologist or had medical experience. Did the prosecutor's aspersions diminish the effect of his testimony? "Not that I saw, because I'd never claimed to be a pathologist or doctor. He was trying to discredit me as much as possible, but it didn't seem to bother the jury. It was just basically smoke and mirrors to try to attack the credibility of the witness somehow and that is all he could do, I guess," Hayes suggests.

There was considerable difficulty conclusively establishing the assailant's exact location because gunshot residue swabs were not taken, nor were stippling patterns recorded from the abdomen of the male, exculpatory evidence that could have scientifically proven how close the attackers were when Hickey fired. Instead, the lack of evidence created a situation in which Hickey's sole testimony had to be weighed against the stories of all three attackers. This made Hayes' interpretation of the available evidence all the more crucial. He had to work from crime scene photos, depositions and statements to police and a set of photos made by family members of the persons who were shot.

Did he have sufficient detail to draw conclusions? "You are never 100% sure, and you never say you are in court, but you say there is a very high probability based on what you saw to testify in court to what you believe occurred," he says now.

In addition, Hayes had to give his testimony out of the regular trial sequence, because he, too, had a prior commitment and was only available to testify on the third day of the trial while the prosecution was still presenting their case. He testified, after which he departed.

The next day Dr. Julie Wynne, the physician who treated the male assailant, was called to describe the gunshot injuries and her treatment of them. Attorney Rosenbluth asked if she observed any stippling on the man's torso, but her answers were inconclusive. Driving home afterwards, the physician felt concerned about her answers and decided to look in her patient's files to verify her accuracy. Opening the files, she discovered photographs taken prior to his treatment.

"Instead of blowing it off, she called the prosecutor that night and told him, 'I have photos that I don't think you ever saw and I think you guys need to see them. I think they could answer that question about ranges and things of that nature,'" Messmer relates.

"It was an honest error, I think, on the prosecutor's part," Messmer estimates. "I don't think he even knew they had the photos. The prosecutor has done numerous cases where people have gone to the hospital, and we have never seen photos like this before. Now we see them all the time because we know to ask for them."

Messmer and the rest of Hickey's defense team found the late introduction of the photographs surprising, as well. "That was really a unique situation. I've been doing this for nine years; my legal assistant has been doing it for 18 years, and Mike Rosenbluth has been doing this for 18 years and that is the first time any of us has seen anything like that happen," he recounts.

The newly discovered pictures were brought into court after Hayes testified to his best estimates of how close the male assailant was standing when he was shot. "I testified to the best of my ability based on the physical damage done to the hand and the lack of photographs of all the wounds on his body. There were three gunshot wounds to his body: two in the torso, one in the hand."

Did the new photos change his opinion? "Yes, we later found out through looking at these photographs that I was probably off base on how the male assailant's hand was struck by a bullet," he confirms. By the time the photos were discovered, Hayes had returned home. He recalls, "I was already back home by when I got the phone call and a frantic email from the defense saying, 'Have you ever seen these pictures? What do you think of these?' I was just livid that I was never given this information to begin with."

Before he left the witness stand, Hayes also testified how easily a person armed with a handgun can be disarmed, and gave the jury a demonstration. During cross examination, Nicolini learned that Hickey was not trained by Marty Hayes, and also learned that Hayes was giving his expert testimony in this case at no charge. When asked why, Hayes answered, "Because throughout my career I have seen people who are being wrongfully prosecuted. I have looked at the evidence and I decided this is simply wrong. If those people don't have the financial resources to hire experts then they still need this type of credible witness, so over the years I've done a few of these without being paid."

Hickey was not a Network member, Hayes explained, and Nicolini asked if the Network's "objective … [is] to challenge prosecution where self-defense is claimed by the shooter?" Hayes responded, "I would say that the mission of the organization is to help people who are being wrongfully prosecuted."

The Prosecutor's Theory

Material experts who testified on Hickey's behalf include several instructors, ranging from the man who taught an early Arizona concealed handgun licensing class Hickey took, to his mentor, James Yeager, from whom he took many classes and for whom he eventually went on to become an adjunct instructor. Initially, Nicolini grilled Hickey about the concepts and principles Yeager taught him, using notes and handouts from classes, and later he went over the same material with the instructor himself, discussing avoidance, de-escalation, gunfight tactics and many of Yeager's similes, acronyms and catchy phrases – tools that the instructor used to help students remember important principles.

Alarmingly, out of context advice from instructors to "always cheat; always win," and the axiom that one should treat every one else in a polite manner while simultaneously having a plan to kill them painted an inaccurate picture about Hickey's outlook on life. Nicolini harvested these quotes from the training notes and handouts, and made much hay with them, especially during his closing arguments in which he described Hickey in highly inflammatory terms.

The prosecutor told the jury not to consider the case from Hickey's viewpoint, from "what was going on in his paranoid mind," but to apply the reasonable person standard. "This is not a case of self-defense, this is not a case of defending a third person, even if you accept his version of how it went down," urged Nicolini.

"He is lying about how it happened. And you know why he is lying? First of all, he …has got the same motivation to lie about these facts that any criminal defendant has in this situation, he does not want to be convicted. But I think Larry Hickey has an additional motivation in this case, he wants to be vindicated, he wants somebody to say, yes, Larry, you exercised your Second Amendment rights to defend yourself and your family like a good American. And you know something else? The same reason why four of his gun instructors have come in here to testify, the people who taught him to use guns, and when to use guns and taught him that aggressive mindset, like Jim Yeager, they want to be vindicated, too. But there is no vindication for Mr. Hickey in this case. It didn't happen as he said it happened," the prosecutor alleged.

"Larry brought a gun to a fist fight and used it to shoot

two unarmed people, and even if you believed his version of facts, I submit that you must convict him of these charges, because the thing is, he was trigger happy. He was a gun-toting, trigger-happy guy, who pulled out his gun in a situation where it absolutely was not required," reads the transcript of parts of Nicolini's closing.

"Reading the transcripts later, I realized this trial was not just about Larry Hickey and his actions," explains Hayes. "This was the Pima County Prosecutor's Office putting the concept of the armed lifestyle on trial because Nicolini attacked the whole concept of taking training, carrying a gun 24/7. He tried to paint the picture that anybody who would do that is really out of whack with society. There was a lot of discussion in his closing about the type of training that Larry took. Nicolini called Larry a liar; he called him a wannabe cop, a wannabe soldier. Frankly, I think it was demeaning to the whole of jurisprudence to see a prosecutor go to those extremes to try to get a conviction when there was nothing in the evidence or record to support his allegations," Hayes notes. "He went overboard."

Messmer reports that he closed out his part of the trial hammering home the fact that, "Larry was never the aggressor. I took the jury step by step through what he did to defuse the situation, to deescalate and try to do everything possible to avoid pulling that gun.

"And then I attacked the prosecution's ridiculous attack about too much training," Messmer continues. "How is it possible for someone to have too much training? I alluded to similar circumstances that you wouldn't want a doctor to avoid going to training and learning the newest medical procedures, you wouldn't want your lawyer to not keep up on his legal education, and that Larry wasn't just going out there to learn this to be some Rambo. He was actually using this to be an instructor for our troops.

"I think that hit home," Messmer relates. As the last point in both cases, he described the attackers as a three-headed monster. In trial transcripts from the first trial, Messmer is quoted as describing the male assailant's entry into the fight, "Now he [Hickey] is not only dealing with two women, but he is dealing with three people attacking him – this monster, this three-headed, six-fisted, six-footed that can stomp you when you fall down monster, – and he adds that the male, a young man in excellent physical condition, is throwing hammer punches to Hickey's head.

"What happens if Larry goes down and they get to his wife?" Messmer says he asked the jury. "We know his kid is somewhere around the area, he is coming out, he is looking. We know he was out sometime shortly after that, not only are they possibly going to beat up the wife, but if Larry goes down and he's knocked out and his gun comes out, then they have a free gun in the hands of these attackers."

Hung Jury

The first trial against Larry Hickey for multiple counts of aggravated assault with a deadly weapon started during on September 29 and concluded with closing arguments on October 7, 2009. When the jury returned, nine voted to acquit and three to convict. They were unable to come to a unanimous decision, and the case closed with a hung jury. Had the jury agreed to convict him, Hickey would have faced a 45-year jail sentence, provided that the convictions on the various charges ran concurrently.

Messmer explains that after trial some of the jurors agreed to talk about the case with the defense team. "The feeling we got was that they just would not come off the fact that three individuals did not have a weapon, and that it was gun versus no gun. They felt that even though these people probably were the attackers, Larry probably didn't have a right to use his gun at that point in time."

Hayes admits that he was not surprised when he received two emails from Matthew Messmer, the first telling him that the trial had ended with a hung jury, and the second that the State intended to retry Hickey.

Hayes remembers his reaction: "Well, I said, that makes sense because there were really two stories being told. While we had the physical evidence to back up Larry's version of the events, they had more witnesses to tell the other story." He says that the jurors had to weigh conflicting information between what the physical evidence showed and what the eyewitnesses said. "The eyewitnesses were also the individuals who Larry shot and they were, frankly, kind of a sympathetic group. There was a lot of evidence on both sides and it didn't surprise me there was a hung jury."

When Messmer emailed a second time, he asked if Hayes would consider helping with a second trial. "He asked, 'Are you up for it again?'" Hayes remembers. "I said, 'Darned right, we are. Let's lock and load.'"

Two scant weeks passed between the end of the first trial and the State's announcement that it intended to try

Hickey a second time. Though the State dropped several of the charges, if his attorneys did not prevail this time, Hickey estimates that he would have faced a sentence of approximately 30 years. Offered the option of pleading guilty to two felonies, Hickey would have probably served two years in jail, expecting a reduced sentence for good behavior.

"At no time did I ever personally entertain accepting a plea," Hickey exclaims. "Counsel told me about the risks [of a second trial], but I was pretty adamant with them. The attorney has to do his due diligence, though, so they told me things like the conviction rate for this county attorney's office was like 92% and on retrials it is like 95%. Then, you don't know what kind of a jury you'll get and the State now knows your testimony, so they will be more prepared.

"They let me know that I had a tougher fight ahead. It worried me," Hickey admits. Still, he elected to go back to trial, noting that although the shorter sentence might be easier to contemplate, "It is not justice, so we turned down the plea offer."

New Trial Strategy

Messmer immediately vowed that in the second trial he would not simply present a re-do of the original arguments, and Hayes offered him an innovative solution. "I said, 'Let me run this idea by you.' I told Messmer that Massad Ayoob could testify to everything I testified to in the first trial, plus talk about weapons retention issues and disparity of force issues to a greater degree. We began planning to have Massad serve in the role that I had in the first trial. Then I volunteered to go to Tucson to as serve as defense consultant to help sort out some of the issues as they came up in court."

Ayoob, who had consulted during preparation for the first trial, joined the second defense effort enthusiastically. "I'm not sure there were things that I testified to that Marty could not have handled," Ayoob interjects modestly. "However, the strategy was to have on the defense team someone who was analogous in their role to the lead investigator who was working at the prosecution table. There you have someone who is deeply familiar with proper protocols for shooting investigations, crime scene reconstruction, bullet trajectories and angles who can advise the prosecutor how to best establish his case in front of the jury.

"Marty fulfilled that role for the defense team. It is rare that a defense team has that and I think it was absolutely critical. The second time around, it allowed a stronger defense to be established." Ayoob notes that he gave testimony about how students are taught to recognize the lethal threat of disparity of force. He told the jury how in Hickey's situation, the male assailant's blind side attack in conjunction with the ongoing attack by the two females tipped the balance creating a deadly situation in which Hickey's decision to shoot was justified.

Civil Suit Settled

Before and during the first trial, Hickey's homeowners insurance began receiving demand letters from Hickey's assailants wanting to tap into his insurance to cover their medical bills and collect damages. Expecting to be acquitted at trial, Hickey directed his insurance company to deny the demands.

Within 30 days after the end of the first trial, his assailants had filed a civil lawsuit for monetary damages. Hickey asked his insurer to obtain a civil attorney for him. Like his insurer, Hickey came to view the settlement as purely a business decision, recognizing that in a civil case, the plaintiffs need only convince a majority of the jurors that their argument is more likely valid than not, unlike the criminal case in which the standards of proof are considerably higher. Recognizing that a loss in civil court could cost more than the $100,000 limit of his insurance, Hickey acquiesced, a settlement was reached and the $100,000 apportioned primarily to the two who were shot in the fracas, although all three had attempted to collect. In attempting to get money from Hickey's insurer, the assailants made a number of depositions, which proved useful later. Messmer calls those depositions ammunition for the defense, "because once again, they changed their story."

To claim monetary damages against homeowners insurance, the trio had to change their stories about where the altercation occurred, from the middle of the street to its actual location, the Hickey family driveway. "That is the problem with having to keep your stories straight," Hickey says, speaking carefully and trying not to sound accusatory.

When police interviewed his assailants, not one admitted to striking Hickey, and they made odd accusations that he didn't say a word to them, only laughed and started shooting. The original female assailant continued with that story through the first trial, but in depositions for the civil case she said that Hickey asked them to return to their home, but she chose not to because she wanted the argument resolved.

In addition, although he had told investigating police officers that he had not hit Hickey, the male assailant testified in both criminal trials that he had hit Hickey in the head. Hickey recalls that testimony: "In my mind, that was like a 'Matlock moment,' an "AH, HA!' like in the TV show *Matlock*. On TV, that is where the judge says, "Case dismissed!" Well, that does not happen in real life! But the jurors hear it and they see this individual squirm on the stand when they are made to read their own testimony. The jury is not stupid, thankfully."

The State Tries Again

Messmer resolved that his defense strategy in the second criminal trial would be much more than a do-over of the first. "I think the prosecutor just thought we were going to do a replay and have the same opening and same closing," he suggests. "We really had to go back and learn this stuff even better. On the second trial it was more important to keep Marty Hayes involved and his suggestion was absolutely great."

Freed of the ordinary trial restrictions through which witnesses are commonly sequestered, Hayes would be free to be in the courtroom all throughout the trial, and, from that broader view, advise on trial strategy. Hayes cites an example of a red herring the prosecutor introduced into the first trial that his advice to the defense helped them avoid in the second. "In the first trial, Nicolini was all concerned about the gun that Larry used. It was a standard Glock 19 loaded with a combination of Silvertip ammunition and some other miscellaneous ammo that was at the bottom of the mag. He was trying to paint the picture of this gun being inherently dangerous, reckless, unsafe, saying 'It doesn't have a safety on it, does it?' I thought it was kind of weird that he was attacking the gun as much as he was, so I just simply answered the questions as honestly as I could and didn't give him any ammunition to work with."

Hayes continues, "In the second trial, I made it clear to the defense team that you need to establish ahead of time what guns the local police use because they all use .40 caliber Glocks which are generally more powerful than 9mm. So in the second trial, we established through a detective's testimony that their gun was a .40 caliber Glock and guess what? Nicolini knew what we had done and he never made the gun an issue in the second trial."

Seated in the courtroom directly behind the defense team, Hayes watched, listened and did his best to judge

how testimony was being received and what the prosecution had up its sleeve. When something concerned him, he
would jot a brief message on a sticky note that he handed
to Messmer's paralegal, Jacqueline Britt, who in turn
passed it on up to Messmer or Rosenbluth at the defense
table with Hickey. "We tried to do it as discreetly as possible so as not to be disruptive," Hayes recalls, noting that
neither prosecutor nor judge challenged the activity and he
believes the jury was all but unaware of it.

"When the prosecution was giving their case, I would
be looking into how to cross examine their witnesses and
look for discrepancies between their testimony and what I
knew about the case," Hayes describes. "Understand that
90 to 95% of the time Messmer or Rosenbluth knew that
and were already on top of it. I told them, 'I don't know
what is in your mind, so I'm going to keep sending these
notes,' and they said, 'Just keep sending them.' Occasionally, I would bring up something they hadn't thought about
and we would get that into the cross examination or the
direct examination for some of the defense witnesses," he
remembers.

"I can't believe that we had such luck!" Messmer
enthuses. "In addition to Mike [Rosenbluth], we have my
legal assistant, Jackie, we have Larry working the trial, but
now we also have Marty who is right behind us and has a
different viewpoint and who can tell us what is going on
with the firearms. That, too, was very important. We delved
into the specifics about the uniqueness of self-defense law
even more than in the first trial."

Messmer drew on testimony from Ayoob, as well as
bringing out testimony from material witnesses Richard Ba-
tory, James Yeager and police sergeant Brian Kowalski, who
had been Hickey's instructors. They testified to information upon which Hickey acted when he defended himself
and his family. Messmer suggests that in the first trial they
expected Hickey's extensive training to speak for itself. "In
the second trial we needed to ask, 'What was this class
about? Why did you take that class? Why was that useful?'"
he explains.

Unfortunately, Kowalski fell seriously ill right before he
was scheduled to testify, and all parties involved agreed
that his testimony from the first trial would suffice. Using
transcripts from the earlier trial as scripts, the judge, prosecutor and a "reader" played the roles. Hayes was selected
to read Kowalski's words, with several odd moments resulting.

Gila Hayes of Armed Citizens Legal Defense Network – at right, talking to a prospective member – wrote this synopsis of Arizona v. Larry Hickey. ACLDN provided substantial assistance to the defense.

The first came when the prosecutor had asked Kowalski to comment on Hayes' testimony in the first trial, which had preceded Kowalski's. The police sergeant responds in glowing terms, which caused Hayes to chuckle, and the prosecutor to break off from his script and ask, "He is talking about you, isn't he?" After that, the court did its best to move on with the testimony. It was going fine until they reached a point in the policeman's testimony in which he gave demonstrative testimony in addition to his spoken words.

Hayes tells the story: "In that first trial, Nicolini had asked Kowalski to demonstrate a retention firing position. Apparently, Kowalski got up and showed the jury what that meant. Because this was demonstrative testimony and not verbal testimony, we were kind of stuck. Knowing me from the first trial, the judge said, 'Well, I think Mr. Hayes is qualified to demonstrate that.' So I got up in front of the

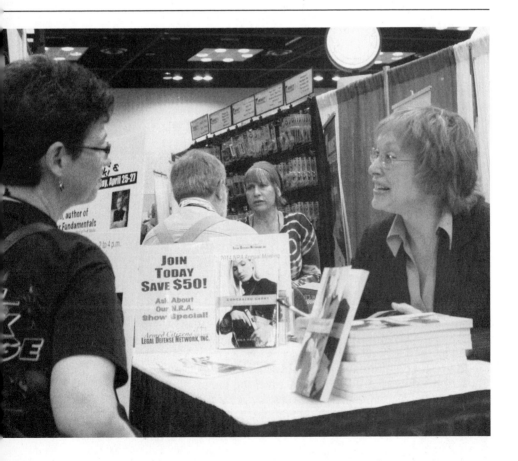

jury and demonstrated some of this demonstrative evidence even though I'd never been sworn in as a witness," Hayes marvels.

"Frankly, I think that would have been an appealable issue if they had wanted to appeal it, though I don't think it would have gone anywhere because it didn't really affect the outcome of the case and it did not prejudice either side," he estimates. "That was a surreal moment. Afterwards, I went back and sat behind the defense and started passing notes again," Hayes concludes.

Of course most of the trial was deadly serious. The expert testimony of Massad Ayoob clarified the very real threat of death or crippling injury Hickey faced on November 17, 2008 when he was set upon by the two sisters and the boyfriend. "We had to explain to the jury that there were multiple issues going on," Ayoob begins. One issue he clarified was Hickey's fast decision when his strategy changed from fending off the blows to drawing and firing his Glock pistol, explaining how the addition of the young man changed the threat to Hickey.

When the young man jumped in to the fight, the circumstances changed "from two females – two fairly good sized, and one very athletic female – against one medium-sized male," he explains. "Now we had not only the tilting of the balance by the very aggressive, buffed-out young male, but with that we had the blind side attack of the sucker punch to the head that Larry with his medical training realized was very close to rendering him unconscious as he sees flashes of white light."

The danger of passing out introduced an additional justification beyond disparity of force and disparity in numbers, Ayoob continues. He explains that disparity of force occurs when an able bodied person attacks a disabled person. That applies even if the disability occurs during the fight. Applying those definitions to Hickey's situation, Ayoob explains, "Larry knows that in a moment he will pass out. There is absolutely no reason to believe that someone who would join in a three-to-one attack and who would throw a sucker punch from an unseen angle would suddenly turn into the Marquis of Queensberry, as the prosecution said, and let it go at the single punch and say, 'Ah, ha! I have taught you to be a gentleman.' That was one of the prosecution's more ludicrous points," he chuckles grimly.

"I explained that once he was down, he would be helpless," says Ayoob. "A reasonable and prudent person in his situation, knowing what he knew, could expect to be stomped to death or horribly crippled. There was no reason to believe these people who would commit such an aberrant, violent three-against-one assault would suddenly turn charitable, merciful, normal and benevolent," Ayoob recounts.

"We had to also explain that Larry knew what they did not: that if they continued to maul him when he was down that they were very likely to find a loaded Glock 19 that he was legally carrying, his wife was not only within the line of physical attack, but also in the line of fire if they got that gun away from him and he had reason to believe that his little boy was threatened, as well. All those things came together in his mind," Ayoob says.

Ayoob's testimony also showed the jury how Hickey's assailants changed their stories from their initial statements, to testimony in the first trial, to depositions for the civil case, to the testimony the jury had heard in this, the second trial. He points out that they had changed their testimony about sequences of events, their locations and what they were doing. "One of the State's witness' testimony about where she was when she was shot was inconsistent with the angle of the gunshot wound and was actually, physically impossible. We used a Ring's Blue Gun with a Crimson Trace laser and that proved to be very effective evidence," Ayoob remembers.

Ayoob takes a deep breath and resumes his narrative, "I think it is another classic example of why certain things need to be articulated at the scene, as I have taught for 30 years. The other side is saying you've done all these horrible things and manipulating the story at will. Here, they said first, 'It happened in the street,' because they realized, 'Wait a minute, we did attack him on his own property. We can't let that come out,' so they said, 'He came out and met us in the street.'

"Really?" Ayoob wonders. "Why are the blood stains on his property?"

The woman testified that after Hickey shot her in the lower leg she hopped up on to the Hickey driveway. "By some magic no blood dripped from the massive, hemorrhaging gun shot," Ayoob interjects sarcastically.

"That was one of the things that I explained on the stand: that it would be virtually impossible for that particular wound that was bleeding copiously not to have bled and have left bloodstains on the street," Ayoob recounts. "When they did their civil suit, in deposition the same witnesses said under oath, 'Did I say it happened on the street? Oh, no, it happened on *his* property,' because the homeowners liability policy won't cover something that happens on a public street," he adds.

"So essentially what you have is these witnesses who blatantly, totally changed their story to whatever served them in whatever setting they were in, criminal or civil. Messmer and his team had to meet it and I believe they met it successfully," he concludes.

Had things gone disastrously wrong and the jury voted to convict Hickey, both Ayoob and Hayes identify issues they believe would have been grounds for an appeal for a new trial.

Ayoob points out, "The judge ignored case law from right there in Arizona, fairly fresh case law in the Harold Fish case, that said that the jury had the right to know anything about the assailant that would cause them to be particularly dangerous even if it was not known to the defendant when they shot them. Now that is a very welcome turnaround from Federal rule of evidence 404B that says prior bad acts by the opponent unless known to you cannot be used in your defense for harming that opponent."

Ayoob continues, "For whatever reason, the judge chose not to go that way and the jury never knew that one of those substantial-sized women was athletic and spent a good deal of time working out in a Brazilian jujitsu dojo and had put on her Facebook page prior to the incident that she 'loved to grapple.' But at trial, she's presented as a helpless June Cleaver in a cocktail dress being attacked by the savage, crazed mercenary gun nut, when in fact she was one of the ones who initiated the attack on Hickey who was attempting throughout to be the peacemaker," Ayoob says.

"The prosecutor won that one," Ayoob accounts. "I think had Hickey been convicted, we would have won on appeal, but it was an uphill fight. That has always been one of the curses of this: attacked by someone with a long, violent history, unless the other side opens the door by blatantly saying you can't believe that someone as nice as the one who was harmed could have attacked this defendant. This prosecutor was wise enough that he did not; he did that by innuendo, but not by statement, so that particular door did not open."

Also kept out of the trial was the videotape of the murder of Constable Lunsford by three considerably smaller suspects during a car search for drugs. "I think we all thought that was an appealable issue that could have set Larry free if he had been convicted," Hayes estimates. "There certainly was case law applicable, but the judge felt the video was too graphic and too prejudicial. Well, this was a prejudicial case, in which he was being accused with three counts of aggravated assault. And this was in front of him, and I think the jury should have seen it. That was a setback."

Hayes muses further, "Having said that, I think that Messmer's closing argument was the pivotal point in the second trial. I remember a lot of passion, and the fact that Messmer really believed that he had a truly innocent individual, which was not the norm for a public defender. He had a lot of passion in his voice when discussing it. In fact, at one point, he had to take a break because he was getting too involved with the argument. He took a break and then he came back and finished up his closing. To me that was the biggest part of the case," he submits.

Hung Again

On May 25, 2010, when the second trial came to an end, eight members of the jury voted to acquit, two to convict and two were unable to reach a decision. This jury was quite different than the first. The State had used all of its challenges to disallow any jury picks that admitted to owning guns, had licenses to carry, or had prior police, military or correctional work experience, Hickey remembers. "Usually the prosecution wants the law-abiding types, cops, people with a sense of right or wrong. Those were the people I wanted on my jury," Hickey comments. This time the State assiduously avoided those types of people, and the jury included a mix of retired folks and citizens who Hayes characterizes as being "antsy, because they just wanted to get back to their jobs."

Messmer relates, "On the second trial, we had a juror that was a lawyer. In hindsight we shouldn't have picked him, because lawyers over analyze everything. He's one of the ones who voted against us and we were absolutely shocked. And he said, 'Hey, I went in there and I said, 'No you can't use a weapon even if there are three on one, if they don't have a weapon,'" explains Messmer.

While Messmer will be the first to say he learned a lot in preparing Larry Hickey's defenses, he stresses that attorneys need to know more about self-defense and the law. "I'm glad you are doing this article. I really do think that the lawyers need to be educated about it because it is different when you read on a page what the law is, but when you see this kind of training that Larry had, the kind of perspective that Marty and Ayoob had about this case, it is a totally different thing than what we are used to."

"We certainly would have talked to people around here, but the knowledge that was available to us through Marty and Ayoob was outstanding and made us able to attack the case and gave us ideas that I don't know as lawyers that we would have picked up, because we don't always know how to start," Messmer admits. "It gave us better arguments because we were not thinking as lawyers, we were more taking our law and applying it to actual firearms and that kind of self-defense training. I don't know that we would have gotten that on our own."

After recounting his ordeal from beginning to end, Hickey emphasizes that he no longer believes that a trial is about right and wrong, crime and justice. "It seems to be about winning and losing," he muses. For example, he cites how a judge arbitrarily controls what evidence to allow in to the trial, and what to keep out.

"People need to understand how it works," Hickey says. "You think you are going to be able to present this evidence and that evidence and everyone will be able to see it clearly. Well, the judge decides what evidence you are going to present."

Because during the fight, Hickey's mind had flashed to the video in which three small people kill a large "line-backer sized" police officer. Hickey and his defense wanted to show the jury the video. The judge would not allow it, though she did allow Hickey to talk about it. "I think the judge was a very fair individual, but that was just a decision that she made."

The defense also wanted to present material from the Arizona Department of Public Safety's required Concealed Handgun Licensing curriculum that specifically addressed disparity of force when attacked by multiple assailants who are unarmed, but were prevented from doing so.

The outcome in a case like Hickey's can also hinge on how the police handle the evidence. Hickey relates that at one point during his first trial, he overheard prosecution members talking about the manner in which Hickey had carried his Glock that night. Something he heard made him worried that the prosecution intended to allege that before the shooting Hickey had his gun tucked in his waistband without a holster, something that would be consistent with running into the house and grabbing a gun.

Concerned, he mentioned it to his lawyers, who casually asked the detective who was sitting at the next table if the prosecution had brought Hickey's holster with them. The detective responded, "There was no holster; he didn't have a holster."

Hickey remembers that, by good fortune, the officer who arrested him was due to testify next. Since in court it is not a good idea to ask a question to which you do not know the answer, Hickey's attorney ran through a series of questions starting by asking if the witness took the defendant into custody, whether he gave him a cursory pat down before putting him in the patrol car, and what, if anything the pat down produced.

The officer answered that yes, he took a holster off Hickey and that he put it in evidence. "That holster could never be found, not that we needed it, because the guy admitted to taking it," Hickey recounts. It was later found after the State released Hickey's firearm. When Hickey went to pick up the gun, the clerk asked offhandedly if he wanted "this other stuff." Hickey asked what it was and the woman gave him some shoes, socks and the missing holster. Further inquiry showed a minor error in the number under which that evidence was logged. Those things just fell through the cracks, Hickey explains.

Hickey characterizes the error as, "Not a huge deal, but if it had gone the other way and the prosecutor was able to convince the jury that I was lying and that I was not carrying a firearm in a holster – that I just went in and stuffed a gun in my pants and went out looking for trouble – that makes me wonder."

Throughout a lengthy interview with Hickey, at no time does he express malice or anger toward law enforcement or the criminal justice system. If pushed, he will acknowledge that the system failed him, especially in the early days of his incarceration, but in admitting that, his tone of voice remains even and dispassionate.

"All of the officers that testified were great," he says. "They got up there and they told the truth about what they observed, their experiences, my demeanor when they responded. I mean, they were great. I don't think there was anything malicious about this prosecution," he concludes.

Reality

Hickey wants other armed citizens to know, though, that real life bears little resemblance to TV or movie dramas. During classes, roundtable discussions, and on Internet forums, people converse about what might happen. "Very rarely, is it about your neighbors attacking you," Hickey points out. "It is about a tattooed gang banger who is robbing the liquor store or the bank. People don't think about your neighbors coming over to kill you or seriously injure you or your family," he stresses. "People think you are going to save the day and people are going to hoist you up on their shoulders and it is not always like that."

"Still, this is the best system we've got," he adds. "You get your chance in court."

"We learn from other's use of force experiences, and you can learn a lot of court stuff from this one. I want to help people avoid the situation I found myself in and avoid the court fight," he emphasizes.

Messmer notes that his defense of Larry Hickey will stand out in his mind as different from other cases in his career. "I thought we did a really good job because we had a great team. Leading up to it, I was absolutely scared for Larry, and worried whether we were going to do the right thing. Once we got to trial, I had no doubts about what we were doing. I knew we were doing it right," he remembers.

"Sometimes, athletes talk about being in the zone," the attorney compares. "I felt during these trials that I was in the zone and that the team we had was in the zone. During the closing, I had no doubt that I was able to reach the jury. At least they were listening, and I could tell, doing this as long as I've done it, that I was reaching them."

Messmer feels pride and satisfaction in the outcome of the two trials. "I think, no matter what, no matter how many good cases that I do in the future, because of the uniqueness of this case and all the hard work and the job that we did and especially the resources that were provided to us, this one it definitely will go down in memory as one of my better cases, one of my personal accomplishments," he allows.

"I would have liked to walk out of there with a jury victory but we still got the victory, so I'm going to hang it up [as noteworthy] because Larry walked away free and he was absolutely innocent," the attorney concludes.

About a month elapsed before the State decided not to take Hickey to trial a third time. "It took two trials, but all my charges were dismissed with prejudice which means they could never come back again. I can't help but think that the same State that dismissed my charges would not have a problem if I had taken a plea and would be sitting in jail today. To me, that is scary," Hickey comments.

As soon as the dismissal was announced, Hickey's attackers had him served with an injunction against harassment, essentially a restraining order that precluded him from owning firearms or coming within a specified distance of them. "We chose the better part of valor and didn't move back into our home right away," he explains. "We knew that as soon as I showed up, this individual would call the police and the police would have to make a decision and that decision would probably be that I would have to go to jail." He hired a civil attorney, and they requested a hearing. "I knew I had to fight this because it was just ridiculous and had no basis in fact. The woman's statement in the injunction was that back in November 2008 in an argument Mr. Hickey shot me, and she also made something up about how my wife would park outside of her house and stare at her, so the judge rubber stamped it," he explains.

On June 14, 2010, following a 2 ½ hour hearing before a city court magistrate, the plaintiff's injunction was quashed. The magistrate took pains to consider all the facts before removing the injunction, retiring to his chambers at one point to consult with Judge Godoy who had officiated at the two previous trials. Oddly, during the hearing, the plaintiff told the magistrate that she really didn't have any problems with Hickey, and that he was welcome to come over to her house to have a soda if he liked so long as he didn't bring a gun along. She stated that she wanted the injunction to prevent Hickey from possessing firearms. The magistrate decided in Hickey's favor. With that decision, Hickey was finally able to return to his home, free of the threat to his freedom and way of life, a black cloud he had lived under since the night of November 17, 2008.

"As an instructor, I teach a lot of foreign weapons classes for a local company that is contracted to teach the military," Hickey explains. "My hearing was on Monday, June 14th, and I had orders to be at Camp Pendleton to teach Marines on Monday and Tuesday the 14th and 15th. I didn't get to teach on Monday, but as soon as the judge quashed the order that I couldn't own firearm, I drove to Oceanside, CA, and taught the next day."

Hickey and his family have now returned to live in their home up the driveway from the place the attack occurred. The sisters and their sons still live across the street.

Chapter 12:
After the Shooting

In the old days, we all went with the standard advice from defense lawyers: "Don't say anything to the police." A few years ago, a law professor's 45-minute lecture went viral on the internet with the same message: never talk to the cops. Interestingly, in three quarters of an hour telling stories of guilty suspects who got hung by their tongue when they tried to outwit trained police interrogators, there's not a single instance of an innocent man getting in trouble for speaking to investigators. There's one case the professor mentions of a mentally ill man whose story was that he confessed to smoke out the real perpetrator. My take: if you're crazy, maybe you *shouldn't* talk to the police. If you're a guilty criminal, talking to the police means that you'll either tell the truth and inculpate yourself, or lie to the cops and get caught in the lie.

Location of spent casings is not consistent, and in author's opinion, can't exactly determine shooter's position. Nonetheless, casings and other evidence should be pointed out at the scene as soon as possible.

The late Jim Cirillo, a friend and mentor of the author, was living proof that after multiple justified homicides, a good person could go on to enjoy life and family.

Never forget that when you shoot someone, however necessarily and justifiably, you look an awful lot like a killer and he looks an awful lot like a victim. The stereotype can take hold quickly if you don't act to let the authorities – from the first responding officer to the designated lead investigator – know what happened. The old saying "You only get one chance to make a first impression" is absolutely true here.

Decades ago, I developed a five-point checklist of things I feel the righteous shooter needs to establish as soon as possible in the aftermath. It has been widely adopted, sometimes with attribution and sometimes without, and is now recommended by entities ranging from the Armed Citizens Legal Defense Network to the US Concealed Carry Association. I'm rather proud of that.

Five-Point Checklist

1. *Establish the active dynamic. That is, let the authorities know immediately what happened here. If you have harmed someone in self-defense, always remember that the active dy-*

*namic is not what you did to him, it's what he
was trying to do to you or another victim. The
active dynamic is his action that forced your
lawful response. It's not, "I shot him." It's, "This
man tried to kill me." Or, "This man attacked
my wife." Whatever it was that led to your use
of force.*

This makes it clear that the guy on the ground doing a
convincing imitation of a victim is in fact the criminal perpetrator. It makes it clear that you, the person with the smoking
gun who just shot someone, are in fact the intended victim.

If one or more of your attackers has left the scene, *explain
that now, and give their description.* It's going to be hard for
people to see you as the innocent party if you failed to let
police know that a violent criminal was at large.

2. *Advise the police that you will sign the complaint. There are two roles open in this particular play: victim and perpetrator. As noted,
   appearances can create mistaken role reversal
   if things aren't immediately clarified. By making a statement to the police to the effect of "I
   will sign the complaint," you reinforce the fact
   that you are the victim-complainant, the good
   guy or gal, and the person you're signing the
   complaint on is the bad guy who forced you to
   harm him in legitimate defense of self or others. (Note: I would not advise using the phrase
   "I will press charges." The reason is that legal
   terminology varies slightly jurisdiction to jurisdiction. While in many jurisdictions it is indeed
   the complainant who presses charges, there
   are some places where the local terminology
   is such that the prosecutor "presses charges." If
   you inadvertently find yourself in one of those
   places and say "I will press charges," it sounds
   to the police as if you have delusions of being
   the elected chief prosecutor, and you won't be
   off to a good start. "I will sign the complaint" is
   neutral and universal.)*

3. *Point out the evidence. The scene will be cha-
   otic. Witnesses will be trampling the scene. So
   will paramedics and police officers. I've seen
   cases of the bad guy's gun being picked up by
   his accomplice or by a well-meaning neigh-*

bor who didn't want to leave it where a child could find it. I've seen spent casings kicked away from their original resting place, or picked up in the treads of emergency personnel's boots or the wheels of an ambulance gurney, thus altering the dimensions of the shooting scene and making it look like something it wasn't. The sooner you point out the evidence to the first responding officers, the more likely it is to be secured. When you've done the right thing, evidence helps you.

No good deed goes unpunished. After killing a gun-armed robber, Zack Rogers was sued by a person whose life he saved in the incident.

4. Point out the witnesses. Witnesses worry about having to lose time from work to testify in court, or being the target for vengeance by criminals. A lot of them "don't want to get involved." Once they leave the scene unidentified, their testimony that would have helped to prove your innocence leaves with them.

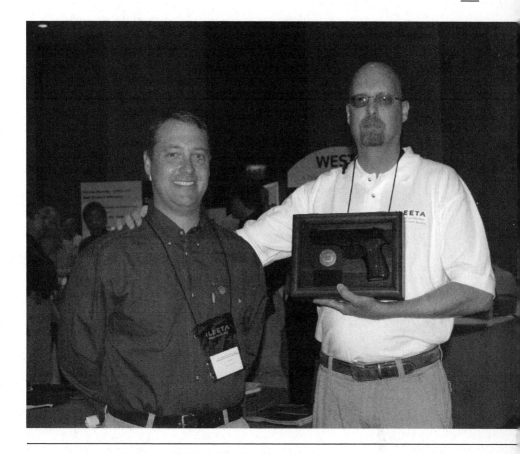

Beretta representative, left, presents Andy Brown with a token of appreciation for his heroism. From some 70 yards, using the Beretta 92 pistol he was issued, Andy slew a mass-murderer who had already killed many with a rifle. His employer did not treat him well in the aftermath.

Point out the witnesses to the police at the first opportunity. (Some have asked, "What if the witness is a friend of the attacker and lies about what happened?" The fact is, he was going to do that anyway, so you haven't lost anything. However, your having pointed him out to the police can be seen as an indication that you believed in your own innocence, or you wouldn't have steered the police to him, and that can't hurt.)

5. Politely decline further questioning until you have consulted an attorney. Studies show that, in the immediate aftermath of a life-threatening encounter, we may forget some things or get some details wrong. The questions to you will come at random as they occur to the officer, and you will answer them in the same

order; in reviewing the cop's notes and his recollection of the discussion later, this can create the false illusion that you were giving a narrative of events in the order in which they occurred, which of course is not the case. But later, when you do narrate events in the sequence of their occurrence, it creates a false perception that you have changed your story. Often, very frightening things that happened are blocked in short term memory by a subconscious that doesn't want to recall them; when you mention something later that you didn't mention at the scene, it sounds made up. You don't want to answer detailed questions as to exact words spoken, distances, or time frames. None of us are human tape recorders. The tunnel vision that afflicts well over half of people caught up in something like a gunfight creates the literal optical illusion that things and people appear closer and larger than they are. If your memory tells you your attacker was six feet away when you shot him but he turns out to have been six yards away, you sound like a liar. Tachypsychia is likewise very common, the sense of things going into slow motion. It seemed to you as if the fight took a whole minute, and you say so, but a security camera shows it was actually only ten seconds, and now you look like a liar. The involved victim who had to fight for his or her very survival is the worst possible witness for measuring things in feet or inches, or counting how many shots were fired.

Experts recommend 24 to 48 hours between one of these "critical incidents," as they are now euphemistically called in the emergency services, and when the participant is subjected to a detailed debriefing. The Force Science Institute recommends "one full sleep cycle."

This is why my recommendation – practical advice, not legal advice – is to establish the active dynamic, indicate that you'll sign the complaint, point out evidence and witnesses known to you...and then stop. Be polite. Do not raise your voice. I for one would answer subsequent questions with, "Officer, you'll have my full cooperation after I've spoken with counsel."

Chapter 13:
Hardware Issues

This book is about the software, not the hardware, of self-defense. Anyone interested in my take on the hardware, I'll refer to my books *Combat Shooting, Gun Digest Book of Combat Handgunnery, Gun Digest Book of Concealed Carry,* and *World's Greatest Handguns,* all from FW Media. At the same time, since the book you're now reading is about self-defense and defending such actions in court, the fact is that choice of gun and ammunition do come into the latter arena. That needs to be discussed here.

If a prosecutor brings you to trial on a charge of reckless driving, do you doubt that he'll make hay with the fact that you were driving a scarlet Corvette Stingray instead of a gray VW bug at the time of the alleged offense? If a plaintiff's lawyer was suing you because your dog bit his client, don't you think he'd play up the fact that your pet was a pit bull instead of a miniature poodle? Why would anyone think it would be any different in a case involving the use of a gun?

The attacks on your choice of gun and ammo aren't based on black letter law; there are no statutes or codes that say you can't carry a gun whose manufacturer named it the Killer Kommando Special, or one with a very light trigger pull. Interestingly, the City of San Francisco, California, at this writing has an ordnance which bans hollow point bullets, and a State of New Jersey law prohibits the handful of concealed carry permit holders there from carrying hollow points, though they can have them at home and police are exempt.

The attacks come from trial tactics, not taught in law school or available on .gov websites. They'll come from unscrupulous – or sometimes clueless – attorneys who are strongly motivated to paint you as bloodthirsty or negligent or both to a jury of lay people expressly selected by those lawyers during the *voir dire* process for their lack of knowledge about weapons and self-defense. Some of those attacks are easy for the knowledgeable defense team and defendant to defeat with logical explanations for the choice. And some are hard to win, making them battles best avoided by choosing different equipment beforehand.

Arguments We Can Win

"He chose an especially powerful gun and loaded it with extra-deadly hollow nosed dum-dum bullets, ladies and gentlemen of the jury. Bullets designed to rend and tear and cause cruel and unusual pain and suffering. And oh, how many bullets he *had,* enough to slaughter a dozen and a half people! What but murderous malice could have motivated him?" That's the kind of argument you can expect. A computer search will get you to the case of *Arizona v. Harold Fish,* in which a retired schoolteacher shot and killed a paranoid schizophrenic who violently attacked him in the desert. Look for the *Dateline* TV episode on the trial, in which some of the jurors who convicted him explain how they bought the prosecution's argument that his use of a 10mm pistol and hollow point ammunition was indicia of malice. His conviction was later overturned on appeal over another issue. When Harold Fish died, he still owed half a million dollars in legal fees to the defense attorney who failed to defeat that argument.

Powerful firearms are defensible. I often carry .357s and .45s on my own time. When I had time to hunt, I used a .44 Magnum Smith & Wesson with 4-inch barrel, which doubled as a defense gun during deer season. I've carried a .45 more than anything else when on duty as a police officer. If asked why I carried "such a powerful gun" – and, yes, I've seen that argument come up with all those calibers – my answer would be that more powerful calibers have historically stopped gunfights faster, and the sooner a gunfight stops the fewer innocent people get hurt or killed.

The research of Dr. Glenn Meyer, a psychologist and professor from Texas who works a lot with mock juries to determine how various issues impact jurors, has done studies which determine that deadlier-seeming "assault guns" make jurors more hostile toward defendants who use them. No surprise: the jury pool is the general public, and the general public for generations now has been bombarded with "assault weapon" propaganda by media and politicians. Does this mean that you should not use an AR15 for home defense? No, it means that you should be able to articulate that you used that light, easy-to-shoot rifle with its telescoping stock because your petite wife and your grandmother could handle it far more easily and confidently than almost anything else if they needed to shoot to save their lives and the lives of their family. It would be worth your time to explain that it's the most popular sporting rifle in America right now, advertised in every hunting periodical on the magazine rack.

When in states where there are magazine capacity limits, I stay within the limit and simply carry more magazines. I often carry a 20-shot Springfield XD(m) 9mm, with a spare magazine. If asked why I chose to carry that many rounds, I would explain (as I already have in Federal court) that the latest study from NYPD showed that 3% of the time their officers needed more than 16 rounds, and the one from LAPD showed 5%. Citizens arm themselves for protection from the same criminals the cops face. 3% and 5% don't sound like a lot, until you ask yourself, "Would I want to be in a situation where there was a 3% or 5% chance that I need this thing to save my life, and NOT have it?" And of course, many more situations go beyond 10 rounds, or six. The history of fighting armed criminals is that many of them can absorb multiple solid hits before ceasing hostility, sometimes from state of rage, sometimes because drugs or alcohol have anesthetized them against pain, and sometimes because they're moving fast in the dark and taking effective cover while they shoot at innocent people. We have more bad guys wearing body armor than in the time of John Dillinger, and that can soak up a lot of ammo before the good guy shooting back realizes it's time to change point of aim.

Why do we use those hollow point bullets, which in my experience opposing counsel will make a point of more times than not in an armed citizen shooting? Not *because* the police do – that would open us up to the "wanna-be cop" tar-and-feathering – but *for the same reasons police do.* Those reasons are:

1. The "mushroom" shape of the hollow point that opposing counsel loves to mention, perhaps hoping to invoke visions of a nuclear cloud over Hiroshima, is also a "parachute" shape intended to slow the bullet down and keep it inside the body of the offender, so it won't pass through and strike an unseen innocent bystander.

2. The cookie-cutter shape of the hollow point tends to bite into hard surfaces and bury itself there, if the bullet misses, instead of ricocheting and going on to endanger innocent bystanders as would the supposedly "humane" bullets the uninformed critics say we should use.

3. *Every single department that issues hollow points will tell you that since the transition from older ammo, these bullets have been more effective and stopped fights faster. Stopping the criminal immediately from stabbing or shooting or otherwise mauling the innocent is the whole reason there is such a thing as "justifiable homicide" in the first place. The sooner he's stopped, the fewer innocents he can harm.*

4. *Finally, we can make a good argument that since this ammunition stops him faster, the Bad Guy will sustain fewer gunshot wounds and may actually be more likely to survive the encounter.*

If the above arguments had been effectively put before the jury, the verdict in *Arizona v. Fish* might have been different.

Arguments to Avoid

In three and a half decades as an expert witness in weapons and shooting cases, I've run across three arguments from the other side which, even though sometimes bogus, are so tough to defeat that it's better not to have to fight them at all. This goes down hard with the naïve folks who believe "a good shoot is a good shoot," which is somewhat akin to the belief that every Christmas a fat guy in a red suit is going to come down a chimney and give them presents, too.

First and foremost among these is what a layman would call a "hair trigger," that is, a trigger pull lighter than what the gun's manufacturer recommends for a defensive firearm. It is within the common knowledge that good people forced to fight criminals with guns are likely to be nervous and shaky. We've known for well over a century that in the grip of "fight or flight response," blood flow is directed away from the extremities and into major muscle groups and internal viscera, to "fuel the furnace" for the strenuous effort primal brain believes is about to take place. It's called vasoconstriction. It's the reason why frightened Caucasians turn visibly pale, and it's one reason we all become extremely clumsy under stress. Mixing that with a "hair trigger" is like mixing fire with gasoline.

What, exactly, is a "hair trigger"? It depends on the gun design, just as the question "what is a safe adjustment of brakes" depends on the specific vehicle. The manufacturer's specification for trigger pull weight on that particular firearm, and the "common custom and practice" for adjusting such guns, constitute the standards. In the timelessly popular 1911 pistol, the Colt company, which has manufactured more of those guns than any other company, tells its armorers that 4.0 pounds is the red-line bottom limit of pull weight for a duty gun used for police, military, or civilian defense purposes. The National Rifle Association requires a 4.0 pound minimum trigger pull on 1911s used in their Distinguished matches, and enforces it with referees equipped with trigger pull weight measurement devices. Do we see a pattern here?

The most popular pistol in the USA today is the Glock. Since its introduction in this country in the early 1980s, this pistol – issued or approved by over 60% of America's police at this writing – had a 5.5 pound standard trigger pull. Some departments have gone heavier: Miami and

Loaded with 185 grain Remington .45 hollow points, Ruger P345 was the death weapon in one of the author's cases. Prosecution made much of the large caliber and the hollow points; defense explained both, and won acquittal.

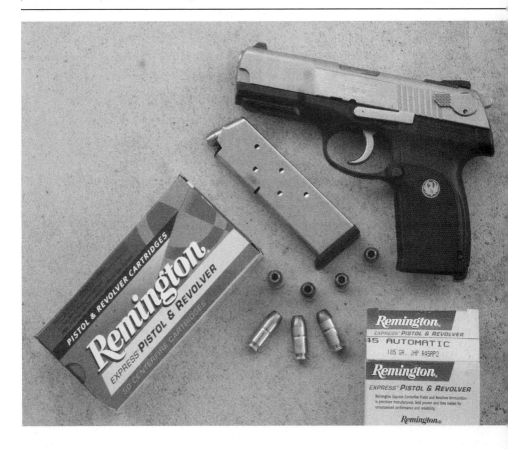

some others went with an 8.0-pound trigger connector. The New York State Police demanded what is now known as the NY-1 trigger, which gives firm resistance from the beginning of the trigger press and brings total pull weight up to around 8 pounds. NYPD demanded more: first called the New York Plus and now known as the NY-2 module, the trigger system in their Glocks approaches *12* pounds, which for this writer passes the point of diminishing returns. The reason, in all cases, was safety against accidental discharges; with thousands of cops using guns under stress, the firearms instructors on those departments wanted a greater safety buffer.

In the late 1980s, Glock came out with a target model sporting a 3.5-pound connector; weighed from the bottom tip of the trigger, that was the pull weight, and leverage being what it is, it ran about 4.5 pounds from the center of the pivoting trigger; they later renamed the exact same part the 4.5-pound connector. However, from the beginning of all that, it was adamant Glock policy that *this trigger pull weight **not** be used in a duty or defense gun*. Their models with this light trigger, then and now, are listed in their

Author has done multiple "cocked revolver/hair trigger" cases, in some of which the allegation was false. He recommends defensive revolvers be rendered double action only.

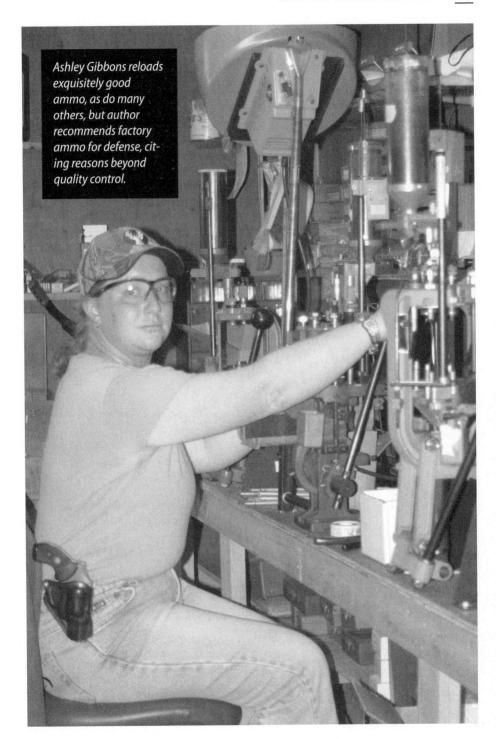

Ashley Gibbons reloads exquisitely good ammo, as do many others, but author recommends factory ammo for defense, citing reasons beyond quality control.

Expansion characteristics of modern ammo are often attacked in court, but author has found those attacks easy to defeat. This is a 230-grain projectile from Federal .45 ACP HST +P load, recovered from flesh and bone after an instant one-shot kill on a hog.

catalogs and websites under "sport," not "duty" or "self-defense" pistols. Target models ordered by police departments are, by policy, shipped with 5.5-pound or heavier trigger pulls.

Would installing a lighter trigger in a duty Glock be a problem? Look up the case of *Santibanes v. Tomball, TX* and see for yourself. The short answer is, "Yes."

Before the Glock, revolvers were standard in American law enforcement. Cocked revolvers with light single-action pulls proved conducive to unintended discharges. Decades ago, LAPD set the trend of converting the guns to double action only. Could, say, a cocked Colt Detective Special with 4.5-pound pull be seen as "reckless and negligent" for taking a criminal at gunpoint? Look up the Appellate Court decision in *New York v. Frank Magliato,* and find out for yourself that the answer is yes.

Why would 4.5 pounds be seen as negligent in a cocked revolver or a Glock, but OK for a 1911? Partly because the 1911 has a passive grip safety and an active manual thumb safety the other two guns don't have, and partly because their own factory literature, court-discoverable, said so.

My own practical advice would be to stay above 4 pounds in a 1911 and 5.5 pounds in a Glock, and render a defensive revolver double action only, an easy gunsmith job.

Why is it an issue at all in an intentional self-defense shooting? Because the hair trigger gives opposing counsel a hook upon which to hang a false allegation, whether criminal or civil. In the criminal case, it's easier to sell a jury on a theory that the gun went off by accident due to a negligently too-light trigger pull, sustaining a manslaughter charge, than to convince them that a good person turned into Mr. Hyde and became a murdering monster. In a civil lawsuit, the motivation is different: plaintiff's counsel is looking for deep pockets. Few defendants have a million liquid, unprotected dollars that the plaintiff can seize to satisfy the judgment if the jury decides in the civil case that you deliberately, maliciously killed the deceased. But most people HAVE a million dollar homeowner liability insurance policy if a burglar was shot, or the same for automobile liability if a carjacker was shot, *and the insurance company has the money!* However, the vast majority

Use of a powerful handgun such as this .45 auto may be attacked by opposing counsel, but is defensible in court.

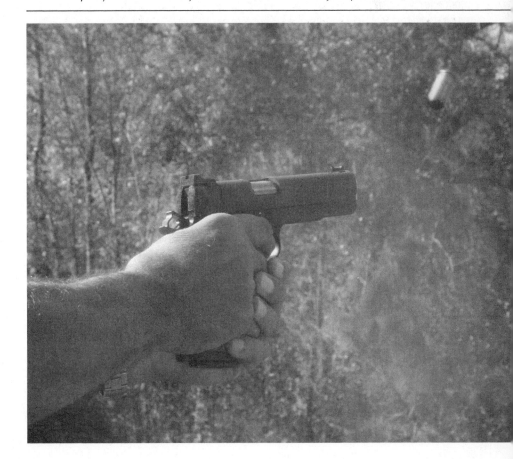

of insurance policies won't pay off on an *intentional tort,* a deliberate act that harmed the plaintiff. But they *will* pay off for a negligent accident. *Voila,* the theory of "he shot my client by accident when he negligently pointed a hair-trigger gun at him" is born.

The second thing I'd avoid is deactivating or removing a safety device: pinning down the grip safety on a 1911 pistol, for example, or removing the magazine disconnector (which prevents the chambered round from being fired if the magazine is out of the pistol) on a Browning High Power. A jury of laymen with little firearms knowledge is deciding the case: do you want to give opposing counsel the argument, "This person is so reckless with firearms that HE DEACTIVATES THE SAFETY DEVICES ON LETHAL WEAPONS." Seriously?

Gun Digest Book of Combat Handgunnery is recommended for more on the "hardware side."

Finally, I would avoid guns with controversial names and decorations. Like the pit bull in the dog bite case, the theory in trial tactics is "the pet reflects the personality of the owner." If you prefer a compact 1911 .45, I'd recommend the Colt Defender, not the Auto Ordnance Pit Bull. I've run across two cases, in one of which I personally testified for the defense, where opposing counsel made a huge deal out of the fact that the defendant had a Colt *Cobra.* I've seen people with cartoon "Punisher" skulls on their grips or the back slide plate on their Glock, and with gun muzzles engraved "Smile, Wait For Flash." People who carried Hornady's novelty ammunition, Zombie-Max, instead of the same company's much more defensible Critical Duty, Critical Defense, and XTP ammo. At the time in your life when you most desperately need to be recognized as responsible, reasonable, and prudent,

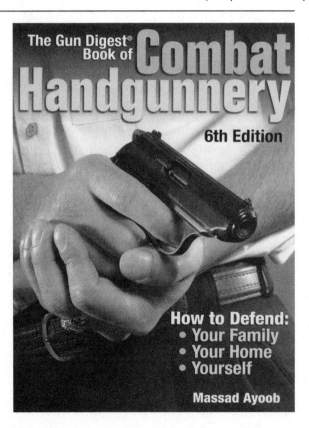

The Gun Digest® Book of Combat Handgunnery

6th Edition

How to Defend:
• Your Family
• Your Home
• Yourself

Massad Ayoob

do you want to be giving that sort of fodder to a silver-tongued attorney who is trying to paint you as reckless and irresponsible with firearms?

I doubt that anyone reading this would defend their family against home invasion by leaving their front door conspicuously open, and place a loaded shotgun inside that door so that when an intruder did enter, he'd be able to grab it and give the homeowner a more challenging gunfight. Some people don't realize that in the "court fight" instead of the gunfight, that's exactly the sort of "firepower" they're handing over to their antagonists when they put "hair triggers" in their defense guns and do any of the other Rambo crap I've discussed above.

A final recommendation on ammunition, from the court defense side: I would most strongly urge you not to put handloaded ammunition in your defensive firearms. Reserve that for practice, hunting, competition, and training. Many self-defense shootings occur at "powder burning distance" and leave gunshot residue on the body or clothing of the opponent.

Combat Shooting, by the author, focuses on tactics, training, and gunfighting history.

If the other side falsely argues that he wasn't close enough to hurt you when you fired, gunshot residue (GSR) on his body or clothes may prove otherwise. But to get that evidence in, your defense team will have to do scientific GSR testing within the rules of evidence, which encompass impartial third-party verification. When you loaded your own ammo and that becomes an issue, you probably won't be able to get it in. The reason is that the other side can argue, literally, "The defendant manufactured the evidence!" "Your honor, how do we know that the fatal shot wasn't a 'special load' he created to fool the crime lab investigators?"

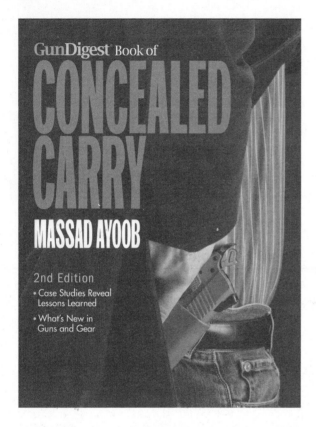

GunDigest Book of
CONCEALED CARRY
MASSAD AYOOB
2nd Edition
• Case Studies Reveal Lessons Learned
• What's New in Guns and Gear

This book covers selection and use of concealed carry methods and related hardware.

I've found this to be the single most contentious argument on the firearms internet. You tell someone the ammo they made themselves may not be the right choice, and they take it personally. I get it. But personal pride has to take second place to family responsibility. If you're falsely accused and can't prove that you're telling the truth, it's your family that will suffer with you through the trial, your possible long imprisonment, and possible terrible financial loss.

I understand your pride in your handloads. When I won a match with ammo I loaded myself, it made me a little more proud, like feeding my family a meal I cooked from scratch instead of having a pizza delivered. But the forensic verification problem is huge: *in almost a decade of internet arguments, no handload fan has ever been able to show me a case where a court accepted a handloader's word or records when it came down to GSR testing to determine distance to figure out which side was telling the truth.* I've been a handloader. But I've also been a son and son-in-law, a husband and father and grandfather, and those responsibilities take precedence. I load my home defense gun, my personal carry guns, and my police duty guns with factory ammunition for verifiability in forensic testing, and also to avoid the argument that "regular bullets weren't deadly enough to satisfy his blood-lust, so he created his own extra-deadly ammunition." I've seen both occur; research *New Jersey v. Daniel Bias* for the forensic side, and *New Hampshire v. James Kennedy* for the "deadly bullets" argument.

It's your life, your hardware, your loved ones who'll go through the ordeal with you…and it's your choice.

Chapter 14:
Concealed Carry Advice

This book would not be complete without some advice on concealed carry. I'd suggest the book I did on that topic, *Gun Digest Book of Concealed Carry*. For now, let's go with something I originally wrote for Harris Publications, who produce two of the magazines I contribute to regularly, *Combat Handguns* and *Guns and Weapons for Law Enforcement*. It went viral a while ago, which I hope I can take as a sign of approval. It is reprinted here with the original publisher's permission.

Black pistol in black holster, with black pants and shirts, is least noticeable "color combination" when handgun is carried visibly.

Ten Commandments for Concealed Carry
by Massad Ayoob

I'm not Moses, let alone God, but the following ten bits of advice are written in stone nonetheless. Not by God, but by the vastly powerful mechanisms of logic, law, and reality.

Commandment I: If You Choose to Carry, Always Carry As Much As Is Possible

Hollywood actors get to see the script beforehand, and nothing is fired at them but blanks. You don't have either luxury. Criminals attack people in times and places where they don't think the victims will be prepared for them. It's what they do. The only way to be prepared to ward off such predators is to always be prepared: i.e., to be routinely armed and

J-frame revolver in pocket can be constantly carried with almost any manner of dress.

While author considers .380 caliber marginal at best, tiny pistols like this Ruger LCP made for that round allow many good people to be armed when they can't carry anything larger.

A gun without spare ammo is a temporary gun; spare ammo is strongly suggested. Here's a spare 10-round .45 ACP magazine for Glock 30 pistol, in Glock's own inexpensive magazine pouch.

"Snag-Mag" pocket magazine carrier, disguised to look like an ordinary pocket knife, was developed by a veteran lawman and firearms specialist.

Safety is critical for everyday carry and accessibility. Here, author demonstrates holstering Ed Brown Custom .45 auto in Ayoob Rear Guard holster by Mitch Rosen. Note thumb is "riding" the hammer, to prevent unintended discharge if something trips the trigger, and index finger is straight so finger won't get caught against trigger during holstering.

Spare ammo is a particularly good idea with a five-shot gun, like this S&W Model 340 M&P. HKS speedloader and Bianchi Speed Strip each hold a full gun-load of five cartridges.

If you can carry one spare magazine, you may not find it hard to carry two. These are .45 caliber Glock 30 mags.

constantly ready to respond to deadly threats against you and those who count on you for protection. It's not about convenience. It's literally about life and death.

Commandment II: Don't Carry A Gun If You Aren't Prepared To Use It

The gun is not a magic talisman that wards off evil. It is a special-purpose emergency rescue tool: no more, no less. History shows us that – for police, and for armed citizens alike – the mere drawing of the

Alertness is paramount if we're to keep danger at bay. Instead of reading like this, with head down in newspaper and head buried like a giraffe at a water hole…

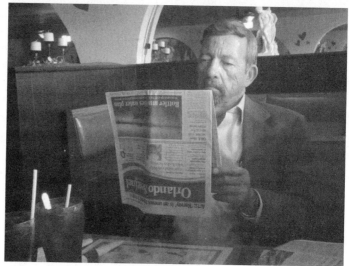

…it's better to sit erect, bringing reading matter up to eye level, to improve the reader's scan of the world around him.

gun ends the great majority of criminal threats, with the offender either surrendering or running away. However, you must always remember that criminals constitute an armed subculture themselves, living in an underworld awash with stolen, illegal weapons. They don't fear the gun, they fear the resolutely armed man or woman pointing that gun at them. And, being predators, they are expert judges of what is prey, and what is a creature more dangerous to them than they are to what they thought a moment ago was their prey.

Thus, the great irony: the person who is prepared to kill if they must to stop a murderous transgression by a human predator, is the person who is least likely to have to do so.

Commandment III: Don't Let The Gun Make You Reckless

Lightweight pseudo-psychologists will tell you that "the trigger will pull the finger" and your possession of your

Don't hesitate to call 9-1-1 at first serious perception of danger.

Common sense: keep fuel tank as close to "full" as possible.

gun will make you want to kill someone. Rubbish. The gun is no more of an evil talisman that turns kindly Dr. Jekyll into evil Mr. Hyde, than it is a good talisman that drives off evil. Those of us who have spent decades immersed in the twin cultures of American law enforcement and the responsibly armed citizenry know that the truth is exactly the opposite. A good person doesn't see the gun as a supercharger for aggression, but as brakes that control that natural human emotion. The law itself holds the armed individual to a "higher standard of care," requiring that they do all that is possible to avoid using deadly force until it becomes clearly necessary. Prepare and act accordingly.

Commandment IV: Carry Legally

If you live someplace where there is no provision to carry a gun to protect yourself and your loved ones, don't let pusillanimous politicians turn you into a convicted felon. Move! It's a quality of life issue. Rhetorical theory that sounds like "I interpret the law this way, because I believe the law should be this way" – which ignores laws that aren't that way – can sacrifice your freedom, your status as a gun-owning free American, and your ability to provide for your family. If you live where a CCW permit is available, get the damn permit. If you don't, move to someplace that does. Yes, it IS that simple. And if you are traveling, check sources such as www.handgunlaw.us to make sure that you are legal to carry in the given jurisdiction. Don't let the legal system make you a felon for living up to your responsibilities to protect yourself and those who count on you. If you carry, make sure you carry legally.

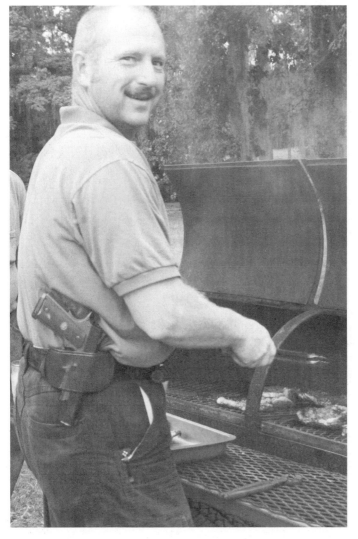

Open carry around the home grill: Springfield .45 is always ready, and in this invitation-only setting, there is little or no alarmed reaction by frightened public.

Legal Heat – 50 State Guide to Firearm Law

View More by This Developer

By Legal Heat

Open iTunes to buy and download apps.

Description

*** THE ONLY APP WITH COMPREHENSIVE CONCEALED & OPEN CARRY LAW SUMMARIES WRITTEN BY ATTORNEYS***

"The Legal Heat app for iPhone is invaluable for people who travel with a gun" – U.S. Concealed Carry Association

Legal Heat Web Site › Legal Heat – 50 State Guide to Firearm Law Support ›   ...More

What's New in Version 1.4.1

Legal Heat would like to thank all of our users for continuing to make the app the top app of its kind. As a reminder, the app is updated fluidly. Meaning, the app content (state laws) will be updated constantly and updates will not come through the App Store unless design or programming modifications are needed. When you click on a

...More

◻ This app is designed for both iPhone and iPad

$0.99

Category: Reference
Updated: Sep 19, 2012
Version: 1.4.1
Size: 18.6 MB
Language: English
Seller: Nelsen enterprises, LLC
© 2011–2012
MyLegalHeat.com
Rated 9+ for the following:
Infrequent/Mild Cartoon or
Fantasy Violence

Compatibility: Requires iOS 4.3 or later. Compatible with iPhone, iPad, and iPod touch. This app is optimized for iPhone 5.

Customer Ratings

Current Version:
★★★★★ 23 Ratings
All Versions:
★★★★★ 142 Ratings

Screenshots

iPhone | iPad

Legal Heat app for smartphones lets you check laws in any jurisdiction.

Commandment V: Know What You're Doing

Gunfights are won by those who shoot fastest and straightest, and are usually measured in seconds. Legal aftermaths last for years, and emotional aftermaths, for lifetimes. Get educated in depth in the management of all three stages of the encounter beforehand.

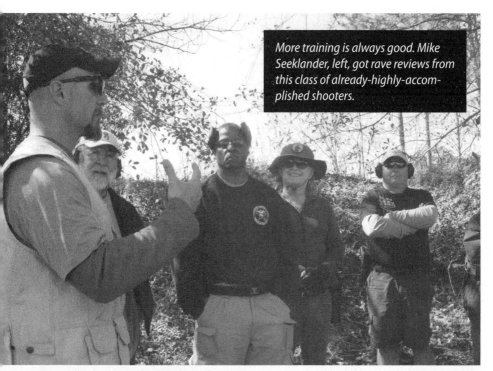

More training is always good. Mike Seeklander, left, got rave reviews from this class of already-highly-accomplished shooters.

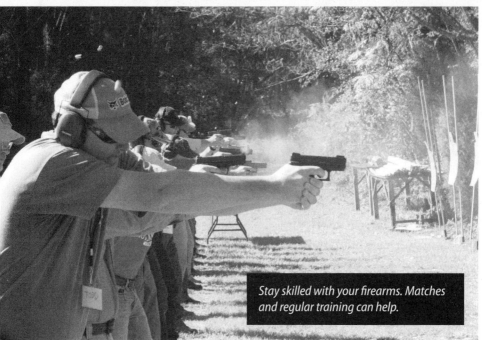

Stay skilled with your firearms. Matches and regular training can help.

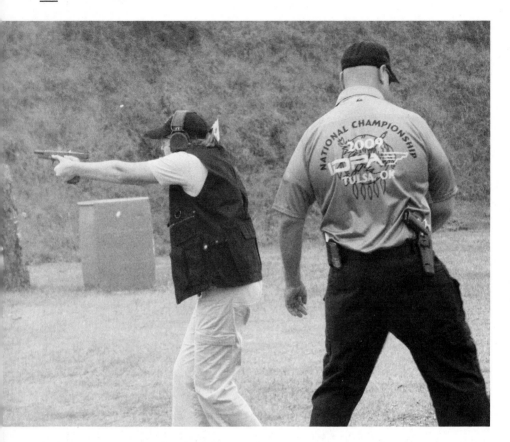

Shooting while moving is a useful skill, demonstrated here by Randi Rogers as she shoots her way to a national championship.

Commandment VI: Concealed Means Concealed

If your local license requires concealed carry, keep the gun truly concealed. The revealing of a concealed handgun is seen in many quarters as a threat, which can result in charges of criminal threatening, brandishing, and more. A malevolent person who wants to falsely accuse you of threatening them with a gun will have their wrongful accusation bolstered if the police find you with a gun where they said it was. Yes, that happens. Some jurisdictions allow "open carry." I support the right to open carry, in the proper time and place, but have found over the decades that there are relatively few ideal times or places where the practice won't unnecessarily and predictably frighten someone the carrier had no reason to scare.

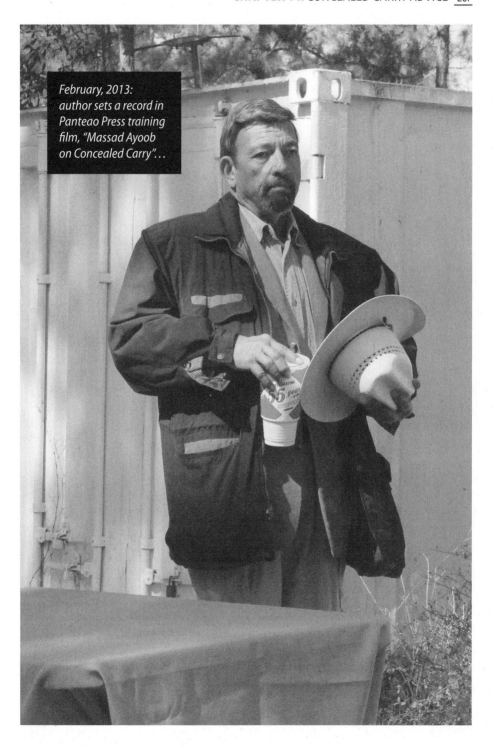

February, 2013: author sets a record in Panteao Press training film, "Massad Ayoob on Concealed Carry"…

...successfully concealing more than 50 loaded pistols and revolvers. Do not tell him it's too inconvenient to carry ONE gun to protect yourself and your loved ones.

Commandment VII: Maximize Your Firearms
Familiarity

If you ever need that gun, it will happen so quickly
and terribly that you'll have to be swift and sure. If
you don't, you'll still be handling a deadly weapon in
the presence of people you love. Making gun manipu-
lation second nature – safety as well as draw-fire-hit
– is thus doubly important.

*Colt .45 has been a classic
American home and personal
defense weapon in one form
or another since 1911. This
one, produced circa 1918, is
still perfectly functional.*

*Powerful, high-tech
firearms can be
controllable. This is a
Colt 10mm modified
with integral recoil
compensator by
master pistolsmith
Mark Morris.*

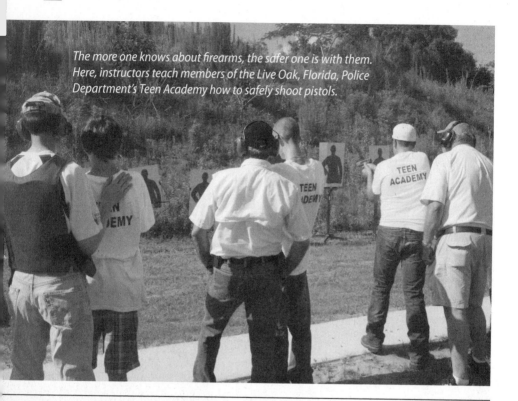

The more one knows about firearms, the safer one is with them. Here, instructors teach members of the Live Oak, Florida, Police Department's Teen Academy how to safely shoot pistols.

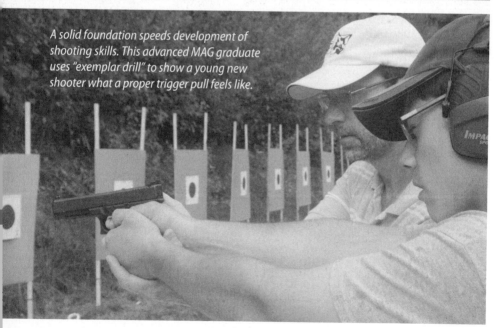

A solid foundation speeds development of shooting skills. This advanced MAG graduate uses "exemplar drill" to show a young new shooter what a proper trigger pull feels like.

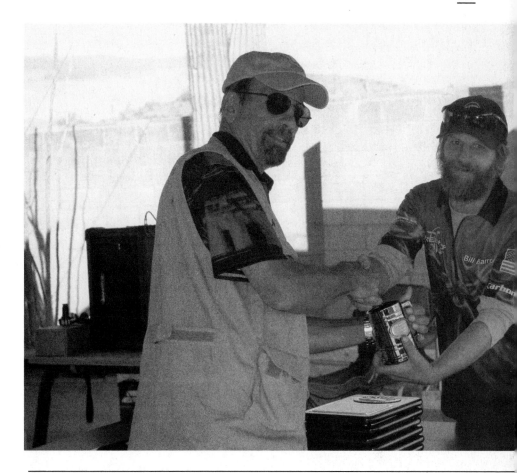

Commandment VIII: Understand The Fine Points

Don't just read the headlines or editorials, read the fine print. Actually study the laws of your jurisdiction. What's legal in one place won't be legal in another. Cities may have prohibitions that states don't. Remember the principle, "ignorance of the law is no excuse."

Commandment IX: Carry an Adequate Firearm

A Vespa motor scooter is a motor vehicle, but it's a poor excuse for a family car. A .22 or .25 is a firearm, but it's a poor excuse for defense. Carry a gun loaded with ammunition that has a track record of quickly

Winning a match feels good. Here, author accepts Stock Service Revolver Champion award from Bill Barron, match director for the South Mountain regional IDPA championship in Phoenix, AZ. International Defensive Pistol Assn. matches help to hone defensive shooting skills.

Gun expert Mark Moritz said, "The first rule of gunfighting is, have a gun." This tiny Browning .25 is easy to carry, but far from first choice for quickly stopping a violent attack.

This Ruger 1911 .45 auto is extremely reliable, and surprisingly easy to shoot fast and straight.

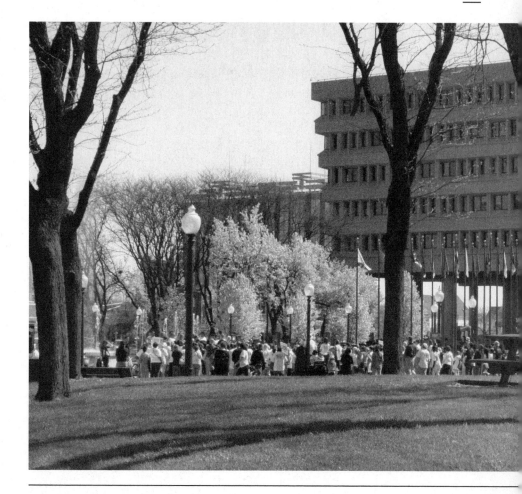

stopping lethal assaults. Hint: if your chosen caliber is not used by police or military, it's probably not powerful enough for its intended purpose.

Commandment X: Use Common Sense

Common sense – encompassing ethics and logic and law alike – must be your constant guide and companion when you carry a gun. Not idealism, not rhetoric. When you carry a gun, you literally carry the power of life and death. It is a power that belongs only in the hands of responsible people who care about consequences, and who are respectful of life and limb and human safety, that of others as well as their own.

Your rights to self-defense are constantly under attack. This anti-gun rally was photographed by the author in Indianapolis in 2014.